STUDIES IN THE ROYAL PRIESTHOOD

KEVIN J. CONNER

STUDIES IN THE ROYAL PRIESTHOOD

KEVIN J. CONNER

Original Edition
© Copyright 2011 Kevin J. Conner

This Edition
© Copyright 2023 Conner Ministries Ltd

It is illegal and a violation of Christian ethics to reproduce any or parts or diagrams in this book without written permission of the author or publishers.

Published by Conner Ministries Ltd

CONNER MINISTRIES

WEB: kevinconner.org
Email: kevin.conner321@gmail.com

Visit www.amazon.com/author/kevinjconner for a list of other books by Kevin Conner.

TABLE OF CONTENTS

FOREWORD 3
PART ONE – EARLY CHURCH HISTORY 5
CHAPTER 1 - THE ORIGINAL PURPOSE 7
CHAPTER 2 - THE EARLY CHURCH 11
CHAPTER 3 - THE APOSTASY AND DECLINE 17
PART TWO – THE REFORMATION PERIOD 29
CHAPTER 4 - THE DARK AGES, RECOVERY AND REFORMATION .. 31
PART THREE - WHAT SAY THE SCRIPTURES? 39
CHAPTER 5 - PROGRESSIVE REVELATION OF PRIESTHOOD 41
CHAPTER 6 - A KINGDOM OF PRIESTS 45
CHAPTER 7 - LEVELS IN THE WILL OF GOD 55
PART FOUR - THE AARONIC PRIESTHOOD 63
CHAPTER 8 – AARON: THE HIGH PRIEST AND HIS SONS 65
CHAPTER 9 - THE PRIESTLY REQUISITES 67
CHAPTER 10 - THE PRIESTLY CONSECRATION 71
CHAPTER 11 - THE GARMENTS FOR AARON AND HIS SONS 75
CHAPTER 12 - PHYSICAL QUALIFICATIONS OF THE PRIESTS 105
CHAPTER 13 - THE CONSECRATION OFFERINGS and ORDER 109
CHAPTER 14 - THE LEVITICAL OFFERINGS 117
CHAPTER 15 - PRIESTLY MINISTRY IN MOSES' TABERNACLE 121
CHAPTER 16 - PRIESTLY MINISTRY IN DAVID'S TABERNACLE ... 123
CHAPTER 17 - PRIESTLY MINISTRY IN SOLOMON'S TEMPLE 129
PART FIVE - AN OVERVIEW OF PRIESTLY GENEALOGY 135
CHAPTER 18 - THE GENEALOGY OF THE ORDER OF AARON 137
PART SIX - CHARACTER STUDIES OF SIGNIFICANT PRIESTS . 141
CHAPTER 19 – AARON: ISRAEL'S FIRST HIGH PRIEST 143
CHAPTER 20 - NADAB & ABIHU: PRIESTS OF PRESUMPTION 147
CHAPTER 21 – ELEAZAR: THE PRIEST WITHOUT FAULT 149
CHAPTER 22 – PHINEHAS: THE PRIEST WITH DIVINE ZEAL 153

CHAPTER 23 - PRIESTS OF HISTORY 155
CHAPTER 24 – ZADOK: THE LOYAL PRIEST 157
PART SEVEN - PRIESTS OF ITHAMAR'S LINE 161
CHAPTER 25 – ELI: THE PRIEST THAT GOD BY-PASSED 163
CHAPTER 26 - HOPHNI & PHINEHAS: PRESUMPTIOUS PRIESTS 171
CHAPTER 27 – ICHABOD: SIGN-CHILD OF A DEAD PRIEST 175
CHAPTER 28 – AHIMELECH: HE DIED FOR DAVID'S SAKE............. 177
CHAPTER 29 – AHIAH: THE PRIEST OF AN IMPATIENT KING 179
CHAPTER 30 – ABIATHAR: THE PRIEST WHO FAILED THE TEST .. 181
PART EIGHT - JEHOZADAK TO BABYLONIAN CAPTIVITY 185
CHAPTER 31 - PRIESTS TO BABYLONIAN CAPTIVITY 187
PART NINE – MESSIAH'S RESTORATION TIMES 189
CHAPTER 32 – JOSHUA: THE PRIEST OF RESTORATION 191
CHAPTER 33 – EZRA: THE TEACHING PRIEST 197
CHAPTER 34 - THE PRIESTHOOD IN MESSIAH'S TIMES................... 201
CHAPTER 35 - THE END OF THE LEVITICAL PRIESTHOOD 205
PART TEN - THE NEW COVENANT PRIESTHOOD 209
CHAPTER 36 - NEW COVENANT TIMES... 211
CHAPTER 37 - THE SPIRITUAL HOUSE 215
CHAPTER 38 - THE SPIRITUAL PRIESTHOOD..................................... 219
CHAPTER 39 - THE SPIRITUAL SACRIFICES 221
CHAPTER 40 - THE FUNCTIONING PRIESTHOOD............................... 229
CHAPTER 41 - A PARADIGM FOR THE NEW PRIESTHOOD 237
SUMMARY 241
CONCLUSION 251
BIBLIOGRAPHY 253
ABOUT THE AUTHOR 255
OTHER BOOKS BY KEVIN CONNER 257

FOREWORD

Both the Old and New Testaments provide many pictures or types of Christ and His Church. In all things, in every picture (or type), Christ is seen to have the pre-eminence (Col. 1:18). In the following table we note a number of these major types that find their fulfillment in Christ and His Church.

	The Church	Christ Pre-eminent
1.	The Family of God	The Firstborn Son
2.	The Temple of God	The Chief Cornerstone
3.	The Body of Christ	The Head
4.	The Bride	The Bridegroom
5.	The Sheepfold	The Chief Shepherd
6.	The Army of the Lord	The Captain of the Host
7.	The Household of Faith	The Chief Steward
8.	The Vine Branches	The Vine
9.	The Kingdom of God	The King
10.	The Discipleship School	The Master
11.	The Spiritual Israel of God	The Prime Minister
12.	The Priesthood	The Great High Priest

Just a glance over the above generally provides an idea where the emphasis has been laid, especially in the fundamental, evangelical and Pentecostal Churches over the years.

There is extensive teaching on the Church being God's Family, God's Temple, the House of God, the Flock of God. There is also much teaching on the Church as being the Body of Christ, the Bride of Christ or the Kingdom of God. Other of these pictures may be dealt with in a greater or lesser degree.

Undoubtedly, the most neglected picture of all listed here is number twelve. That is, the Priesthood and more particularly, **The Priesthood of All Believers**, Christ being our Great High Priest.

This, of course, provokes the question: Why is this so? The Church of Rome and some of the Protestant denominations have taken this Old Testament picture and developed a heavy emphasis on Priesthood with its Priests, Bishops, Cardinals and Monks, the Papacy and so forth.
One wonders if so-called Protestantism has allowed itself to be robbed of the truth of the "Priesthood of All Believers" because of Romanism, some High Anglican Churches and some Orthodox Churches. The authors of this text think so! To speak of Priesthood could speak of Romanism and so forth.

So! This is what this textbook is all about: **The Priesthood of All Believers.**

Our prayer is that there will come a fresh reformation to the Church and that both leaders and people will rediscover and recover this evidently neglected, almost forgotten and lost truth of the believers' priesthood.

Kevin J. Conner
(with assistance from Jeff Cameron)
2011

PART ONE – EARLY CHURCH HISTORY

Chapter 1 The Original Purpose
Chapter 2 The Early Church
Chapter 3 The Decline and Apostasy

CHAPTER 1 - THE ORIGINAL PURPOSE

With the death of Christ on the cross, the veil of Jerusalem's temple was torn from top to bottom. It was a supreme act of God (Matt. 27:50-54). It must have been a great shock to the priests on duty on that Passover occasion!

This act of God signified the end of the old dispensation and the Law Covenant and the opening of the new dispensation and the ushering in of the New Covenant.

The veil of Christ's flesh was 'rent' in conjunction with the 'rent veil' of the temple (Heb. 10:19-21). The sacrifice of Christ forever abolishes animal sacrifices. The blood of Christ forever does away with the blood of animals. The priesthood of Christ forever does away with the Aaronic and Levitical Priesthood, which will never be established again, in this age or the ages to come.

This is the whole teaching of the Book of Hebrews, especially Hebrews chapter 7 through chapter 10. For anyone to seek, in any way, to establish or re-establish a priest-class or priest-craft is to despise the work of the cross of Jesus and to fly fully in the face of the New Covenant Priesthood. This will be seen more fully in a subsequent chapter.

With the inauguration of the New Covenant, there is the inauguration of a new priesthood – the priesthood of all believers. This was the original purpose in Jesus ratifying the New Covenant with His own body and blood (Matt. 26:26-28 with Heb. 8).

Under the Old Covenant, only men could be priests. Under the New Covenant, both men and women can be, and are, priests, having access to God through Christ. Denominations debate, argue and divide over the matter of 'ordaining women as priests'. The matter has already been settled by Jesus at Calvary. "In Christ", Paul says, there is neither male nor female (Gal. 3:27-29).

Under the Old Covenant, only one tribe out of the twelve tribes of Israel was chosen to be the priestly tribe and that was the tribe of Levi. Out of that priestly tribe, the house of Aaron was chosen to be the High Priestly line. Under the New Covenant, all believers, both men and women, out of every kindred, tongue, tribe and nation, are called to be priests unto God. Christ is our Great High Priest, and the members of Christ's body are believer-priests under Him, who is both Priest and Sacrifice in the one person of our Lord Jesus Christ.

Under Old Testament times, the offices of Priest and King were separated, divided to two of the tribes of Israel. The priesthood was given to the tribe of Levi; the kingship was given to the tribe of Judah. Any who dared to presume to unite these two offices were severely judged by the Lord God, and that, very swiftly. Under New Covenant times, our Lord Jesus Christ unites in Himself these two offices. He is both KING and PRIEST, sitting enthroned with the Father (Zech. 6:12-13). Here Joshua (type of Jesus, our Savior) was to sit and rule on his throne, and be a priest on his throne, and the counsel of peace shall be both of these offices (Refer. Amp. O.T. of Zech. 6:12, 13). As such He is King-Priest, our Melchizedek.

This truth extends also to the Church, the Body of Christ. Note the following Scriptures, written under inspiration of the Holy Spirit by the apostles Peter and John.

"... a holy priesthood" (1Pet. 2:5). "But you are a chosen generation, a royal priesthood ..." (1Pet. 2:9). "... and has made us kings and priests (a kingdom of priests), to His God and Father ..." (Rev. 1:6). "And has made us kings and priests to our God. And we shall reign on the earth" (Rev. 5:10). "... but they shall be priests of God and of Christ and shall reign with Him one thousand years" (Rev. 20:6 NKJV).

The prophet Isaiah confirms the same calling. "But you shall be named the priests of the Lord. They shall call you the ministers (servants) of our God ..." (Isa. 61:6. NKJV/NIV).

To be "kings and priests" to God and His Christ, or a kingdom of priests, is nothing less than the Order of Melchizedek. Christ is THE King-Priest after the Order of Melchizedek. The Church, which is His Body, is called into and after the same order.

It is called to be a holy priesthood, a royal (kingly) priesthood. Head and Body constitute the same order of Melchizedek. "For both He who sanctifies and those who are being sanctified **are all of one,** for which reason He is not ashamed to call them brethren ..." (Heb. 2:11).

This was God's original intention, His original purpose, in the building of His Church, the New Testament Church.

The challenge is this: Is the Church, as a whole, fulfilling God's original purpose, His original intention? Are believers fulfilling their ministries as "kings and priests unto God and His Christ"? What does it really mean to be a king, or a kingdom of priests unto God and His Son and are we fulfilling that calling? Or has the king-priestly ministry been suppressed or supplanted by a hierarchical form of government in the Church? Where is the Order of Melchizedek in the earth of which Christ is the head and High Priest? Just what has happened over the years of Church History?

But this brings us to our next chapter!

CHAPTER 2 - THE EARLY CHURCH

There are many, many books which deal with early Church History, and the reader is referred to these for fuller details. But, before considering the decline and the cause of this decline, a brief overview of early Church History will be helpful.

It is to be remembered that, over time, in early Church History, there was a complete break that took place between the Old Covenant Priesthood and the New Covenant Priesthood of all believers.

The greatest influencer in these days was the apostle Paul. To him was given the revelation of the Church being "the Body of Christ". There was not to be a Jewish body and a Gentile body. Pauline revelation declared: "By one Spirit are we all baptized into one body, whether we be Jews or Gentiles" (1 Cor.12:13). No other apostle was particularly given this "Body revelation". It permeates Paul's writings as no other apostolic writings, as these references show (1 Cor.12:1-31; Rom.12:1-8; Eph 4:4-6, 11-16; Col.1:15-20).

The Church was seen as a functioning body, members one of another, members witnessing the Gospel, proclaiming Christ wherever there was opportunity. To use the language of our textbook, it was a functioning priesthood, the priesthood of all believers, reconciling man to God.

A. Church Growth

Within a few decades after the cross this new religion called Christianity touched its world. The blood of its Founder had not yet finished falling to the ground when the first fruit was reaped. Jesus was still alive to see that first precious soul, first of countless millions that would follow. The hardened heart of the career-criminal on the cross next to Jesus was smashed and broken as he saw the Lamb of God dying with such dignity a death that normally degraded men to the utmost. What he saw and heard caused him to cry out. "***Lord,*** *remember me when You come into Your kingdom!*" (Luke 23:42). That was one!

As Jesus breathed His last, the centurion who oversaw these dreadful proceedings was moved to exclaim, "Truly this man was the Son of God." (Mark 15:39). That was two!

Fifty days later most, if not all the remnant of His followers were sitting wondering what to do next … and in the words of an old song, ***then the Spirit came!*** The result was beyond the wildest dreams of these pioneers of the faith. Peter preached his first sermon and three thousand came into an experience with Jesus their Christ (Acts 2:41). The trickle is turning into a river.

Days later another five thousand were added (Acts 4:4). In Acts 5:14 we see multitudes coming in. In Acts 6:1 and 7 the numbers are greatly multiplied ... and this is only a matter of days, weeks and months after the cross. The river is becoming a flood. Note that Acts 6:7 says a great number of the priests became obedient to the faith. It is a powerful move indeed when the religious people are touched and transformed by God's grace. The rest of Acts and a number of historical documents give us an indication of the explosive growth of the New Testament Church. The writer of the old hymn captures some of the feel of this move of God:

On the mount of crucifixion,
Fountains opened deep and wide
Through the floodgates of God's mercy
Flowed a vast and glorious tide
Grace and love like mighty rivers
Poured incessant from above
And heaven's peace and perfect justice
Kissed a guilty world with love.

This incredible flood of God's saving grace and mercy caused a flood of souls to come pouring into the Kingdom of God.

B. Tertullian – Early Church Father

Hear the words of the greatly respected Tertullian, one of the "early Church fathers" writing about the number of Christians in the Roman Empire (Time – approximately 150 years into the Christian era).

"We are but of yesterday, and we have filled everything you have – cities, tenements, forts, towns, exchanges, yes! and camps, tribes, palace, senate, forum. All we have left to you is the temples! ... Why! without taking up arms, without rebellion, simply by standing aside, (in modern parlance we would say going on strike) by mere ill-natured separation, we could have fought you! For if so vast a mass of people as we had broken away from you and removed to some recess of the world apart, the mere loss of so many citizens of whatever sort would have brought a blush to your rule – yes, that it would, and punished you too, by sheer desertion! Beyond doubt, you would have shuddered at your solitude, at the silence in the world, the stupor as it were of a dead globe. You would have had to look about for people to rule. You would have had more enemies left than citizens. For, as things are, you have fewer enemies because of the multitude of the Christians when nearly all the citizens you have in nearly all the cities are Christian." **A New Eusebius, Doc 140.**

C. New Covenant Ministers

The New Testament tells the story of the birth of something new in God's creation. For approximately 1500 years before the coming of Jesus the Aaronic and Levitical priesthood had sacrificed its innocent victims to temporarily cover the sins of a stiff-necked, self-willed and rebellious people who had missed their calling in God. These sacrifices could only cover sin but never cause it to cease. Animal blood could not cleanse sin. It could only cover sin! The tribe of Levi were designated by God and ordained to do the priestly work. They did the God-business while the other eleven tribes went about their own business. The eleven tribes supported the Levitical tribe of priests with sacrificial offerings and tithes of all they acquired.

When Jesus came, He didn't do much to vindicate the role of the established priesthood and religious leaders. He found fellowship with fishermen, tax gatherers, rich people and poor, but the priests, scholars and religious authorities were not so often found in His entourage. His crucifixion and death ushered in the end of the Levitical priesthood and its sacrifices. The curtain in the temple was ripped from top to bottom, destroyed by the hand of God, and along with it the priesthood as it then was.

In that one supreme moment in His life when Jesus did offer sacrifice once and for all, He gathered into Himself the whole meaning of priesthood and sacrifice and obliterated forever the need of a priestly caste. The result of that action, and his entirely original contribution was, for the first time in the history of religion, to enable an entire people to be priest. Is this not one of the biggest differences between Christianity and all other religions on the face of the earth? (The Liberation of the Laity, Ann Rowthorn, p12 quoting Vincent J Donavan, **Christianity Rediscovered: An Epistle from the Masai**, 1976 p140).

Fifty days later (Acts 2) the Spirit of God fell on the remnants of Jesus' ministry. These were a motley bunch, but they were the ones God had chosen. They had no ordination other than the new wine and oil of the Holy Spirit. They were not men and women of scholarly note, but they had walked closely with the Master on His earthly pilgrimage and they knew His Words and His ways. They picked up the mantle discarded by the early pioneers of their nation. They became the royal priesthood God was seeking in Ex. 19:1-6. They became God's interface with the world. It truly was a new day ... the day of a *new creation*.

The Old Testament priests centered their activities around tabernacle or temple and religious observances. The New Testament priests (each and every believer) were integrated with and embedded in their world. The old priesthood remembered endless days of sacrificial offerings, but this new seemingly ignorant and uneducated "priesthood" spoke of one perfect sacrifice which forever did away with the need for further offerings for sin. The old had truly passed away and the new had come (2 Cor. 5:17).

For fifteen hundred years the old priesthood had consistently failed to keep its own nation on track with God, let alone fulfill its calling to bring the nations of the earth before God. Yet within just a few decades this new priesthood had impacted their world.

The old priesthood held a monopoly on Jewish political, civil and religious power (subject of course to the Roman Empire) but the new priesthood transcended these powers with the power of God, and in the exercise of the new and royal priestly ministry was subject to no one, other than an accountability to each other and to a mantle of authority that seemed to be laid upon those who had walked closely with Jesus.

Conflicts inevitably arose. In Acts 3 and 4 we see the old priesthood in power trying desperately to bring the new priesthood into order and under control. The casual reader today gets no sense of import or perspective on this meeting. Peter and John stand before the power-brokers of the nation. It is somewhat akin to an uneducated worker of our day standing before a board of lawyers, politicians and philosophers. In fact it is even more powerful than that because these people are not only highly educated leaders and rulers but until this point they were seen as representing God in the earth. Everything Peter and John have been previously taught said that these people were to be listened to, respected and obeyed.

The meeting is opened, the charges are laid, but Peter is filled with the Holy Spirit (Acts 4:8) and there ends the contest. In its innocence, simplicity and power the new blows the old away.

The ministry of the new priesthood has begun by showing its superiority over the old. Fishermen, tax gatherers, common people and even a few rich, educated and privileged are the new people of God and will, in the power of God, achieve what the old never could.

The very disciples themselves were, significantly, laymen, devoid of formal theological or rhetorical training. Christianity was from its inception a lay movement, and so it continued for a remarkably long time … in contrast to the present day when Christianity is highly intellectualized and dispensed by a professional clergy to a constituency increasingly confined to the middle class. In the early days the faith was spread by informal evangelists and had its greatest appeal among the working classes. (Michael Green, Evangelism in the Early Church, Grand Rapids MI: Eerdmans Publishing Co., 1970 PP. 172, 175)

Oh the effectiveness and fruitfulness of so many of those early Christians! Normal everyday believers who until that point had never amounted to much in their world were doing outstanding exploits. They elected some of their number to serve tables, but the power, grace and urgency of God couldn't be confined to such administration, necessary as it was. It spilled over and poured out of these "un-ordained by man but anointed of God" newly installed royal priests as they went out and ministered in power, great wonders and miracles (e.g. Acts6). The sick were healed, the dead were raised and the hungry were fed.

There was no talk of a priestly caste doing the work of God. Far from being the prime movers of these things the priests were the ***recipients*** of the ministry (Acts 6:7). The preachers and power-brokers were God's ***Laos***, God's people … the farmers, fishermen, tax gatherers, labourers, etc., *ad infinitum*, who had for generations been subjugated to the priesthood in all matters religious, but now were chosen by God to carry His gospel to the world. The priests were allowed to take their place *in* the ***laos*** of God, but they didn't bring their priesthood titles, rank and ministry with them. Like everyone else they had to count it all but dung that they may win Christ and be found in Him (Phil.3:8-9). Priests and paupers, high priests and harlots; all stood on equal footing, for the ground is always level at the foot of the cross.

Some would argue that we can't make any valid remarks about how the old priesthood fitted in with the new Church because there is no historical evidence which addresses that issue. We would say it is one of the few situations where an argument from silence can be used with great confidence. The mere fact that in all the New Testament there is no mention of such a priesthood operating in the New Testament Church is plain evidence that the old priesthood was a non-issue.

In Acts 6:7 we see **"a great company of the priests became obedient to the faith."** But they were not in the Church as "old covenant priests" but as "new covenant believers" and members of the new covenant priesthood "in Christ" – not "in Aaron" and not "in Levi".

Most of the New Testament epistles are written to address difficulties in the churches. It is infeasible that the writers would not have addressed the priests to do something if they had any authority whatsoever. But instead, the old priesthood is counted as though dead. All the New Testament writers address their letters and appeals to the saints (who are the *hagioi*, the holy, the normal everyday believers who have embraced salvation through Christ), the elders and deacons, or combinations thereof. The idea of a priesthood set apart from the common believer is unknown in the New Testament, and in fact at odds with it.

In the New Testament (Covenant), all believers are called to be in that "**holy priesthood**", that **"royal priesthood"** of which Peter and John write (1 Pet.2:4-9; Rev.1:6; 5:9-10). All are citizens of that "**kingdom of priests**".

CHAPTER 3 - THE APOSTASY AND DECLINE

Having seen what God's original intention and purpose was in early Church History, we note that within a few centuries the Church declined from the purposes of God, just as did Israel of Old.

With the death of the apostle John in the first century, apostasy began its evil work and within a couple of centuries or so, a "Clergy/Laity" system arose which paralyzed the priesthood of all believers.

A. The Apostasy Foretold

The apostasy (Grk. *"apostasia"*) had been foretold by Old Testament writers, Jesus and His apostles, as the following confirms.

1. Falling stars symbolized the apostasy both in Old and New Testaments (Lke.10:17-21; Isa.14:12-14; Rev.12:4; Dan.8:9-12).

2. Jesus warned His disciples that, because of abounding iniquity, the love of many would grow cold (Matt.24:10-13).

3. Paul also warned the saints, by the Spirit, of the departure and apostasy from the faith and the giving heed to seducing spirits (1 Tim.4:1-3; 2 Tim.3:1-9).

4. Peter foretold the rise of false teachers and false prophets (2 Pet.3:1-3).

5. Jude also spoke of the departure from the faith that had been once and for all times delivered to the saints (Jude 3-5).

6. Paul also warned the Thessalonians of the great apostasy, the great falling away, that would take place in the Church, the Temple of God (2 Thess.2:1-12).

B. The Decline into 'Clergy/Laity'

In brief we consider the rise of the clergy and the decline of the laity into two different grades or classes of believers. This is a major part of the apostasy from the faith once delivered to the saints. But we need to define these words and what they have come to mean in our times.

1. **Clergy** = "those ordained for religious duties". The word is related to 'Cleric', a member of the Clergy. (Grk. "klerikox" from "kleros", meaning lot, heritage" (Oxford Dictionary).
Clergy = men ordained for the public service of God; the body of ordained ministers, as distinguished from the laity.
Clergyman = an ordained minister; one of the clergy.
Refer also to cleric, clerical, clericalism.

Many expositors see the interpretation of the name 'the Nicolaitans' (Rev.2:6 & 15), as foreshadowing a priest-craft arising in early Church times.

'Nico' means 'to conquer', and 'Laos' means 'the people'. Thus Nicolaitanism means 'to conquer the people'. That is exactly what the clergy have done in numerous places; conquered the laity.

2. **Laity** = lay people, as distinct from the clergy (Oxford Dictionary).
   Laity = the people, as distinguished from the clergy (Collins Dictionary).

Such distinctions were unknown in the early Church. All were "priests unto God". All were members of the Body of Christ. How then did we come to this point where the clergy system has strangled the life out of our churches and the laity is happy with the idea? If we rely only on the Bible as most Protestants do, the clergy as we know it today should not exist. But earlier generations of the Church were not stupid people. How can they have started with the Scriptures and ended up with what we now have? A short walk-through history will inform us a little on this matter.

C. **Church History – Apostles, Elders and Deacons – Threefold Ministry**
In the very early church immediately following Pentecost, it seems the apostles were in charge (Acts 1:13, 15; 2:14, 42-43; 4:32-37; 6:2; 9:27; 11:1; etc).

Servers/waiters/administrators, later interpreted by many to be deacons, were quickly added to administrate over material matters (Acts 6:2ff).

The first mention of elders in the Christian context is in Acts 11:30. However, it was a thorough going term long used to describe a group of people within the Jewish system. It seems the Christians simply adopted the term and office that was already in existence in Judaism. In Acts 14:23 the apostles ordained elders in every church and in Acts 15:1-4, 22, we see the apostles and elders sitting in the seat of authority.

Two words from the original Greek are translated "elder".

1. ***presbuteros***. The basic meaning of this is "a person of old age". In ancient times authority was given to older people with wider experience. The term implies seniority by reason of age (1Tim.5:1; 1 Pet.5:5).

2. ***episkopos** = **overseer*** which is also translated as "elder" by most Bibles although the KJV translates it as "bishop". In Acts 20:17 and 28 we see the elders/presbyters are supposed to be overseers over the church (also 1 Pet 5:1-3). So in Acts 20:17 and 28 and 1 Pet 5 ***episkopos*** is to do with ***overseeing***, which is an action ... a job ... something they ***do*** rather than being an office or title.

Elders are to play the part of ***overseers*** and shepherd (***poimano***) the flock. But in Phil.1:1 it has become an ***office*** ... which is translated "*together with the bishops and deacons.*" The act of overseeing has at this early stage become an office. In Titus.1:5 and 7 we see the terms used interchangeably.

Wherever these elders are mentioned in the New Testament they seem to be located in a given local church along with the deacons (servants or waiters at tables). It is commonly stated that the service of deacon is that of the seven in Acts 6, although some dispute any connection. Those who dispute this would argue that in 6:2, the function of these was to 'serve' tables but we should note that 6:4 speaks of the 'serving' of the Word by the apostles.

So we may serve/deacon by waiting on tables or we can serve/deacon by preaching and teaching the word. Thus language alone does not equate these with deacons. Without endless argument and hair splitting, we will settle for the traditional understanding where Acts 6 shows us the beginning of the deacon ministry.

It would seem then that if we are to take church government from the New Testament picture, the apostles and elders were the spiritual guides, overseers and teachers. The ***apostles*** often traveled and had input to a number of local churches, but the ***elders*** were related to local church government only. It seems that ***deacons*** were there to serve, probably in a variety of practical ways. The system seems to have worked well until the death of the apostles.

D. Local Church Ministry: Elders/Bishops & Deacons – 2fold Ministry

From the inception of the New Testament Church there were problems. Most of the Epistles testify to this fact, i.e., they are written to address problems in the churches. 3 John shows us that there were even major problems with church leaders (Diotrephes = nourished by Jupiter or Zeus).

While the original apostles were present, problems could be sorted out by appealing to their knowledge and authority. But after their passing, self-appointed and would-be-if-could-be apostles, prophets, teachers, etc. abounded and, quite naturally, along with this proliferation of preachers came problems.

Who had the knowledge and authority to sort these things out? Better to have hand-picked locals who had the church at heart rather than unknown claimants to privilege and position ... hence the investiture of power into the hands of the elders or bishops.

Speaking of this very situation the Lion Handbook, The History of Christianity, p117 says, "This Spirit-gifted leadership had largely disappeared by the early second century. The *Didache* shows that, in one region, some prophetic teachers were settling down, others had become self-seeking, and 'bishops and deacons' were gaining new prominence."

Note: The *Didache* is the earliest existing document written by the New Testament Church, dated C90-100AD. We can read part of this in Doc.8 New Eusebius.

"Local leaders emerged at an early stage. Congregational life was directed by a team or group, commonly known as 'presbyters' – that is, elders or fathers in the faith ... or 'bishops' – that is, guardians or overseers ... Other titles were used – pastor or shepherd, teacher, deacon or servant, ruler or president. The status and function of the different posts were still flexible. There was no counterpart to 'the minister' of today in earliest Christianity. Churches met in small, house-based gatherings until at least the third century." (Lion, p117).

See New Euseb. Doc 7 (Clement of Rome, c96) for the claim to Divine validation for the twofold ministry (an interpretation of Isa 60:17 which we may not consider valid).

So their answer to the problems was to put more power in the hands of the local leadership. This aided the emergence of the twofold local church ministry; that of Elders/Bishops and Deacons.

E. Local Church Ministry: One Bishop, Presbyters & Deacons – 3fold
In an historical document written about or shortly after the time of the **Didache**, we can see the beginnings of the emergence of one senior bishop above the local eldership.

"Avoid divisions, as the beginning of evil. Follow, all of you, the bishop, as Jesus Christ followed the Father; and follow the presbytery as the apostles. Moreover, reverence the deacons as the commandment of God.

Let no man do aught pertaining to the Church apart from the bishop. Let that Eucharist be considered valid which is under the bishop or him to whom he commits it. Wheresoever the bishop appears, there let the people be, even as wheresoever Christ Jesus is, there is the Catholic Church. It is not lawful apart from the bishop either to baptize, or to hold a love feast. But whatsoever he approves, that also is well-pleasing to God, that everything which you do may be secure and valid". Doc 13 A New Eusebius.

"… only that Eucharist which is under the authority of the bishop (or whomever he himself designates) is to be considered valid …" (Bulley, The Priesthood of Some Believers, pp57-58, quoting Ignatius from Smyrnaens 8:1).

To further quote Bulley P319, " … especially from c.200, the ordained increasingly took over the power and public ministry in the church at the same time as their priesthood was being taught and emphasized, while the laity lost power and opportunities for public ministry, as their priesthood was being devalued and/or largely ignored … Further, the charismata, whilst still experienced by non-leaders as late as Cyprian, were increasingly being restricted to the ordained, particularly in the vital area of teaching which was regarded as a priestly ministry … Power, both spiritual and 'political', was becoming concentrated in those who claimed a special priesthood and authority from God, as was most, if not all, exercise of public ministry in the church. **It seems fair, then, to conclude that both the understanding of the general priesthood and the active participation of the laity in the church's life, and above all in its public life, ministry and mediation of God's grace, were significantly limited, diminished, and harmed by the rise in the clergy's specialized priesthood and the clergy's domination of the church's power and public ministry** (Emphasis ours). The rise in the specialized, and the diminution and dilution of the general priesthood were integral to these developments. In so far as these developments involved limitations on the Spirit's use of the non-ordained in public ministry and the exercise of power, rather than enhancing the Spirit's ministry, they diminished it and restricted it increasingly to the ordained. Although the church gained the benefits of clearer and more effective order, these increased the danger of the misuse of power, as Origen especially attests, and of the passivity of the laity, as he also attests."

Bulley, page 125, speaks of a 3rd century document called the Didascalia Apostolorum. Quoting from this … "You also then today, O Bishops, are priests to your people, and the Levites who minister to the Tabernacle of

God, the holy Catholic Church, who stands continually before the Lord God" (p127-8).

Also ... "... you then are to your people priests and prophets, and princes and leaders and kings, and mediators between God and His faithful, and receivers of the word, and preachers and proclaimers thereof, and knowers of the Scriptures and of the utterances of God, and witnesses of His will, who bear the sins of all, and are to give any answer for all." (p128).

The reader will pardon the lengthy quotes, but it helps to see the apostasy and the gradual decline in it. These, along with other documents, show the emergence of the threefold ministry of the one bishop, multiple presbyters (or, elders) and deacons.

This pattern became universal before the third century. About AD 250, the Church at Rome had "... 1 bishop, together with 46 presbyters, 7 deacons and 7 sub-deacons, as well as 42 'acolytes' or attendants (acolyte = follower, or the highest of the minor orders, including laity, who do altar attendance, candles, etc), and 52 exorcists, readers and doorkeepers" (Doc 207 A New Eusebius, c250, and Lion, The History of Christianity p.117-118).

F. The Exaltation of the Bishop

In discussing the trend towards one bishop being selected out of multiple presbyters, The Lion Handbook, The History of Christianity, p.118 says, "The bishop gradually emerged as undisputed leader of the Christian community;" and goes on to state some reasons for this trend:

- Congregations often needed one from the group of presbyters or bishops to take the initiative, or represent them – for example, by presiding at the Lord's Supper, contacting other churches, teaching, or guarding church property and offerings.
- One-man leadership was suggested by the roles played by the founding apostle or missionary, especially if he had settled in one place for an extended period

(The Lion Handbook, The History of Christianity, p.118)

The argument for a succession of teachers traceable back to the apostles also led towards one-man leadership. Cyprian (200-258 AD, Bishop of Carthage) championed the apostolic succession idea. "Now the apostles were seen as the first bishops, and bishops were called apostles." (*Lion, p.119*).

In the teaching of the twelve apostles as seen in the Didache, (see Doc 8, A New Eusebius) we read, "Elect for yourselves bishops and deacons worthy of the Lord, despise them not …". In that early teaching we see no hint of any so-called apostolic succession. The leadership was to be elected by the church members. But in Doc.203 we see Cyprian has moved a long way from that early apostolic teaching. Now he speaks of …

- The bishop having mounted to the lofty summit of the priesthood.
- the bishop being made up by the judgment of God and His Christ and the college of venerable bishops.
- the bishops chair being *traceable back to Peter.*
- the bishop's chair being a *sacerdotal chair.* Sacerdotal = pertaining to priesthood, to do with doctrines which assert the existence of an order of priests charged with sacrificial functions and invested with supernatural powers transmitted to them in ordination … (Oxford Universal Dictionary).

Jerome (347-420 AD) said, "With the ancients presbyters were the same as bishops; but gradually all the responsibility was deferred to a single person, that the thickets of heresy might be rooted out. Therefore as presbyters know that *by the custom of the church,* they are subject to him who shall have been set over them, so let bishops be also aware that they are superior to presbyters *more owing to custom than to any actual ordinance of the Lord* (J R Cohu, The Evolution of the Christian Ministry, p.27).

Local churches were now fully under the command of one senior elder or bishop and the trend towards the clergy as we know it is nearly complete.

G. Emergence of the Bishop of Bishops

Along with this trend towards the exaltation of the bishop, came another movement towards establishing one bishop above all others. Tertullian writes scornfully of this move (C 217-22).

Christian modesty is being shaken to its foundations … I hear that there has even been an edict set forth, and a peremptory one too. The Sovereign Pontiff (!) – the Bishop of bishops – issues an edict. (New Eusebius., Doc 154).

Cyprian also speaks scathingly of the movement … "For no one of us sets himself up as a bishop of bishops, or by tyrannical terror forces his colleagues to a necessity of obeying … " (Doc. 218. N.E., Cyprian, 256AD). By the mid 300's Rome is claiming pre-eminence (Doc.4 Creeds, Councils and Controversies).

By 367-77 AD, Rome is really gaining ascendancy. In AD336-7, Jerome appeals to Damascus, the Bishop of Rome ...

"I think it is my duty to consult the chair of Peter, and to turn to a Church whose faith has been praised by Paul. I appeal for spiritual food to the Church whence I took upon myself the garb of Christ. Rome is the fruitful soil that bears a hundred-fold, in the East the seed is choked. The West has the light of the Sun of Righteousness, the East has the light of Lucifer, who has once more set his throne above the stars (Isa. 14:12). Yet, though your greatness terrifies me, your kindness attracts me. From the priest I demand the safe keeping of the victim, from the shepherd the protection due the sheep ... My words are spoken to the successor of the fishermen, to the disciple of the Cross. As I follow no leader save Christ, so I communicate with none but your blessedness, that is, with the chair of Peter. For this, I know, is the rock on which the Church is built. This is the ark of Noah, and he who is not found in it shall perish when the flood prevails. (Doc 143, Creeds, Councils and Controversies).

Finally, hear the Roman Emperor Valentinian III, 445 AD, order even civil leaders to obey the authority of the Roman Pontiff (Doc 234, Creeds, Councils and Controversies). The journey to the dark side of things is now complete! Here is the loss of laity in the pulpits and government of a Church which was founded on tax gatherers, fishermen and carpenters.

"The long history of the church, until the Protestant Reformation (for some churches) and the mid-twentieth century (for others), is, with few exceptions, the tale of the takeover of the whole Church by an increasingly powerful – and at times ruthless and corrupt – clerical minority. Overbearing clerical power gradually but steadily and relentlessly forced the lay majority to relinquish their place in the priesthood of the Church in favor of those who were masters of ritual, clothed like kings, who alone had access to the world beyond the chancel steps and the rood screen. And as the laity lost their understanding of themselves as the priestly people of God, clergy developed for themselves 'a whole sacramental theology of worship and a mystique of priestly consecration'." (Anne Rowthorn, "The Liberation of the Laity", p.21)

By the time of the Reformation the clergy had all but destroyed the Church and its royal priesthood – the priesthood of all believers.

"The full-bodied understanding of the Christian community as the loving fellowship of the priesthood of all believers had been buried under a thousand years of increasing clericalism, excess, corruption and abuse" (Rowthorn, p.37).

The above is an attempt at a skeleton outline of the process which saw the sidelining of the **laity** and the emergence of the **clergy** into the situation which we know so well today.

H. Ordination

One final word needs to be added to finish this chapter. It is the word "ordain" or other related words, such as ordination. As noted in several of the quotes above, the words "ordained" or "ordination" came to be especially applied to those "ordained into the clergy". Over the centuries there arose false concepts of ordination which gave superior ecclesiastical authority and power to the clergy – those who were ordained.

The word "ordain" is a New Testament word, but over time, words lose meaning, or the meanings are changed. This is what happened to the word "ordain".

Ordination = "the public setting apart of someone to ministry, or the solemn induction by the Church into leadership". Such is the basic definition of its meaning in Church manuals in our day.

- Paul and Barnabas ordained elders in every church (Acts 14:23).
- Titus was told to ordain elders in every city (Titus 1:5).
- Timothy was also told by the apostle Paul never to be in a hurry to ordain an elder (1 Tim.5:22).
- Jesus ordained the Twelve before sending them out to preach the Gospel of the Kingdom (Mrk.3:14).
- He told them they were ordained to bring forth fruit (Jhn.15:16).
- Paul says he was ordained to be a preacher and teacher (1 Tim.2:7).

Ordination was the setting aside of someone to responsibility in the Church, but it was not the setting aside to be in any spiritually superior or dictatorial position of power and control over the people of God, such as is seen in some denominations today, e.g., Romanism, High Anglican Churches, and some of the Orthodox Churches.

Following are some brief quotations which show the abuse of this word "ordination" and the usurpation over believers, robbing them of their priestly ministry in the Body of Christ, and the Priesthood of all Believers. It shows the abusive power and control by the clergy over the laity, of those thus ordained.

1. **Pope Gregory XVI** – AD. 1831-46
   "No one can deny that the Church is an unequal society in which God destined some to be governors and others to be servants. The latter are

the laity; the former clergy" (Anne Rowthorn, The Liberation of the Laity, p.8).

2. **From a Papal Encyclical** – Pope Pius X – AD.1906 basically follows the same as Pope Gregory.
"The Church essentially is an unequal society. That is, it is a society formed by two categories of persons: pastors and flock ... As far as the multitude is concerned, they have no other duty than to let themselves be led". (Anne Rowthorn, The Liberation of the Laity, p.8).

3. **From Vatican II**
"The priesthood of the ordained is different from that of the whole church 'in essence and not only in degree'. This essential difference is defined in terms of a 'sacred power' to bring about the Eucharistic sacrifice and rule God's people."

And again, "... there will never be a time when laymen and women are not on their knees before the altar and sitting before the pulpit ... lay people will always be a subordinate order in the Church". (Both quotes from Bulley, The Priesthood of Some Believers, pp10 and 11).

4. **Protestant Churches**
As a general rule, Protestant Churches, be they Evangelical or Pentecostal, do not hold ordination as seen in the above. Though there may be some kind of inauguration service, with exhortation and prayer, and possibly the laying on of hands, there is not that mystical power given to any leader, be they senior minister, elder or deacon, as in the Roman, Anglican or Orthodox Churches. There is a basic belief in "the priesthood of all believers", though it may not be emphasized or practiced.

However, the danger of a 'Protestant-form-of-Romanism' is always present and many cases of abuse could be referred to. Some exercise power over their flock by saying "I'm the pastor, and you do what I say'. Some are 'loners' and have no checks and balances in their leadership. Some churches have gone to the other extreme and have a 'Board of Deacons' or 'Business Board' which may 'hire or fire' the dominant leader on a yearly basis. Others reacting against this kind of bureaucracy move to a 'democratic' type of Church government, the rule of the people.

But enough has been written relative to Church History, showing as briefly as possible, the apostasy from that Faith once delivered to the saints, and the decline over Church History to where the Church is generally at today. The issue is: "The Priesthood of All Believers" has been almost lost to the Church and God desires to see this restored.

All believers are redemptively equal though they may be functionally different according to their place as members of the Priestly Body of Christ in the earth.

PART TWO – THE REFORMATION PERIOD

Chapter 4   The Dark Ages, Recovery and Reformation

CHAPTER 4 - THE DARK AGES, RECOVERY AND REFORMATION

With the apostasy from the faith once delivered to the saints and the rapid decline of the Church into two classes of people – Clergy and Laity – the Church lost its power and divine influence.

A. The Dark Ages

One of the Reformers is reported as referring to this period of time, from the 4th and 5th Century to AD.1500 (approximately) as the Church's "Dark Ages". This period lasted over some 1000 years. This same period is also spoken of as the Church's "Babylonian Captivity", because of the suppressed condition of the people of God. A major factor in this suppression was the people of God becoming known as "the laity", which automatically gave them a rank and function inferior and subordinate to the "ordained ministry". In the following we see a brief sketch of the characteristics and conditions over this time.

Words, true or false, good or bad, accurate or inaccurate, paint pictures in our mind's eye. Sadly, many Bible words through misuse, abuse and lack of knowledge, paint false pictures in our minds. ***"Priest"*** is one such word. What images are evoked in your mind when you hear this word? The chances are, pictures of men with round white collars, or wearing flowing robes and strange head gear, or waving candles or containers of incense come before you. This would be an accurate image if we consider the way the word is normally used, but is it Biblically true and accurate, and does it really matter anyway?

It is the conviction of this study that these images are not only inconsistent with the Biblical concept but are a major limiting factor in the life, health and expansion of the New Testament Church. Roman Catholic, Episcopalian/Anglican, the ethnic Orthodox denominations and various other churches have priests who to some degree fit the traditional images mentioned above. It is of course from such sources that we get these images. This is not a criticism of such denominations, but simply the way it mostly is. The clergy have been set apart from the laity in dress, vocation and function. They are ordained by their denomination and there is a clear difference between the two parties.

This difference is seen by many as qualitative (once ordained they are actually in a different class or species of minister) rather than merely quantitative (same in kind but different in degrees of skill). The priest is paid to preach and pray while the parishioners parade their attributes, skills and abilities mostly outside the church. The priests are the professionals who are expected to do the 'God-business', thereby releasing adherents to pursue secular careers and come along to the Sunday gathering to contribute with their earnings and their presence. Many in Christendom believe this is a convenient arrangement. All too often (there are of course many exceptions) under the clergy-priestly system little is required of the laity other than to show up, put some money in and not disturb the smooth running of the group. We see this concept of the priesthood emerging in most of the quotes in previous chapters.

Within Evangelical and Pentecostal/Charismatic Christianity (which generally embraces the idea of the "every-believer-priesthood") the leaders of Churches have a variety of styles. Some are highly autocratic and directive, and in a theology not far removed from clericalism, see themselves as standing between God and their people. *"Their people need them ... how else can the sheep hear from God or get His counsel?"* Others strenuously reject this idea and expend no little effort encouraging their people to seek God for themselves.

B. The Recovery of Truth

But things were not to remain as they were in the period of the "dark ages". The Lord had promised through the prophets and apostles that the truths which had been lost over this period would be restored to the people of God. Lost truths would be recovered.

Hear the Prophet Joel (Joel 2:25). "So I will restore to you the years that the swarming locust has eaten, the crawling locust, the consuming locust, and the chewing locust …" (NKJV). The years of the "dark ages" were years that were lost. The priesthood of all believers, the gifts of the Holy Spirit, justification by faith, along with many other truths – all seemed to have been eaten away by the spiritual locusts that had gotten into the Church, destroying the truths. But God promised to restore those lost years.

Hear the Apostle Peter (Acts 3:19-21). "Repent therefore and be converted, that your sins may be blotted out, so that times of refreshing may come from the presence of the Lord … whom heaven must receive until the times of restoration of all things, which God has spoken by the mouth of all His holy prophets since the world began". Thus there were to come "**seasons of refreshing**" and "**times of restoration**" from the presence of the Lord. There would come times of restoration of lost truths, and lost years, to the Church. The faith once delivered to the saints would be recovered. All would be restored to His Church. This recovery of lost truth began with the period of the Reformation. Many were the Reformers. Martin Luther seems to be the bright star in the Reformation period.

C. The Reformation Period

Scholars of the Reformation speak of three great principles coming out of that movement. These three principles were:

1. The Authority of the Word of God – the Bible
2. Salvation by Grace alone,
3. The Priesthood of every Believer.

During research prior to this study, one major Christian bookshop was visited. There was not one single book on the shelf which dealt with the topic of the **Priesthood of the Believer**. Over a period of time, two different assistants were asked for help. They had never heard of such a thing. They were both very helpful and scanned the computers looking for anything on the topic. After a diligent search they came up with three titles which contained the words "priesthood" and "believer"; one of which was no longer in print, the others not immediately available. This speaks for itself, showing that this is indeed a neglected or forgotten subject among believers, and more especially Church leaders.

In any Protestant, Evangelical, Charismatic or Pentecostal church on any given Sunday, we are likely to hear reference to two of the great reformation principles, namely the ***authority of God's Word*** and ***salvation by grace alone.*** But when was the last time we heard someone teach on the ***priesthood of the believer*** and the hindrance of the clergy to Christian life and growth? And even if this topic is actually mentioned, it is often dealt with in such a way as to enforce the idea of a graded spirituality where the laity still has some dependence on the leadership to do their 'God-business'.

It may be asked: Why is there such a plethora of preachers and books dealing with two of the three great Reformation principles and such a dearth of the third? If one lets one's mind wander, it would be very easy to come up with some possible reasons, but none of these would be edifying.

On this doctrine of the priesthood of all believers, one of the most famous of the reformers, Martin Luther, is quoted as follows:

"Where the Word of God is preached and believed, there is true faith, that (certain) immovable rock; and where faith is, there is the bride of Christ; and where the bride of Christ is, there is also everything that belongs to the bridegroom. Thus faith has everything in its train that is implied in it, keys. sacraments, power, and everything else." … and …

"All of us who are Christians have this office of the keys in common."
… and …
"Every Christian has the power the pope, bishops, priests and monks have, namely, to forgive or not to forgive sins …"   … and …

"For clericalism tends to identify the church with the priestly-sacramental clergy to such an extent that it is no longer, in fact or conception, the people of God. Modern Roman Catholicism, for example, finds it most difficult to interpret the church as the people of God when, by defining it as the corpus Christi mysticism, it bases its reality on the sacraments and the priests … the sacraments can be and are celebrated even if there is no congregation present".
        Wilhelm Pauck, in "The Heritage of the Reformation", pp105-106

Pauck comments, "In other words, a man of faith has all the spiritual powers which in Roman Catholicism belonged to the clergy alone. (p.105).

So at the time of the reformation, and still even now in this modern age, in many branches of Christendom, the New Testament imagery of the Body of Christ consisting of all the individual members, all playing their part, no matter how insignificant they may be, was all set aside. The Church, the Body of Christ as we know it, doesn't even have to be present. Any ordained cleric dispensing sacraments to silent seats constitutes the Church.

Reading the History of the Reformation, one cannot help but be shocked and impacted by the abuses which emanated out of this understanding of the Church. When Biblical truth, the very truths of God, are lowered to the point where they are subjugated to the words and authority of the clerics, any abuse is possible. This is not to say all the clergy were bad or corrupt. They were just so indoctrinated with the theology of the Church they knew little or nothing of Bible truth and didn't really care anyway. The Reformers took strong exception to this state of affairs. Many began to take issue with Church theology which attributed so much power and authority to clerics, regardless of their Biblical knowledge and lifestyle.

Hear the remark of one man who risked his life to translate the New Testament into English:

William Tyndale noted the ignorance of the local clergy and said to one cleric, "If God spare my life, ere many years pass, I will cause a boy that drives the plough shall know more of the Scriptures than thou dost". (The

History of Christianity, p.370).   Such was the clerical and religious system of that era.

IN SUMMARY:
The New Testament teaches about Church Office and Church government, but it leaves absolutely no room whatsoever for any priestly class who stand between God and His people. There is intercession; there is government; there are specialized gifts of ministries; but as for clergy/laity in the institutionalized religious way, there is absolutely no basis for their existence in the New Testament! In fact the very word translated as "**clergy**" is the Greek **kleros** and this is seen in various texts as applying to the rank-and-file Christian believer.

For example:
1. Acts 26:18 a *share* (from **kleros**) among those being sanctified by faith
2. Col.1:12 the *inheritance or allotment* (from **kleros**) of the saints (all believers)
3. 1 Pet.5:3 those *allotted or assigned* (from **kleros**) to your care.

Are you born anew of the Spirit of God? Have you taken your place in the New Testament Church? Then you have an *inheritance, share* or *allotment* (all from **kleros**) in Christ along with every other believer from popes to paupers. You are God's clergy. He knows of no priesthood other than the one you have taken your share in. There will be others who know more than you and are perhaps further advanced in their spirituality and service than you, but none of them can lay claim to any more authority with God than is available to you. By birthright you belong to God's royal priesthood.

To have a priestly caste as the religious professionals who do the 'God-business' for others is wrong on at least six counts.

1. It has no New Testament basis and is in fact contrary to the mood of the Scriptures.

2. It badly weakens and limits the ministry of the New Testament Church. There are many people who are blessed with gifting from God but if these have to put their gifts aside in deference to the clergy those gifts are nullified, and the Church is weaker for it.

3. It makes the same mistake as the Israelites who were content to put someone between them and God and thereby forfeit their high and royal calling.

4. It devalues the potency of the supernatural new birth experience. Christians who have experienced this life transforming phenomenon are children of royalty … children of the King. As such they have access straight to their Father who delights in meeting with them all individually. As soon as someone steps in between them and their Abba Father one of the main privileges of the regeneration experience is lost and the Spirit-born Christian never occupies his/her proper place.

5. It also explains why and how some who express their Christianity by laying claim to membership in their particular denominations can live an evil lifestyle all week, spruce up nicely for the Sunday gathering and not see any problem with the large gap between their faith and their behavior. To the un-churched, such people are hypocrites. Those who believe the Bible to be the ultimate authority in matters of life and faith would also see an inherent hypocrisy in such professors of Christianity. But to the person who has taken a position underneath the clergy and who trusts that authority implicitly, there is no problem. They believe, in keeping with the quote from Pius X, that by giving the clergy free reign, by following their lead and by faithful attendance, they have fulfilled their religious obligations. Many neither know nor care what the Bible says about moral and ethical issues. To them it is Church membership, the sacraments administered by the clergy and regular, faithful attendance which matters. While many Christians see this as incredibly blind and deluded, many members of clergy-controlled Christendom have no such concerns.

6. Lastly, and worst of all, the idea that any believer needs anyone other than Christ to mediate between her/him and God is an insult to the mediating work of Christ on the cross. We may intercede for one another before God, but the worst sinner who has "put on Christ" has as much right to appear directly before God the Father as the archbishop, pastor or pope. *"For there is one God, and one mediator between God and men, the man Christ Jesus"* (1 Tim.2:5).

Every Christian is meant to be a royal priest. Every Christian has access to God. Every Christian can and must do his/her own 'God-business'. Every Christian must employ their gifting to minister to others. We may all seek help at times. We may all take counsel, teaching and advice. But to put anyone between us and God, other than the man Christ Jesus is to do what the Israelites did in evading their spiritual calling and responsibility.

The Anglican teacher and author Michael Green in his book "Freed to Serve", Hodder and Stoughton, 1994, p.31 writes of: "… no hard and fast distinction between clergy and laymen in the New Testament. All alike are the servants and ministers of God. The New Testament offers us a Church full of ministers!"

But this brief history of the Church through the Reformation now brings us to **"What Say the Scriptures"** on the Priesthood of all Believers?

PART THREE - WHAT SAY THE SCRIPTURES?

Chapter 5   Progressive Revelation of Priesthood
Chapter 6   A Kingdom of Priests
Chapter 7   Levels in the Will of God

CHAPTER 5 - PROGRESSIVE REVELATION OF PRIESTHOOD

In our previous chapters, we have seen God's original purpose in and for the Church in this dispensation of the Holy Spirit.

We considered the apostasy and decline of the Church over its history, from the faith once delivered to the saints. The Church entered the period of the "dark ages", or, as it was also called "the Church's Babylonian Captivity."

But God, in His grace and mercy called His faithful remnant 'out of Babylon' (spiritual and religious confusion) and began to restore the truths lost over the years in that decline. The Reformation period was the beginning – and only the beginning – of the recovery of truth.

But this brings us to our present and future chapters: "What Say the Scriptures?" especially concerning the Priesthood, and here, the theme of this textbook, "The Priesthood of All Believers".

A. Progressive Revelation

A study of the Scriptures, as a whole, shows us that there was a progressive revelation and unfolding of the truth of Priesthood. It is seen first in the Old Testament and then follows through in a new manner in the New Testament.

1. Patriarchal Priesthood

The offering of sacrifices to God and prayer for family constituted Patriarchal Priesthood. The father of the house acted as priest of the household, the house of faith. This is seen in the examples as given here.

- Job offered sacrifice and intercessions to God on behalf of his family, his sons and daughters (Job 1:1-5).
- Adam, after the Fall, must also have told his sons Cain and Abel that the only way of approach to God was through blood sacrifice. The very fact that God clothed Adam and Eve in the coats of skin provided through sacrifice actually constituted priesthood in the household. Abel accepted the 'gospel of blood atonement' and Cain rejected it (Gen.3-4 with Heb.11:4 and 1 Jhn.3:10-15).
- Noah, after the Flood, built an altar to the Lord and offered clean sacrifices to God on that altar (Gen.8). This was by the commandment of the Lord.

- Abraham, Isaac and Jacob, as the 'three fathers of Israel' also had their altars built to God and made offerings to God as was required.

These were the Patriarchs, the fathers of the whole race, Adam, Noah and then Abraham, the father of the chosen race. As the fathers, they were responsible to God for their families.

2. **Melchizedek Priesthood**

    In Gen.14:18-20, Melchizedek met Abraham as he was returning from the battle of the kings. This mysterious person ministered to Abraham (Abram then) communion – bread and wine – and Abraham gave him tithes of the spoils of the battle. Note the timing of this event. This time in Abram's life and this section of scripture is rich in covenant language and symbol. There is God's promise to Abraham in Gen.12:1-3 and 7 along with the blessings pronounced by Melchizedek in 14:18-20. There is the making (literally, "cutting") of the covenant (15:17) which involved the promise of the land (15:18). And at this significant time of the forming of the Abrahamic Covenant which would affect the world until the closing of the age, the mysterious figure of the king-priest Melchizedek arrives upon the scene and receives tithes from Abraham. Melchizedek is not mentioned again in Scripture until Psalm 110 and then the truth is developed more in the Book of Hebrews. This will be seen more fully in a later chapter. Melchizedek was a King-Priest. By this time, there were other nations who held the concept, office and function of King-Priests.

3. **National Priesthood**

    Israel was chosen as a nation. God's purpose was that this nation be unto Him and in the earth "a kingdom of priests." Israel was called "the Church in the wilderness" (Acts 7:38; Ex.19:1-6). God wanted the nation to obey His voice, keep His covenant and they would be God's peculiar treasure. But a whole chapter needs to be given to this matter.

4. **Aaronic and Levitical Priesthood**

    For reasons dealt with later, God chose the Tribe of Levi to be the priestly tribe to the rest of the 12 tribes of Israel. And within the tribe of Levi was the house of Aaron, chosen to be the High Priestly line. The prophecy of Moses over Levi was that the Urim and Thummim would be there, they would teach God's laws and judgments to Israel, sacrifice on God's altar and offer incense to

Him (Deut.33:8-11; Read carefully Num.1-2-3). This priestly tribe was to be supported by the tithes and offerings of Israel (Num.18). Aaron and the priests would wear the priestly garments.

5. **New Testament Priesthood**
   - Christ – The Head
     The theme of the Book of Hebrews is Christ, our Great High Priest (Heb.5-6-7). He is also priest upon the throne. He is King-Priest and this after the Order of Melchizedek (Psa.110). He is our 'Joshua', and He builds the Temple of the Lord, the counsel of peace being between both offices of King and Priest (Zech.6:9-15 Amp). But more on this in a later chapter!

   - Church – The Body
     The following Scriptures show that the Church, the Body of Christ, is also called to be a "kingdom of priests" (or "kings and priests") to God and to His Christ. This under the New Covenant includes both men and women (1 Pet.2:9; Rev.1:6; 5:9, 10; 20:4,6). It is a holy priesthood, a royal priesthood to offer up sacrifices to God. The prophet Isaiah says that they would be called priests of the Lord and servants of our God (Isa.61:6).

   In the New Testament the Gospel of Matthew shows Christ as King and the Book of Hebrews shows Christ as Priest. As we consider these things, we discover a progressive revelation and unfolding of the Priesthood (Prov.29:18 Swedish Translation with Hab.2:1,2).

On the cross, the veil of the Temple was torn from top to bottom. The Old Covenant Priesthood of Aaron and Levi was fulfilled and abolished, the New Covenant Priesthood of Christ and His Church came into effect. It is a Priesthood after the order of Melchizedek and all that that means. The enemy of Christ and His Church has opposed the Church coming fully into this ministry of Kings and Priests and thus we have seen the decline into the dark ages of Church History. But all that was to change in the mind of God!

B. The Covenants
Each of these 'priesthoods' involved God's progressive revelation and unfolding of His covenants to His people also. Priesthood belongs to covenant.

- Patriarchal – Adam – Priest in his house – Adamic Covenant
- Patriarchal – Job – Priest in his house
- Patriarchal – Noah – Priest in his house – Noahic Covenant
- Patriarchal – Abraham – Priest in his house – Abrahamic Covenant
- Melchizedek – King and Priest in the one person
- Aaronic and Levitical – Priestly tribe in a chosen nation – Covenant of Levi – Mosaic Covenant
- Christ – Priest after the Order of Melchizedek (Psa.110 with Heb.7). The New Covenant
- The Church – the Body of Christ, kings and priests to God and Christ after the Order of Melchizedek. To bless all nations. The New Covenant.

SUMMARY:

We see from this that the doctrine of the Royal Priesthood is not some new idea of God's. It has always been in His purposes and there has been a progressive unfolding and revelation of the priesthood from the beginning until now in this New Testament age.

CHAPTER 6 - A KINGDOM OF PRIESTS

Scriptures to Read: Ex.19:1-6 with Acts 7:38 (KJV/NKJV).

INTRODUCTORY:
In the Book of Exodus, we see how God delivered the nation of Israel from Egyptian bondage with a strong and mighty hand. He took a nation from the midst of another nation, and the nations, by the power of redemption (Deut.4:32-36). He wanted to work in them and through them to bless the nations of the earth. Redemption always has a purpose.

Israel was called "the CHURCH (or Congregation) in the wilderness" (Acts 7:38). The Greek is *"ekklesia"* the congregation or the Church. The nation was chosen to be the instrument for the revelation and demonstration of the kingdom of God in the earth. Paul tells us that various things happened to them for types and examples to us and these things are written for our admonition upon whom the ends of the previous ages have come (1 Cor.10:6,11).

A consideration of the passage in Ex.19:1-6 provides much food for thought. The apostle Peter basically takes the same purpose of God for Israel and then applies it to the New Testament Church as "the royal priesthood."

Note: When Israel left their captivity in Egypt (Ex.12) God told them to celebrate that great event with a feast ... called the Feast of Passover. Fifty days later they came to Mt Sinai (Ex.19) and God gave them the ten commandments (Ex.20). This great event where they received the Law became celebrated as the Feast of Pentecost (*"Pentecost"* means the *fiftieth day*) or "the Feast of Weeks". So Pentecost comes fifty days after Passover.

A. The Feast of Pentecost – Ex.19:1,2
   1. **The Mountain**
      Israel's spiritual life was governed by the Feasts of the Lord. The nation experienced the power of redemption in Egypt in the Feast of Passover. The nation has been brought miraculously through the Red Sea, led by the Cloudy Pillar of God to camp before Mt Sinai. This was according to the word of the Lord spoken to Moses by the Lord out of the burning bush (Ex.3:1,2). Mt Sinai was also Mt Horeb, the mount of God and the token given to Moses. Israel would serve God at this mountain.

   2. **The Third Month**
      As noted, Passover was in the first month, the beginning of months, the beginning of the sacred year (Ex.12). This meant deliverance through the Passover lamb. Pentecost (as we know it – Acts 2:1), took

place in the third month (Lev.23). All pointed to Christ our Passover Lamb (1 Cor.5 with the Gospels), which meant deliverance from the bondage of sin. Then Pentecost pointed to the descent of the Holy Spirit, our Pentecost (Acts 2).

B. The Purpose of Pentecost – Ex.19:3,4

1. Egypt's Judgments

God talked to Moses in the Mount. He reminded him to tell Israel what He had done to the Egyptians and how He had judged the gods of Egypt in the plague-judgments (Ex.7-12, especially Ex.12:12). It was a judgment on the false gods of Egypt. Here at Mt. Sinai the Lord wanted to declare His purpose for the nation, and this at the Feast of Pentecost.

2. Eagles Wings

The Lord bore Israel on 'eagles' wings' out of Egypt. This was symbolic of His delivering power. The Lord used the eagle in its role with the young eaglets to describe His own dealings with Israel. "I bare you on eagle's wings …" (Deut.32:11).

As the eagle stirs its comfortable nest, picks it to pieces, so that the eaglets would fly, so the Lord did to Israel. They were almost getting comfortable in Egypt, so the Lord picked their nest to pieces. They would be brought on His wings to Sinai to hear the purpose of their redemption.

3. Unto Myself

His desire was to bring Israel "unto Myself". The whole purpose of delivering Israel from Egyptian bondage was to bring the nation into a personal relationship with Himself. He would be their God. They would be His people. It was symbolic of the marriage relationship by covenant, and He would be "a husband to them" (Jer.31:31-34). Unto Him would the gathering of the people be (Gen.49:10). Such also is God's purpose in New Covenant relationship.

C. The Purpose of God for Israel – Ex.19:5,6

In these verses, we see God's plan and purpose for Israel, the Old Testament Church in the wilderness. Israel, as the Old Testament Church, was called to be the instrument for the revelation and demonstration of God's kingdom in earth, and all that is meant by that word. Note seven particular things in this purpose of God for Israel which God spoke through Moses.

1. **Obey My Voice**
   "Now if you will obey My voice ... then ..." (Ex.19:5 with Jer.7:21-28). The issue here as the foundation for relationship was obedience. If you will obey My voice. It is the first law of the kingdom. Adam disobeyed the word of the Lord (Gen.2:16, 17; 3:1-6 with Rom.5:12-21). By one man's disobedience, all were made sinners. By one man's obedience, we can be made righteous. There would be blessings upon obedience. A. Murray writes: "Christ died to bring us back to the obedience from which Adam fell." Read also Isa.42:24; Gen.22:12,18; Heb.5:8; Jhn.14:15-23; 1Pet.1:2,22; Isa.1:19,20. God wanted Israel simply to "obey My voice". If we love Him, we will keep His commandments. It is the obedience of love.

2. **Keep My Covenant**
   It may be asked: Which covenant is the Lord talking about? The Mosaic or Law Covenant had not yet been given. The only covenant they knew about mainly was the Abrahamic Covenant. It was on the basis of this covenant they had been delivered from Egypt (Ex.2:24,25; 3:11-16; 6:1-8). God is a covenant-making and covenant-keeping God. Israel was to keep the covenant, even as Abraham, Isaac and Jacob did (Gen.17:9-14; Acts 7:8). It was called the Covenant of circumcision and it was to be kept in their generations. If they failed to do this, they had broken the covenant. The Abrahamic Covenant was a covenant of grace and faith. The seal of covenantal relationship was circumcision (Gen.17:1-11; 18:19).

3. **A Peculiar Treasure** – Psa.135:4; Deut.14:2; 26:18; Eccl.2:8)
   Israel was to be a peculiar (special, as a jewel) treasure to the Lord above all people. He had chosen Israel for Himself, to be His special treasure. Israel was, in Old Testament times, like "the treasure hid in the field" (Matt.13:44). Peter speaks of the New Testament Church as God's treasure also. The "peculiar treasure" of the Old Testament becomes the "peculiar people" of the New Testament (1Pet.2:5-9). The people of God are special to Him, being beyond the usual, belonging exclusively to God.

4. **All the Earth is Mine**
   The earth is the Lord's, the fullness thereof, and all those who dwell in it (Psa.24:1-2). The earth is His possession. He gave to the different nations their inheritance, according to the number of the children of Israel (Deut.32:8; Acts 17:26-28). Israel is God's chosen nation, but all the earth and the nations of the earth are His. They are under the sovereignty of the Lord. God's purpose for Israel is that they bless the nations of the earth. All nations were to be blessed through the chosen

nation. Israel was actually chosen to be the 'missionary nation' to the nations of the world, not merely to be blessed (Rom.9:1-6; 3:1-3). They were blessed above all nations of the earth; blessed to bless!

5. **A Kingdom**

Israel was called to be "a kingdom …" The word "kingdom" = "kingdom", or king's domain, a king's subject. Israel was to be God's kingdom in the earth; His subjects, His citizens, over which God would rule and reign as their King. It was to be a theocratic kingdom. Israel was His Church, yet also to be His Kingdom. The Lord wanted to establish His kingdom in earth and have Israel to illustrate and demonstrate the laws and the power of that Kingdom of God in the earth. His rule, His reign, His power and authority would be seen in the chosen nation. His Laws would be obeyed. God gave them His laws for the kingdom to run harmoniously. There was the Moral Law, the Civil Laws, the Health and Hygiene Laws and the Ceremonial Laws. Israel would be a blessed, healthy and happy nation as they obeyed the laws of the Kingdom (Psa.144:12-15). All the Gentile nations would see what a great and blessed nation Israel was because of obedience to His kingdom laws. It would be a just and moral nation, law-abiding citizens of God's kingdom. It would be a practical demonstration of the kingdom in the earth. The kingdom of God is righteousness, peace and joy in the Holy Spirit (Rom.14:17).

6. **Priests unto God**

The concept of priests and priesthood was common in ancient cultures. The Israelites would have been familiar with the idea. Priests were religious specialists, the specially gifted and knowledgeable ones about the gods and their worship. But God wanted Israel to "know their God" and His character of holiness. And here God wanted the whole nation to be "kings and priests" unto Him. Or, in other words, a "kingdom of priests." The other nations would take notice of Israel and say, What a great and holy God they serve! Note these references that show God's intended purpose for Israel was "that the people would know the true God of Israel (Deut.4:6; 26:17-19; 1Kgs.8:41-43,60; Isa.43:7,21; 44:23; 60:1-3; 61:3; Jer.13:11).

The only priesthood they knew about was the visit to Abraham of Melchizedek, who was a King-Priest unto God. Therefore they were to be a "kingdom of priests" unto God. In other words, they were offered the "Order of Melchizedek". This would be the fulfillment of being a kingdom of priests. Kingship would mean rule, reign, dominion, authority, government. Priesthood would mean prayer, intercession, sacrifice and worship. All this is what God presented to Israel in this passage.

7. **A Holy Nation**
The nations of the earth, the Gentile nations, were anything but holy. "Holiness unto the Lord" was to be impressed on the nation of Israel. Other nations were evil, unholy, corrupt, immoral, idolatrous and under demonic influence. Holiness was to be stamped on the chosen nation of Israel. Israel was to be a holy nation. The word of the Lord in Leviticus to Israel was: "Be holy, for I the Lord your God am holy" (Lev.11:44; 20:26). The same word is spoken to the New Testament Church also (1Pet.1:15, 16). The Lord is holiness personified (Ex.15:11; 28:36; 39:30). He wants a holy people. They would worship the Lord in the beauty of holiness (1Chr.16:29; Psa.29:2). The revelation given to the prophet Isaiah was that of a thrice holy God. "Holy, holy, holy …" (Isa.6:3). They would have holy garments, holy days, holy feasts, a holy place as a holy nation. Without holiness no man would see the Lord (Heb.12:14).

In summary we may say: At the beginning of God's dealings with His people on earth He chose a nation to be uniquely His above all other nations on earth (Ex.19:1-6). He mightily delivered them from slavery in Egypt and revealed His desire for the whole nation. *"I brought you to Myself; out of the nations I took you to be my treasured possession, I want you to be a kingdom of priests and a holy nation."*

The concept of kings, priests and priesthood was common in ancient cultures. The Israelites would have been entirely familiar with such an idea. Priests were the religious specialists, the specially gifted and knowledgeable about the gods and their worship. But from the very beginning, this was not to be so in God's chosen nation. God wanted a body of people where there were no human religious specialists. Every individual Israelite was to be a priest in his own right. But if they all were priests, on whose behalf did they act? If a priest is meant to come before God and do religious things on behalf of other people who would these other people be? The bottom line is that every Israelite was to walk with God and be a living demonstration of the attributes and values of a Holy God in a corrupt and fallen world.

The moral and ethical standards they embodied would set them apart and cause them to shine like a beacon in the darkness. The other nations of the world would then take notice and glorify God.

Inasmuch as they were to represent (re-present or present again) God to the nations, they had a high and royal calling and a royal heritage, thus fulfilling the royal or kingly aspect of Exodus 19:6. In their mediatory function where they could lead other nations and peoples into the presence of God, they would fulfill their priestly function. So God's original heart's desire and intention was for a unique people to be His royal priesthood amidst all the nations of the world and glorify Him.

D. Their Failure to Fulfill God's Purpose

Something tragic happened in Israel! Instead of the whole nation becoming a kingdom of priests after the "Order of Melchizedek", God instituted the Aaronic and Levitical Priesthood and this through one single tribe out of Israel, the tribe of Levi! Was this what God meant by Israel becoming a "kingdom of priests"? Certainly not. But this needs to be considered before moving to our next chapter.

A careful reading of the following verses and their context provides the basis for our thoughts. Moses has been in the Mount of God. God has spoken these tremendous words concerning His purpose for the nation. Moses comes down from Mt Sinai. He calls the elders and the people and told them the words of the Lord (Ex.19:7). What is their response?

These references tell us.

1. "All that the Lord has spoken we will do ..." (Ex.19:8)
2. The people said to Moses, " ...you speak with us, and we will hear; but let not God speak with us, lest we die" (Ex.20:18-21).
3. And again, "All the words which the Lord has said, we will do" (Ex.24:3).
4. And again, "All that the Lord has said we will do and be obedient" (Ex.24:7).
5. And once more the people say to Moses, "You go near and hear all that the Lord our God may say, and tell us all that the Lord our God says to you, and we will hear and do it" (Deut.5:27).

Note the two recurring themes here.
(i) Don't talk to us – talk to Moses, and (ii) All that the Lord says, we will do.

And what is the response of the Lord to their words?
"I have heard the voice of the words of this people which they have spoken to you. They are right in all they have spoken. <u>Oh, that they had such a heart in them</u> that they would fear Me and always keep all My commandments, that it might be well with them and their children

forever!" Read carefully Deut.5:22-31, especially verses 27-30 and Deut.18:15-19).

There was nothing of dependence on the GRACE of the Lord. All they had experienced up to this time was God's grace. Bringing them out of Egypt, preservation through the plagues, the miraculous crossing of the Red Sea, the Cloudy Pillar of Fire leading and guiding them to Mt. Sinai – the manna and the waters from the rock – all had been by the GRACE of God. They did not even say they would keep His commandments and do all the words the Lord spoke to them *"by His grace!"* They are so self-sufficient.

They can still trust in themselves. They just do not understand the depth of their fallen and sinful human nature. They boastfully say, "All that the Lord says, we will do …" They just don't seem to realize that, apart from Divine grace, human nature is incapable of doing all that the Lord says.

A carefully reading of these passages as given show that, during and after the giving of the law the Israelites showed an incredible propensity towards self-will, disrespect and outright rebellion against God. Instinctively they knew that to stand in the direct presence of God and exercise this self-will would mean death. It was therefore far less dangerous and much more comfortable to send Moses up the mountain to deal with God while they pursued their own agendas and awaited Moses' return. They could then (so they thought) deal with Moses without standing in the terrible, exposing light of the perfect and holy God.

They exposed their need for a mediator – someone to stand between themselves and God. Typologically speaking, this elevation of Moses spoke of the coming Prophet (Jesus) who would take up His place between humanity and God as the one and only true Mediator between God and mankind. But in its original context these verses show a very human response to the holiness of God. Human nature is the same today. Every revival and visitation of the Lord proves the same.

The self-willed and self-sufficient Israelites could not bear the all-exposing searchlight of God's direct and immediate presence, so they sent Moses up the mountain to do the 'God-business' for them. Let another person deal directly with God and let them be released from their spiritual and personal responsibilities.

When they as a people said, anything God says, we will do, they forfeited their high calling to be a "kingdom of priests" – a royal priesthood – that God so desired. They settled for God's second best, namely, a priest caste who would stand between themselves and the Lord God. Thus God now chooses the tribe of Levi to be the priestly tribe and fulfill the priestly ministrations on behalf of the twelve tribes of Israel. They dropped to a secondary level in the purposes of God.

But God's purposes were not to be frustrated forever. The Levitical Priesthood was to be a temporary priesthood. God would still have a people who would fulfill His original plan and intentions. God never gave up on His original purpose. It was just put aside for a while. There would come another group of people, the spiritual Israel of God, and they would fulfill what Israel of old failed to fulfill. When Jesus came, He would fulfill and abolish all that was temporary in the Aaronic and Levitical Priesthood. He would build "His Church" against which the gates of Hades would not prevail (Matt.16:15-19). This New Testament Church would be brought back to the level of God's perfect and full will and do what "the Church in the wilderness" never really fulfilled. It would be by and through the grace of God in Christ.

The following comparisons of Old Testament Israel and the New Testament Church show how the New Covenant Church would fulfill what God's original intention was for the Old Covenant Church. The Scriptures listed in the appropriate columns confirm this along with a reading of these Scripture references.

God's people would be priests of the Lord and they would be called the Servants (the Ministers) of the Lord. They would be trees of righteousness (Isa.61:1-6; 1Pet.2:5-9; Rev 1:6; 5:9,10; 20:6). The New Covenant people would be called out of darkness into God's marvelous light to show forth His praises and be the light of the darkened world (Matt.5:14-16).

Old Testament Israel	New Testament Church
The Prophet Moses – Ex.19:1-6	**The Apostle Peter – 1 Pet.2:1-10**
1. Obey My Voice 2. Keep My Covenant 3. A Peculiar Treasure to Me 4. All the Earth is Mine 5. You shall be a Kingdom 6. Of Priests unto Me 7. And a Holy Nation	1. Obedience to the Lord's words 2. Keep My Covenant (New Covenant) 3. A Peculiar People to Me 4. Make disciples of all Nations 5. Royal (a Kingdom) 6. A Holy Priesthood 7. A Holy Nation

Without doubt, Peter is referring to God's original intention for the Nation of Israel. Most of Peter's language, under inspiration of the Spirit, is adapted from the passage in Exodus. God's purpose, though apparently side-tracked for a time, will be fulfilled. The New Testament Church is called to be "a kingdom of priests", or "kings and priests" after the Order of Melchizedek. It is a holy and royal priesthood, God's holy nation in the nations of the earth. It is God's 'missionary Church' to the nations of the earth. Out of every kindred, tongue, tribe and nation there will be those who are called into that kingdom of priests, as the Scriptures here confirm. They will be named the Priests and Ministers of the Lord.

What a high and holy calling, what a noble calling is placed upon every believer who is in New Covenant relationship with God through our Lord Jesus Christ, to be a king and priest unto God.

CHAPTER 7 - LEVELS IN THE WILL OF GOD

Scripture: Rom.12:1-2

The more one studies the Word of God; it appears that there are different levels in the overall will of God as the following study hopefully shows.

A. The Sovereign Will of God
Sometimes spoken of as "the pre-determinate will of God", where the will of God will be done in heaven or earth or in the universe, regardless of angelic beings or humankind. God is absolutely sovereign. He rules and reigns over all things. He can cause men or rulers to do His will regardless. Two examples illustrate this fact.

1. The crucifixion of Jesus was in the determinate counsel and sovereign will of God as these Scriptures confirm (Jhn.19:10-11; Acts 2:23-24; Lke.22:22; Acts 4:27-28; 13:29-31; 17:26-27). He also determined beforehand the bounds of the nations before they even existed (Deut.32:8).

2. The ten kings of the Anti-Christ kingdom fulfill God's sovereign will as seen in Rev.17:17. "For God has put it into their hearts to fulfill His will (purpose), to be of one mind, and to give their kingdom to the beast, until the words of God are fulfilled."

Thus, without falling into fatalism (what will be will be), faith in the living God shows that God Himself is sovereign over all things, over the nations of the earth, and His will shall be done in spite of and regardless of man's free will.

B. God's will and Man's free will
When God created man (Adam and Eve), He created each with a free will, a will of their own. They had the power of choice. The Fall demonstrated this fact. Man chose to exercise his free will which was in reality self-will, which was also indirectly Satan's will (Gen.3:1-6). The angelic realm also had the power of choice, the exercise of free will. When Lucifer sinned, he exercised his free will as seen in the five "I will's" of Isa.14:12-14. Self-will is the root of all sins in the universe, both in heaven and on earth.

The purpose of God in redemption is to bring mankind back to the **good, acceptable and perfect will of God** (Rom.12:1-2).

With regards to mankind, especially those of us who are redeemed, there appears to be two levels in the will of God that one may walk in. These are: the perfect will of God and/or the permitted will of God.

1. **The Perfect Will of God** – Rom.12:1-2
   Paul speaks of the   (a) Good,
                              (b) Acceptable and
                              (c) Perfect (full or complete) will of God.

   God only wishes that which is good for His people. The good will of God is (should be) the acceptable will of God. It is the full or complete will of God. Because God is our Creator and we the created, and because of His redemptive love, God has a plan and purpose for each of our lives (Prov.20:18; Eccl.3:1,17; 8:6; Acts 26:16-17; Rom.8:28-29; Eph.1:11; 3:11).

   In redemption, we move from the low level of self-will to the higher level of the good, acceptable and perfect will of God. It is "not my will, but Your will be done" (Matt.6:10; 7:21; 12:50; 26:39-42).

   Our responsibility is to submit and surrender our free will to the good, acceptable and perfect will of God. In this the believer finds rest, joy and fulfillment, in doing the will of God and not living a life of self-will. Numerous are the saints in both Bible times and human history who can testify to this truth.

2. **The Permitted Will of God**
   This was formerly referred to as the "permissive" will of God. However "permissive" has taken on a bad meaning living in a "permissive society". The word "permitted" is used as a more appropriate word for our study.

   By "permitted" will of God, we speak of man falling to a lower level in the will of God. It is where God accommodates to man's free-will and the hardness of the human heart. The diagram and several illustrations confirm this to be so.

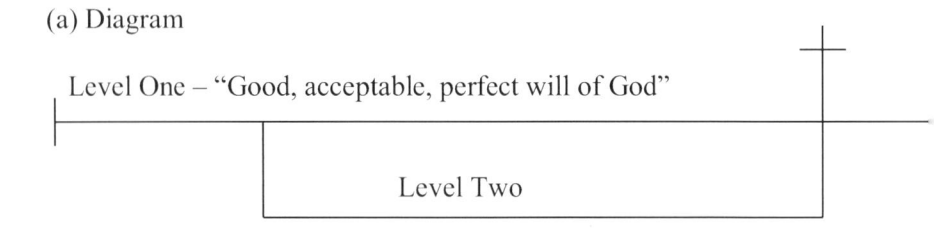

   (a) Diagram

   Level One – "Good, acceptable, perfect will of God"

   Level Two

   Permitted will of God

(b) Illustrations

1) Marriage, Divorce and Remarriage – Matt.19:2-8
The Pharisees tested Jesus about Moses allowing Israelites to divorce. Jesus directed them back to "the beginning", to the Book of Beginnings, the Book of Genesis.

"In the beginning God made them male and female. For this reason: the man leaves his father and mother and cleaves to his wife. They two become one flesh". Two become one. What God has joined together, man must not separate (put asunder). This was God's perfect will. In the beginning, Adam, Noah, Isaac, Joseph and others were all "a one-woman-man". Marriage was between a man and a woman "in the beginning" (Gen.1:26-28; 2:7, 15-25; 6:18; 7:7; Gen.24; Gen.41:44-45). This was the **perfect** will of God.

But the Pharisees persist, trying to pit Jesus against Moses or Moses against Jesus. They now refer to Deut.24:1-3; Isa.50:1; Jer.3:1). This was a law Moses gave years later that permitted divorce and remarriage. Jesus perceived their wickedness and answered accordingly. "He said to them, Moses, because of the hardness of your hearts, **permitted (suffered)** you to divorce your wives, but **from the beginning** it was not so" (Matt.19:7-8).

Thus the principle of the two levels in the will of God is illustrated here.

Edenic Covenant	Perfect will of God	New Covenant
Gen.1-2 The Beginning Male & Female One man/woman		"As at the beginning" Jesus
	Permitted will of God Mosaic Covenant – Hardness of heart Divorce and Remarriage	

2) The Entrance of Sin – Gen.3:1-6, 22
Undoubtedly one of the questions most believers have in mind is why did God allow the entrance of sin into the human race, let alone the angelic realm? It can only be said that God permitted sin to enter. It was not God's perfect will. God Himself knows good and evil and He intended mankind to know good and evil, but not by tragic experience. He permitted all this to happen but had the plan of redemption in place for when man would exercise his free will to partake of the forbidden

tree of the knowledge of good and evil. After being deceived by the serpent, man came to know good and evil but could only be and do evil because of this tree. God knows good and evil and can only be good because of His perfectly sinless and holy nature. Paul in Romans 7-8 deals with these two trees.

When Adam chose to eat of the tree of the knowledge of good and evil, he was in effect saying, "I want to know good and evil for myself so I can make my own choices. I don't want to depend on God to tell me what is good or bad, or right or wrong". Self-will was enthroned and all creation has ever since been eating the bitter fruits of that decision. God foresaw it and permitted it but was even then preparing for something better. The first Adam chose self-will and fell to this lower level of existence. The last Adam – Jesus – chose not to do His own will but the will of the Father; that will which was good, acceptable and perfect (1 Cor.15:45; Rom.12:2).

3) Hagar and Sarah

Abram started out in hope as a "young man" of 75 with some great promises. Gen.12:2-4,7,16. These promises were confirmed once again in 15:1-5. While God always intended for Abram to have a son by Sarai (Sarah), they took the lower level and path of their own choosing and Abraham took Hagar as his secondary wife. Originally it was the perfect will of God for a man and his wife to cleave together and become one flesh. This was a monogamous marriage. Departing from God-ordained monogamy and stepping down into a permitted but lower level of the will of God (the bigamous relationship) immediately brought conflict and pain. See Gen.16:4ff.

4) Ishmael and Isaac

Ishmael was the fruit of Abram and Hagar's union. From the beginning Ishmael was in conflict with Isaac who was the son of promise. History shows this conflict to be alive even in our times as seen in the hostile relationship between the Arab nations and the Jews. The son of the flesh and the son of promise also became the allegory of the two births: our natural birth according to the natural processes of the flesh and our new and heavenly birth according to the Spirit of Promise. Read Jhn.1:12-13; Gal.4:22-31; 1 Pet.1:23-25).

5) Saul and David

This same truth of God's permitted and perfect will is seen in Israel's first two elect kings, Saul and David. God had foreseen and foretold of the time when Israel would cry for a king and told them to set up a king, but of His choosing (Deut.17:14ff). Then in due time God

Himself chose and appointed Saul (1 Sam.9:16-17 and 10:1) as king and leader to govern the people.

The scriptures are clear that their demanding a king was an affront to God. Read carefully 1Sam.8:4-22; 10:17-19; 12:12-20). It is evident that God appointed Saul as king so they would get what they deserved for rejecting God's kingship; for their rejecting the theocracy (God's rule) and wanting a monarchy. Saul was God's permitted will as it was not God's perfect timing for a king. As Saul showed himself progressively unworthy to lead God's people, God began to move David, of the kingly tribe of Judah, towards kingship. Saul was then permitted to reign for some forty years, but it was God's perfect will to establish the shepherd David, the man after His own heart as king. King Saul, operating on the lower level of God's will tried many times to kill David who had become God's first choice for a king. Once again, we see the permitted will of God in conflict with His perfect will, resulting in pain for all involved.

6) **Priesthood – Melchizedek or Levitical**
The same truth is seen once again in the matter of the Priesthood. As we have seen in our studies so far, in Ex.19:1-6 God's perfect will for Israel as a nation was to be in the Order of Melchizedek, a royal priesthood or a Kingdom of Priests (cf. also 1Pet.2:1-10). Because of Israel's self-confidence (All that the Lord says, we will do) their boasting and their reluctance to stand accountable in the divine presence, God permitted the nation to drop to the lesser level of His will, the Aaronic and Levitical Priesthood. This order lasted for some 1500 years (Ex.19-20, etc).

Jesus came to bring the New Testament Church up to the level of the Order of Melchizedek, an order of kings and priests under Christ; He, the Head; the Church, His body (Psa.110; Heb.7; Rev.1:6; 5:9-10; 2Pet.2:1-10).

The Lord knows the depravity of fallen human nature. He knew the depravity of heart even in the chosen nation of Israel. Because He foreknew it, He also foretold it previously through His servants, Jacob (Gen.47-48) and Moses (Deut.33).

This was the separation or the dividing of the two offices of King and Priest. Instead of the Order of Melchizedek, which was the union in the one person of King AND Priest, God divided these two offices to two different tribes in Israel. The Tribe of Judah was given the Kingship. The Tribe of Levi was given the Priesthood. When anyone tried to unite these offices or usurp either office, there was immediate judgment executed from the Lord.

King Saul tried to be a King-Priest when he presumed to offer the sacrifice instead of the prophet Samuel. For this, he forfeited the kingdom over Israel (1Sam.13).

King Uzziah presumed to enter the office of the Priest and offer incense in the Temple of the Lord. He was struck with leprosy until the day of his death (2Chr.26 with Isa.6:1).

When the Kingdom of Israel divided into two kingdoms or two houses, the Southern and the Northern Kingdoms, the Kings of Israel were never God's perfect will. God permitted them to reign. The prophet Hosea says: "They have set up kings, **but not by Me**" (Hos.8:4). That is, "without My consent" (NIV). It was God's permitted will to have Kings over the House of Judah, but it was never His perfect will when Saul was chosen. God's tribe, the kingly tribe, was Judah. Saul was of the tribe of Benjamin.

The same is true concerning the Priesthood. It was God's permitted will to have the Aaronic and Levitical Priesthood in Israel. It was never His perfect will.

When, in the fullness of time (Gal.4:4), Messiah Jesus came, in Him is seen the personification of God's perfect will being done in the earth. He is God's King of the Tribe of Judah, to whom all Judah's kings pointed. He is the King of kings, and Lord of lords. Because He is the central one in the Godhead, He is the Mediator between God and man. He has been made a Priest after the Order of Melchizedek, the very order offered to Israel as a nation, which order they forfeited. Jesus is both KING and PRIEST, forever, after the Order of Melchizedek (Psa.110 with Heb.7).

When Jesus died on the cross, the veil of the temple was torn from top to bottom, signifying it was an act of God. It also signified that the Aaronic and Levitical order of priesthood was finished. It became obsolete, along with the whole sacrificial and priestly function and system of things.

When Jesus came to bring to birth the new and royal priesthood, it was the old, the permitted and imperfect priesthood which opposed Him and had Him crucified. Together Jews and Romans sent Jesus to the cross. Jealousy and envy stirred the murderous hostility of the then ruling priesthood which demanded the death of Christ (Jhn.7:32; 11:47ff; 12:10; 18:3; 19:6 and 15). The voice of the priests was heard above the voice of the people as they became agitators for the death of God's priest, the Lord Jesus Christ (Lke.23:4-5, 10, 13-24).

When Caiaphas the high priest tore his priestly garment, he actually brought himself under the death penalty and pronounced by this act the death of the Aaronic and Levitical priesthood. Read carefully Matt.26:57-67 with Ex.28:32 and Lev.21:10. The priest's garment must not be torn.

When Jesus died on the cross, the veil of the temple was rent from top to bottom, signifying that the old priesthood was abolished, done away with, along with the old Mosaic sacrificial system. The way into the Holiest of All was now open for all to enter "within the veil" into the presence of God Almighty (Matt.27:50-53 with Heb.9:1-9).

By the work on the cross the new order was brought in – the Order of Melchizedek. This order was extended to the Church, the Body of Christ, as already noted previously. No wonder "a great company of priests became obedient to The Faith" (Acts 6:7). Sad to say, it was the old Aaronic and Levitical priesthood still operating under the permitted will of God which became the greatest opposition of the new order, the Church after the Order of Melchizedek. Acts ch. 3-5 illustrate this. They threw the apostles into prison and forbade them to speak any more in the name of Jesus.

Sad to say, once again Church History shows in principle the same type of thing taking place. The clergy-class has often suppressed and stifled the truth of the priesthood of all believers. So-called "ordained ministry" has not always been willing to release what is called "the laity" into the purposes of God to fulfill their ministry after the Order of Melchizedek. But this is what this textbook is all about!

It may be asked: Why then, has God given numerous chapters to that of the Kings and the Priestly functions? Is it only for that which is historical? It indeed includes that, but Paul tells us that "All these things happened to them for types and examples and are written for our admonition upon whom the ends of the age have come" (1 Cor.10:6,11). So there are numerous lessons to be learnt by a study of the Kings of Israel and Judah, as also a study of the Priesthood of Aaron and Levi.

The reader is referred to the Bibliography to the text "***Kings of the Kingdom***" which deals with character studies of all the Kings of Judah and Israel. Many are the lessons found in the text. The present textbook deals with "***The Royal Priesthood***" and many are the lessons to be found in the study of Priestly ministry.

The Lord Jesus wants His people to indeed be a Kingdom of Priests, a holy and royal priesthood; Kings AND Priests unto our God and His Christ. This is the full, complete and perfect will of God. He wills to have, and will have, a Church – the many-membered Body of Christ – that will be all that the Order of Melchizedek was meant to be in the earth. The challenge to all believers is to move from the lesser level to the high level in the perfect will of God.

Operating in the permitted will of God rather than the perfect will of God opens the door to needless conflict and pain in the Body of Christ. Whenever God permits this to happen, believers depart from the good, acceptable and perfect will of God to the lesser and lower level of His will. The purpose of the ascension gift ministries in Eph.4:9-16 is to bring the members of the Body of Christ to where they function in their proper ministry, and in the picture below we see that is the Priestly Order of Melchizedek.

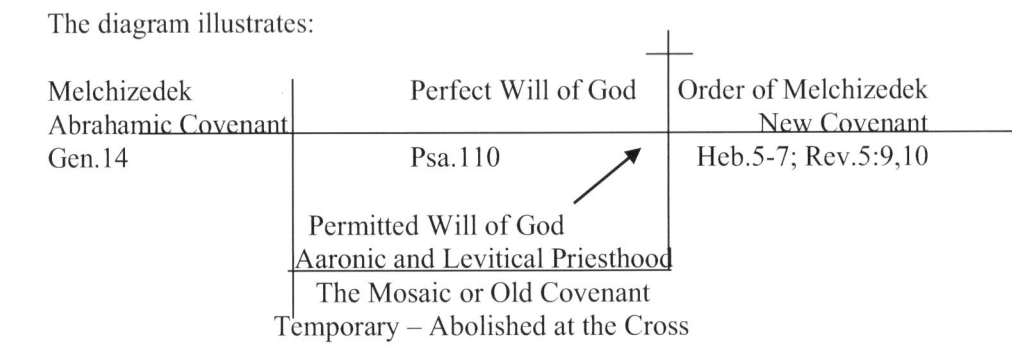

The diagram illustrates:

Melchizedek	Perfect Will of God	Order of Melchizedek
Abrahamic Covenant		New Covenant
Gen.14	Psa.110	Heb.5-7; Rev.5:9,10

Permitted Will of God
Aaronic and Levitical Priesthood
The Mosaic or Old Covenant
Temporary – Abolished at the Cross

PART FOUR - THE AARONIC PRIESTHOOD

Chapter 8   Aaron, the High Priest and his Sons
Chapter 9   The Priestly Requisites
Chapter 10   The Priestly Consecration
Chapter 11   The Priestly Garments for Aaron and Sons
Chapter 12   The Physical Qualifications of the Priests
Chapter 13   The Consecration Offerings and Order
Chapter 14   The Levitical Offerings
Chapter 15   Priestly Ministry in the Tabernacle of Moses
Chapter 16   Priestly Ministry in the Tabernacle of David
Chapter 17   Priestly Ministry in the Temple of Solomon

CHAPTER 8 – AARON: THE HIGH PRIEST AND HIS SONS

Introductory:

By way of introduction to **Part Four, "The Aaronic Priesthood"**, it will be helpful to have an overview of the larger picture from Pentecost (Ex.19) to the closing chapter of the book (Ex.40).

1. The Purpose of the Pentecostal Covenant – Ex.19
2. The Ten Commandments – Ex.20
3. The Laws and Judgments – Ex.21-24
4. Revelation of the Tabernacle of the Lord (Moses' Tabernacle) – Ex.25-27
5. The Priesthood of Aaron and his Sons – Ex.28-29
6. The Revelation of the Tabernacle furnishings and the builders – Ex.30-31
7. The Golden Calf Idolatry – Ex.32-34
8. The Construction of the Tabernacle of the Lord – Ex.35-38
9. The Priesthood Robes – Ex.39
10. The Tabernacle erected and the Glory of the Lord – Ex.39-40

In theological order it would be:
1. The Covenant (Ex.19-24)
2. The Sanctuary (Ex.25-27, 35-38, 39, 40)
3. The Priesthood (Ex.28, 29, 39 with Lev.8-10; Num.3-4)
4. The Sacrifices (Lev.1-7; Lev.16; Num.19)
5. The Feasts of the Lord (Lev.23)

The logic is: If there is a Covenant, then there must be a Sanctuary. If there is a Sanctuary, there must be a ministering Priesthood. If there is a Priesthood, it is of necessity that they offer Sacrifices. This is the flow of Heb.8:1-6). That is somewhat of the order of the chapters above in the Book of Exodus, and the flow on into the Book of Leviticus.

A. Aaron – the High Priest and his Sons

Here we consider God's election and selection of the Aaronic and Levitical Priesthood. It was to be a Priesthood of temporary nature. It would last some 1500 years, until the first coming of the Lord Jesus Christ, until the work of the cross of Calvary.

Aaron and his sons would constitute the High Priestly line and every future High Priest would and could only come from the line of Aaron's lineage (Ex.6:23; 24:1,9; 28:1). The tribe of Levi, of which Aaron came, was chosen by the Lord to be the priestly tribe and they would serve as the diakonate to the House of Aaron. There would be the High

Priest, Aaron, and his sons and the tribe of Levi would be as "under-priests". This is the overview of the Aaronic and Levitical Priesthood.

A thoughtful study of Ex.32:25-29 would seem to point to the reason why God chose the tribe of Levi. That tribe stood with Moses in the judgment by the sword of judgment in Israel as they destroyed those who were involved in the golden calf idolatry. This tribe gathered themselves together and stood with Moses against that terrible sin of idolatry.

1. Aaron's Tribe

Aaron was of the tribe of Levi, as was his brother Moses, and his sister, Miriam. Levi was chosen as the priestly tribe, while Judah was chosen as the kingly tribe. Levi would minister to the twelve tribes of Israel (Ex.28:1 with Num.ch 3-4).

2. Aaron's Calling

The Lord told Moses to take his brother Aaron and his four sons, Nadab, Abihu, Eleazer and Ithamar and set them aside to the priestly office (Ex.28:1). The writer to the Hebrew believers tells us, "No man takes this honor to himself, but he that is called of God, as was Aaron …" (Heb.5:4). Aaron did not take this office presumptuously. His calling and election were of the Lord.

3. Aaron's Ministry

In Ex.28:1-4 we have Aaron's specific ministry spelt out. Three times in this passage the Lord told Moses why Aaron was chosen to be Israel's High Priest. "… that he may minister to **Me** as priest …" (Note vss.1, 3, 4 with Heb.5:1). Aaron and his sons were taken from among men to minister to the Lord in the priest's office.

B. Aaron's Sons

Aaron had four sons, as noted above: Nadab, Abihu, Eleazer and Ithamar. Their mother's name was Elisheba (Ex.6:23; along with Ex.24:1; 9; 28:1-4; Num.3:2; 3:4; 26:60-61; 1 Chr.6:3). Each had the greatest honor and calling before God and with their father, to minister to the chosen nation of Israel.

Because of the sin of presumption, Nadab, the firstborn, and his brother Abihu, were both slain before the Lord as they offered strange fire and strange incense (Ex.30:9; Lev.10:1-2; Num 3:4). In due time, after Aaron's death, Eleazer became the succeeding High Priest in Israel. This will be seen in due time.

CHAPTER 9 - THE PRIESTLY REQUISITES

Introductory:
The word "priest" means "A Prince, a Minister" in the priestly office. The Hebrew word is "Kohen". Collins Dictionary says it also means "Presbyter: one who officiates at the altar and performs rites of sacrifice. The word can also mean "Presbyter" or "Elder".

The word "Priest" also involves "Mediator", one who comes between God and man and between man and God. The approach of a Priest is inward, representing man to God and also outward, representing God to man. The New Testament clearly shows that the Lord Jesus Christ is THE one and only Mediator between God and man (1Tim.2:5). In Him is the union of two natures: the human and the Divine, the nature of God and the nature of man. Only as such, being the God-Man, can He truly be the Mediator. A Mediator must have the nature of both of the conflicting parties, in order to bring about reconciliation. Jesus is the beginning of the new creation of God. This is the truth set forth in Old Testament Priesthood. All points to Christ and then His Church.

A. Qualifications for Priestly Ministry
The Lord set the standard in His word for all who would minister in the Priest's office. The Lord was very particular in His instructions to Moses as to the way of approach for priests into His Sanctuary. They could not approach in any way they wanted to, or the way they liked, or even in any attire they desired. It must be His way of approach or else death would strike the presumptuous. All requirements had to be perfectly met because the conditions set out in the Aaronic and Levitical Priesthood point to and find their spiritual fulfillment in Christ and His Church, or that which is after the Order of Melchizedek. It is first the natural, then that which is spiritual (1 Cor.15:46).

We note four most important requisites for priests of the Levitical Order.

1. One must be born into the Priestly Tribe
No one could be accepted as a priest or minister in that office unless they had been born into the priestly family or born into the priestly tribe of Levi. Their names had to be found on the Register of the tribe of Levi (Ezra 2:36, 61-63; Num.3:5-51, espec. v10). They must be able to trace their genealogy or pedigree back to Levi, the father of the priestly tribe called after his name (Neh.7:39, 63-65).

Levi was the third son of Jacob/Israel. His name means "joined" (Gen.29:34; Num.18:2, 4). This pointed to the New Testament believer who must be born again, born of the Holy Spirit, who is the third person in the Godhead. One must be born from above in order to function in priestly ministry in the New Testament Church (Jhn.3:1-5; 1:10-12; 2Cor.5:17-21). They must be 'joined to the Lord' as these references show. They must be 'added to the Church' (Acts 2:41, 47; 5:14; 11:24).

Aaron was born into the priestly tribe of Levi. He could trace his genealogy under God. No stranger could come near the office of a priest on pain of death (Num.3:10; 18:4, 7). The stranger was called an "outsider" in NKJV. "In Christ" the believer is no longer a stranger or foreigner. They are no longer counted an 'outsider' (Eph.2:11-22) but fellow-citizens of the household of faith.

2. **One must be in Covenantal relationship with God** – Gen.17
The sign and seal of covenantal relationship with God was through the rite of circumcision. This was the sign and seal of the Abrahamic Covenant. God sought to even kill Moses, after He called him, even though he was of the priestly tribe of Levi. This was because Moses' own sons were not in covenantal relationship with God and had never been circumcised (Ex.4:24-26). How could Moses, in priestly ministry, bring Israel out of Egypt on the basis of the Abrahamic Covenant when his own sons were not covenant children?

Later on, through the Prophet Ezekiel, God reproved the priesthood for allowing the stranger and the uncircumcised **in both heart and flesh** to minister in His Sanctuary (Ezek.44:4-8, 9-14).

The Covenant of Circumcision (Acts 7:8) involved several things:
    1. The shedding of blood
    2. The cutting off of the flesh
    3. The invocation of a person's name
    4. This took place on the eighth day

Only then was an Israelite in covenant relationship with the Lord God and entitled to the blessings, privilege and ministry of the covenant. The same was true for the priesthood. Those of the priestly tribe needed to be in covenant with the Lord through the rite of circumcision.

In the New Testament Paul is clear that true circumcision is of the spirit, and of the heart, not just of the letter or of the flesh (Rom.2:24-29; Col.2:11-14). The born again believer must know this inner circumcision by the cross and the work of the Holy Spirit. All that which was typified and shadowed forth in the rite of circumcision is involved in new birth, water baptism and Holy Spirit baptism. This is the seal of God in the name of God. Only then may a New Covenant believer minister as a priest unto God and His Christ.

3. One must have experienced Redemption

The Levite was also redeemed by the ½ shekel of silver, the standard of the Sanctuary (Num.3:1-51; Ex.30:11-16). It was the price of the soul. It was the ransom money, or the atonement money. It was then they could be numbered among the priests unto God. All must know the price had been paid for them.

New Covenant believer-priests must know that redemption which comes through the precious blood of Christ. We are not redeemed with corruptible things such as silver or gold, but with the precious blood of Christ, who is the Lamb and the Priest of God (Job 33:24; Psa.49:7-9; Matt.20:28; 1Tim.2:5-6; 1Pet.1:18-20). It is the blood of God (Acts 20:28).

4. One must be thirty years of Age

The Levitical priests could minister as priests from 30 years of age to 50 years of age, a ministry span of twenty years (Num.4:3, 23, 30, 35, 39, etc). Though born a priest and in the priestly tribe of Levi (Num.3:12-16), he was but a babe. As such, he needed training, teaching, discipline and preparation by instruction in the things of God, in the Word of the Lord. This would be learnt through the ministry of other and older priests.

Thirty is the number of consecration to ministry, to function: It is the time of maturity for ministry.

- Joseph was 30 years of age when he came to throne ministry (Gen.41:46)
- David was 30 years of age when he came to the throne over Israel (2Sam.5:4)
- Jesus was 30 years of age when He was baptized and entered ministry (Lke.3:23)
- The Ark of Noah was 30 cubits in height (Gen.6:15)
- Levitical Priests must be 30 years of age to begin anointed ministry (Num.4:1-4)
- Jesus was sold for 30 pieces of silver (Zech.11:12, 13; Matt.27:3).

Even though one was born to be a priest, he could not presumptuously rush into Tabernacle ministry unless trained in Divine things. All pointed first to Christ, and then to spiritual maturity in the believers in the Church. Paul put it this way and the principle is true today. The child, though he be a prince, is under "tutors and governors" until the time appointed by the Father (Gal.4:1-4 with Eph.4:9-16). God has set in the Church apostles, prophets, evangelists, shepherds and teachers to bring the saints – believer priests – into the work of their ministry and maturity.

This is pictured in Aaron and his four sons, five in all (Ex.28:1-2). The Levites were given to Aaron and his sons to serve in the Tabernacle (Num.3:1-3, 5-13; 18:1-7). The priestly son must be teachable, submissive, and able to receive correction and discipline in the training period. He must learn to discern the difference between the clean and the unclean, the holy and profane, by the Word of the Lord through older priests in ministry. He must learn the divine order of sanctuary services and ministrations of the articles of furniture as well as the sacrifices and oblations to be offered to the Lord. All this is training for ministry in the appointed time. Babes in ministry are not capable of handling divine things. Paul saw many believers yet as "babes in Christ" (Heb.5:11-14; 1Cor.3:1-7).

B. Examples to Us

Such are the lessons to be learned from the requisites of the priesthood. All these things happened to them for types and examples and are written for our learning, our instruction, our understanding and admonition (Rom.15:4; 1Cor.10:6,11).

All these things were shadowing forth truths in the external form from which New Covenant believer-priests may learn (Rom.2:20). The shadow has passed away but the TRUTH that was hidden in the external form remains and by these things we learn the spiritual laws of the Lord.

CHAPTER 10 - THE PRIESTLY CONSECRATION

Introductory:
The consecration or inauguration of Aaron and his sons to the priestly office was quite a detailed affair. There were particular animal sacrifices and unleavened bread used in the consecration of them all before they could minister in that office. A chapter will be given concerning these details.

The details of this orderly arrangement are gathered from Ex.ch. 28-29, as well as Lev. ch.8-9). These chapters should be read in order to familiarize oneself with the intricate details of the ceremony of consecration.

However, with relation to Aaron and his sons personally, in this consecration service, we note "**the three witnesses**" of the Lord before they began their ministry. The apostle John speaks of these "three witnesses" as "the witness of the water, the blood and the Spirit" (1Jhn.5:6-8).

The number three is the number of God, or the Godhead and this is stamped upon the consecration of Aaron and his sons.

- The Bible reveals that the eternal Godhead is seen in the Father, the Son and the blessed Holy Spirit (Matt.28:18-20).
- Man was made in the image and likeness of God and is also a triune being; spirit, soul and body (1Thess.5:23).
- Believers are baptized in water into the triune Name of the triune God, into the Name of the Lord Jesus Christ (Acts 2:36-38).
- In the Feast of Passover, there was a triune application of the blood of the lamb on the side-posts and the lintel of the door (Ex.12).
- In the revelation of the Name 'Christ', we have three Greek words, "chrio", "charisma" and "Christos", speaking of the Anointer (the Father), the Anointing (the Spirit) and the Anointed (the Son), our Messiah, the Lord Jesus Christ (1Jhn.2:20, 27).
- So it is in the consecration of Aaron and sons to priesthood. There are three that bear testimony; the Water, the Blood and the Oil, as seen in the above Scriptures.

This triune witness is seen in the cleansing of the leper (Lev.ch.13-14), in "the day of his cleansing". It is also seen in the consecration of the priests in "the day of his consecration" (Ex.28-29 with Lev.8-9).

A. The Day of Consecration for the Priests

1. The Witness of the Water – Ex.29:4; Lev.8:6

The first thing Moses did, as the congregation of Israel was gathered for the occasion at the Tabernacle door, was to wash Aaron and his sons with water.

2. The Witness of the Blood – Ex.29:20-21; Lev.8:23-24

In the consecration there was also the witness of the blood. The blood of the sacrifice was taken and placed on three parts of the body, a triune application of the blood.

It was placed on: (a) the tip of the right ear,
(b) the thumb of the right hand,
(c) the big toe of the right foot.

It was indeed a triune application of the one sacrificial blood. First the water, then the blood. A study of Gen.3:1-6 shows us how all three were defiled by the entrance of sin and needed cleansing in order to serve the living God in priestly ministry (1Jhn.1:9 with 1Jhn.5:6-8; Heb.9:11-22).

3. The Witness of the Oil – Ex.29:7, 21; Lev.8:12, 30

Next came the oil of anointing. The oil was placed upon the blood-sprinkled priesthood. The oil in Scripture is ever the symbol of the Holy Spirit. The oil was placed on them and on their garments.

B. The Day of Cleansing for the Leper

For the cleansing of the leper, there was a slight difference in the order of "the three witnesses". The reason is evident as the leper had been defiled and needed total cleansing in order to be restored to the fellowship of the Camp of Israel, the "Church in the Wilderness" (Acts 7:38).

1. The Witness of the Blood – Lev.14:1-7, 14, 25

The blood was mingled with the water. The leper had a triune application of the blood with water.

It was placed on (a) the right ear,
(b) the right thumb,
(c) the right toe.

It thus repeated the truth of the above that these things were defiled by the entrance of sin and each needed the cleansing of blood and water.

2. **The Witness of the Water** – Lev.14:1-7, 8, 9
   The leper then was wholly bathed in water. It was the cleansing of himself as well as the cleansing of his clothes. Once again, we have the witness of the blood and the water.

3. **The Witness of the Oil** – Lev.14:15-18, 26-29
   Upon the blood and the water there was a triune application of the holy oil. The oil was then placed on:

   (a) the right ear,
   (b) the right thumb
   (c) the right toe
   (d) the remnant of the oil was poured upon the head.

   Thus the leper was totally cleansed in the day of his cleansing and welcomed back into the camp of the saints of Israel. It is worth noting the significance of all this when Jesus cleansed the leper and told him to offer the offering Moses commanded as he showed himself to the priest (Matt.8:1-4).

C. The Day of Cleansing and Consecration for Believers

Without doubt, the significance of all this – both the cleansing of the leper and the consecration of the priests – finds its significance and real and spiritual fulfillment in the believer's life and in the corporate Body of Christ, which is the New Testament Church.

1. **The Blood**
   Every true believer must have the witness of the blood, that his sins of the former leprous life has been cleansed by the blood of Jesus (Jhn.1:29, 36; 19:34-35; 1Jhn.1:7-9; Rev.12:11; Heb.9:22).
      (a) The ears – hearing
      (b) The hands – serving
      (c) The feet – walking …. Must now be given to serve the Lord.

2. **The Water**
   Every true believer needs the washing of water by the Word (Grk. Lit. Laver. Eph.5:26), as well as the washing of regeneration (Titus.3:5; Jhn.3:5). Read also Matt.28:19-20; Jhn.19:34-35; Acts 2:36-42; 1Cor.6:11; Heb.6:1-2; Heb.10:22. Believers will obey the Lord in the commandment of water baptism also.

3. **The Spirit**
   Every true believer will know the witness of the Holy Spirit, who is "the oil", the unction within, as they seek to serve the Lord now in

priestly ministry in the Body of Christ (Note the Scriptures on the importance of the Holy Spirit in new birth and the baptism of the Holy Spirit. Matt.3:16-17; Matt.4:1; 12:28; Lke.1:30-33; Jhn.3:1-5; Jhn.3:34; Acts 11:25; Rom.8:14; 2Cor.1:21; Titus.3:5; 1Jhn.2:20,27).

There must be:
(a) the anointed ear to hear what the Spirit is saying
(b) the anointed hand to serve the Lord and people
(c) the anointed walking before the Lord in the light of His Word.

The believer is cleansed from the leprosy of sin, and now becomes a priest unto God and His Christ, to serve in His Sanctuary, the Church, for the glory of His name. This is the whole purpose of redemption.

CHAPTER 11 - THE GARMENTS FOR AARON AND HIS SONS

Introductory:

In this chapter, we consider the priestly garments of Aaron and the garments of his sons. Aaron, as High Priest alone, is distinguished from his sons and all others of the priestly tribe of Levi. He alone has "the garments of glory and beauty", the holy garments. The garments are listed out for us in Ex.28:1-4; 29:5-9; Lev.8:6-9. We will consider them in the order Aaron would put them on. He would certainly be decked out as the High Priest (Isa.61:10).

The Garments of the High Priest according to the Order in which they were placed on Aaron

1. The Linen Breeches (Trousers) – Ex.28:42; 39:28; Lev.16:4
2. The Broidered Coat – Ex.28:4, 39; 29:5; 39:37
3. The Girdle of the Broidered Coat – Ex.28:40; 29:8-9; 39:29
4. The Ephod Robe of Blue – Ex.28:4, 31-35; 29:4; 39:22-26
5. The Ephod itself with the Chains & Onyx Stones – Ex.28:4, 6-14; 39:1-7
6. The Curious Girdle of the Ephod – Ex.28:8; 39:5
7. The Breastplate of Judgment – Ex.28:4, 15-30; 29:5; 39:8-21
8. The Twelve Stones of Israel – Ex.28:17-21
9. The Urim and Thummim – Ex.28:30; Lev.8:8
10. The Mitre (Turban) – Ex.28:4, 36-39; 29:6; 39:28
11. The Golden Plate of the Mitre – Ex.28:36-38; 39:30, 31
12. The Ribbon of Blue – Ex.28:28, 37; 39:21

A. The Garments of Aaron the High Priest

The Garments of Aaron as High Priest in Israel will be considered in the order listed above. As seen in the Bibliography above, there is much detail given to the garments of the High Priest. These garments were made by the women of Israel, by the wisdom and Spirit of God on them as skilled people.
- The materials are given in Ex.28:4-6
- The Spirit of wisdom came upon the various women workers – Ex.28:3; 35:22, 25, 26, 29; 36:6.
- The manner of work was specialized work; the weaving, the needlework and the embroidery – Ex.35:35.

B. Significance of Garments in Scripture

Garments in Scripture always have great significance. They speak of the character, the office, the dignity and nature of a person's function or ministry. Hence we have God's exactness in the garments or clothing that His priests wore in service to the Lord.

Note some of the major references to garments in Scripture.
- The rough garment of a Prophet – Zech.13:4
- The Babylonish garment that brought defeat to the camp of Israel – Josh.7:21-24
- Joseph's garment of many colors used as evidence of his supposed death – Gen.37:1-4, 23-33.
- The garment with the plague of leprosy in it - Lev.13:47-59; 14:55 with Jude 23.
- The garments of the Israelites with the hem of blue – Num.15:38
- The garments of Jesus – Psa.22:18; Psa.45. The garments of the King and Queen
- Let your garments always be white – Eccl.9:8 with Rev.16:15
- Put on your beautiful garments O Zion – Isa.52:1
- The garments of vengeance – Isa.59:17; 63:1-4
- The garments of salvation, praise and righteousness – Job 29:14; Isa.61:3, 10
- The garment of sackcloth – Psa.69:11
- The garment of light – Psa.104:2
- The man without the wedding garment – Matt.22:2-14
- The garments of glory and beauty for Aaron and his sons – Ex.28:2; Ezek.44:17-19; Ezra 2:69

There are many other Scriptures that may be seen in a study of Strong's Concordance. The Lord was very particular about the garments His priests wore. There were no weird clothing styles or Canaanitish culture clothes on them. What a person wears tells a lot about that person, or what group they may identify with. A good principle is to dress for the occasion. It we are in the house of the Lord, dress for the occasion; if at work, or in service, dress for the occasion. The Priesthood must be clothed with proper garments as they serve in the Tabernacle of the Lord (Other references may be read in Gen.35:2; Josh.9:5, 13; Isa.9:5; Lke.24:4; Matt.9:16, 20, 21; 14:36; 21:8; Jhn.13:4, 12; Rev.3:4; Deut.22:11; Ruth 3:3; Lke.15:11; 10:35-37; Rev.19:7-8).

The Church as the Body of Christ, thus representing Him in the earth, should be clothed spiritually with the garments of salvation and the garments of righteousness, serving the Lord. The earthly robes of Aaron point to these spiritual garments – the Old Testament natural things pointing to New Testament spiritual things.

C. **The Holy Garments of Glory and Beauty – Ex.28:2, 40**
The garments that Aaron and his sons wore were holy garments, garments of glory and beauty. Aaron's name means "very high, lofty"

and his name points to our Lord Jesus who was highly exalted to the throne of the Father. As Aaron, He is our GREAT High Priest!

1. Garments of Glory

The Hebrew thought is "weight, in a good sense; splendor" and the Hebrew word is translated as "glorious, honorable" (SC.3519).

So upon Aaron there was the weight of responsibility as High Priest. His garments were glorious, and honorable to wear as representative of the people of God in the presence of the Lord.

2. Garments of Beauty

The word "beauty" has the thought of "ornament" and is translated by various words, such as, beauty, beautiful, comely, fair, honor, and majesty. (SC.8597). "Let the beauty of the Lord our God be upon us" (Psa.90:17 KJV). David wanted to behold the beauty of the Lord (Psa.27:4).

3. Holy Garments

Holiness is the very nature of God. He is perfectly holy. Aaron wore holy garments. So Jesus, our great High Priest is absolute holiness. He is the sinless Son of God. He is most holy (Lke.1:35; Matt.1:23). Without holiness, no one can see the Lord (Lev.11:44; 1Pet.1:15-16; Heb.12:14).

In Revelation Chapter One, John sees Jesus in His glorified state. This is a picture of Jesus as our great High Priest, standing in the Sanctuary, standing to minister to the golden lamp-stands, as did Aaron of old. Jesus is totally clothed in "the garments of glory and beauty". He is clothed in light and glory. John, when he saw this post-resurrection, pre-incarnate glory, fell at His feet as one dead, until the right hand of Jesus brought him back through resurrection life (Rev.1).

On the great Day of Atonement, Aaron would lay aside his garments of glory and beauty and be clothed wholly in pure white linen garments as he performed the work of atonement (Lev.16). So Jesus, in order to fulfill every type of the Law, laid aside His glory as the pre-incarnate Christ, and took upon Himself the pure, white linen garments of a perfect humanity, in order to fulfill the work of atonement on the cross of Calvary. Then Jesus, having finished the work the Father gave Him to do, asked the Father to glorify Him with the glory He had before the world began. When He ascended to heaven He was clothed once again in the garments of glory and beauty, which He had before the incarnation (Jhn.17 with Phil.2:1-11).

D. The Garments of Aaron
  1. **The Linen Breeches (Trousers)** Ex.28:39, 40-43; 39:28
  There were several of the garments of the Priests that were made of fine linen. There were the linen breeches (or trousers), the linen coat, the linen girdle (or belt), the head-gear (or turban). All these were made of fine twined linen and all teach the same symbolic truth. Linen was made by the Egyptians. It is always and ever in Scripture the symbol of righteousness (Rev.19:7-8).

  a. Pure linen – God wants purity, absolute purity. He is a holy God and does not look upon sin. He turned His face away from His only Son on Calvary when He was made sin for us.

  b. No mixture – There was not to be a mixture of wool and linen (Deut.22:11; Ezek.44:17-18). Linen speaks of pure grace; wool speaks of that which causes sweat; sweat is produced by works of self-effort. Sweat is the result of the curse in the Fall of Adam and Eve (Gen.3:19; Lke.22:44). The Galatian Churches were a mixture of works and grace; in the spiritual sense, a mixture of "wool and linen". Saved by grace, they tried to perfect themselves by works of the law.

  c. To Cover Nakedness – the main purpose of the linen breeches was to cover their nakedness. God Himself is covered with light as a garment (Psa.104:2). Jesus was clothed with light, glistening light shone through His garments on the Mount of Transfiguration (Matt.17:2; Mrk.9:3).

  Adam and Eve lost their garment of light when they sinned. They were discovered naked and tried to hide and cover their nakedness to be accepted of the Lord God (Gen.3:1-6). Man needs a covering to be accepted of God. God provided a covering for Adam and his bride, through the substitutionary death of an innocent victim (Gen.3:22-24).

  An unredeemed spirit is a naked spirit for all eternity. This will be hell for the unregenerate. The redeemed will have a glorified body clothed with light (2Cor.5:3).

  Many nations at that time included in their worship to their gods much which was obscene. Nakedness was often part of their conduct. God requires modesty and decency. Nudity or exposure of the body was forbidden in Israel. No 'flesh' is to be seen in His presence. They were to worship the Lord in the beauty of holiness (Psa.29:2. 2Chr.20:21; 1Chr.16:29).

In the "last days", this move towards indecency is intensifying, with increasing exposure of the body, and nudist colonies around the globe. Dress is constantly tending towards more indecent exposure of the body. It is a symbol of revolt and rebellion against God and His Word that declares man needs to be covered. The reproductive part of the human body has to be covered (Read the evils of such indecency in Rom.1:24-32).

- An awareness of nakedness came about through responding to the Satanic temptation and the Fall (Gen.3:15). Adam and his wife made fig-leaves to cover themselves in an effort to make themselves presentable to God. It was a bloodless covering, of self-effort and works, totally unacceptable to God. Shame comes on man because of this nakedness (Gen.2:25; 3:7-10). God clothed them in the coats of skin (Gen.3:21).
- Noah also became naked in his drunken state. Ham came under a curse because of talking about his father's nakedness (Gen.9:21-25).
- God warned Israel never to approach His altar in any form of nakedness (Ex.20:24-26). Egyptian High Priests often had their priests lead the way in indecent exposure of the body. This became the signal for all manner of immorality: filthy orgies, incest and so forth. Such took place in heathen temples. Eli's sons were priests at God's altar, yet sons of Belial at the same time (1Sam.2:12-17, 22, 34-36).
- God gave strictest instructions to Israel concerning nakedness (Lev.18 with Lev.20).
- Man is born naked and needs immediate covering (Job 1:21).
- The Israelites danced themselves naked before the golden calf and were judged for it (Ex.32:25).
- God warns the Church against spiritual nakedness also (Rev.3:17; 16:15; with Ezek.16:7, 22; Isa.58:7; 2Cor.5:3).

The natural points to the spiritual. Man needs covering. Man is 'flesh'. Man is naked without spiritual covering. This is true naturally before mankind and spiritually before God.

d. Foundational garments. Aaron and his sons would put these garments on first. They were not seen by man but seen by the Lord God. The linen breeches were foundational garments and placed on the priests' bodies first, and then the other garments

came next. So inner righteousness is seen by God as first and foundational to any other garments.
e. Righteousness by Faith – Linen, as noted, is ever and always the symbol of true righteousness. The Bible speaks of three kinds of righteousness:

- Self-righteousness ((Isa.64:6)
- Legal-righteousness, of the Law (Phil.3:6-9)
- Faith-righteousness (Phil.3:9-10; Rom.10:1-4).

This faith-righteousness – faith in the Lord Jesus Christ who is "Jehovah Tsidkenu" (The LORD our Righteousness) is the only righteousness acceptable to God. We "put off" the filthy clothes of self-righteousness and we "put on" the Lord Jesus Christ, who is made righteousness to us (Rom.13:14; Eph.4:22-24; Col.3:8-14).

We are now covered. We are no longer naked in His sight. It is that inner righteousness, internal, inwrought and then to be outworked. We can now "work out" what God "works in" (Phil.2:12-13).

It is first of all:
- Imputed righteousness – It is judicial, and internal, and righteousness by faith in the Lord Jesus Christ (Isa.59:17; 61:10; Jer.23:1-6; 1Cor.1:30; 2Cor.5:21). It is glorious within (Psa.45:13). It is what we are in God's eyes.

Then it is:
- Outworked righteousness – It is practical, external and seen in our lives (Rev.19:7, 8; Matt.5:20; Rom.8:1-4). Here we cleanse ourselves from all filthiness of the flesh AND spirit (2Cor.7:1). It is what we are in man's eyes.

f. White Raiment – the color of faith-righteousness is white, white as light, as seen in these Scriptures.

- Clothed in white raiment (Rev.3:4-5)
- The 24 elders clothed in white (Rev.4:4)
- Saints who have washed their robes white in the blood of the Lamb (Rev.7:14)
- Saints are to keep their garments white (Rev.16:15)
- The fine linen is the righteous acts of the saints (Rev.19:7-8)
- God's priests are clothed in righteousness (Psa.132:9, 16)

- He has covered us with the robe of righteousness (Isa.61:10). Margin – Decked as a priest.

g. The Lord Jesus Christ – Aaron, as Israel's High Priest, was a type of our Lord Jesus Christ, who is our GREAT High Priest (Heb.5:1-5). All the above pointed to Him, who is the "Righteous One", or "The LORD our Righteousness" (Jer.23:6). Many Scriptures confirm that He is God's perfect and righteous One, and it is only as we are clothed in His righteousness that we are acceptable to God. It is "in Christ" and then "Christ in you".

- Pilate found Him righteous (Jhn.18:38; 19:4-6)
- Pilate's wife found Him righteous (Matt.27:19)
- Herod declared Him innocent (Lke.23:13-15)
- Judas testified also (Matt.27:3-5)
- The repentant dying thief also (Lke.23:39-41)
- The Roman Centurion (Lke.23:46-47; Mrk.15:39)
- Stephen also (Acts 7:52)
- Peter (Acts 3:14; 1Pet.2:22)
- John (1Jhn.3:5)
- Paul (2Cor.5:21; Heb.4:15)
- Ananias (Acts 22:14)
- Demon spirits (Matt.8:29; Lk.8:28; Mk.1:23-24; 5:6-7)
- The Holy Spirit (Jhn.1:32-33)
- The Father God (Matt. 17:5; Heb.1:8-12)
- Jesus Himself (Jhn.8:46)

The Epistle to the Romans declares clearly the truth of Justification by faith. It is right standing before God and man. This is true faith righteousness (Rom.5:1; 9:30; Phil.3:6-9; Heb.7:1-2; Jer.23:5-6; 33:16; Isa;59:17). He is the LORD our Righteousness!

h. That they die not – in conclusion, the linen garments were to be on Aaron and his sons whenever they entered the Sanctuary that **they die not!** (Ex.28:42-43). It would be on pain of death that they entered God's Tabernacle without the under garments on, so serious was God about these foundational garments. How much 'spiritual death' takes place in many 'churches' today because saints have the outward garments that all see, but the inner garment of faith righteousness is not there, where God sees!

Aaron and his sons could have put on the outer garments of glory and beauty, but without the "unseen by man, but seen by God" under garment, they could have died! It is what we are on the inside that counts with God. Otherwise, like the Pharisees, we are 'white-washed' but not 'washed white' (Matt.23:27). The Pharisees were righteous externally, like the white-washed sepulchers, but they were not clean on the inside.

Jesus said: "Except your righteousness exceeds that of the righteousness of the Scribes and Pharisees, you will be no means enter the kingdom of heaven" (Matt.5:20). Theirs was an external righteousness of the Law, but they rejected the faith righteousness in Jesus Christ (Rom.9:30-33).

2. **The Broidered Coat** – Ex.28:4, 39; 29:5; 39:37
According to Strong's Concordance (SC.8665 from SC.7660), the word "broidered" means "checkered stuff". It means "to inter-weave (colored) threads in squares; by implicit. (of reticulation), to enclose gems in gold: - translated, embroider, set (Ex.35:35; 28:23, 39)". SC.7551 also is "to variegate color, i.e., embroider; by implication, to fabricate: - translated, embroiderer, needlework, curiously wrought."

The broidered coat was also of fine twined linen. It was like a long oriental garment, a tunic of linen and worn next to the person himself. Both Aaron and his sons wore this broidered coat. It was distinguished from the other garments which were for glory and beauty.

The broidered coat was needle-worked with a kind of "checkered stuff", woven throughout the coat. Joseph had a **coat** of many colors (Gen.37:23, 31-33). The priests have an embroidered **coat** (Lev.8:7, 13). It is the same Hebrew word for both.

With regards to Jesus Himself, our High Priest, He was on the outside what He was inside. Woven throughout His perfect humanity was His Deity, as the God-Man. His character, His love, His motives, His ministry, His kindness to people, His anger against hypocrisy – all was, as it were, "needle-worked" (woven) throughout His whole life, as symbolized in the embroidered coat. He was not like the Pharisees, who were one thing on the inside and another thing on the outside. The religious looked clean on the outside, but inwardly they were full of dead men's bones and uncleanness (Matt.23). Jesus was outwardly what He was inwardly.

3. The Girdle of the Broidered Coat – Ex.28:40; 29:8-9; 39:29

This was like a belt. There were actually two girdles, or two belts; one for the broidered coat and one for the Ephod, which is called the "curious girdle". This was also made of fine twined linen. The girdle was used in service. The long flowing garments were gathered up and about them and the girdle was used to "gird up the loins". Garments too loose would hinder movement or progress in the service of Divine things. Bringing the loose folds of the garment together would make movement easier.

Various girdles are mentioned in Scripture which illustrate these thoughts.

- Elijah had a leather girdle (1Kgs.18:46; 2Kgs.1:8) John the Baptist also (Matt.3:4).
- Jeremiah used a girdle for a sign (Jer.13).
- Christ and the angels had golden girdles (Rev.1:13; 15:6).
- There is a girdle of righteousness (Isa.11:5).
- They used Paul's girdle as a sign of binding him (Acts 21:11).
- We must have our loins girt with the girdle of truth (Eph.6:13-14; Ex.12:11).
- Servants must gird up their loins (Lke.12:35, 36; Jhn.13:4).

Refer also to these references for other examples (1Sam.2:18; 2Sam.6:14; Psa.30:11; Psa.93:1; Jer.1:17; Dan.10:5; Joel 1:13; Acts 12:8; 1Pet.1:13).

The girdle is the symbol of righteous service whatever that may be. It is the symbol of faithfulness, strength, gladness and righteousness in the service of the Lord. Our motives, our attitudes, our desires must all be pure and righteous before the Lord (Eph.2:8-10; Matt.5:16; Psa.18:32; 30:11; Deut.28:47).

Apparently, woven within the girdle were the four colors as in the curtains and the embroidered coat. In spiritual sense they point to the Four Gospels in the life and ministry of Jesus, our great High Priest, as illustrated here. These colors are mentioned some 24 times in Exodus, and always in the same order, which we follow here.

Fine White Linen	Blue	Purple	Scarlet
Gospel of Luke	Gospel of John	Gospel of Matthew	Gospel of Mark
Christ the Righteous One	Christ the Heavenly One	Christ the Royal One	Christ the Sacrificed One
Son of Adam	Son of God	Son of David	Son of Man
The Priest	The Judge - God	The King	The Prophet
Righteousness Himself	Grace and Love	Blend of Human-Divine	A Worm and no Man

Such is woven throughout the Four Gospels in the life of Christ. The Holy Spirit is the Divine embroiderer and wove these things (colors) into the life and ministry of our Lord Jesus Christ in earthly function.

It is worthy to note that each of these colors were associated with the Lord in His death on the cross and His burial in the tomb.

- His body was wrapped in linen – Matt.27:59; Mrk.15:46; Lke.23:53; Jhn.19:40
- He had a gorgeous robe, blue hem – Matt.27:35-36 with Num.15:37-41
- He was clothed in a purple robe – Mrk.15:17-26; Jhn.19:2, 5
- He was clothed also in scarlet – Matt.27:28

The same colors as in the garments of Aaron and sons, and the veil and curtains of the Tabernacle of the Lord are identified with HIM who is THE Tabernacle of God Himself (Jhn.1:14-18).

4. **The Ephod Robe of Blue** – Ex.28:4, 31-35; 29:4-5; 39:22-26
   The Ephod robe of blue is not to be mistaken for the Ephod itself, with its chains and onyx stones on the shoulders. The Ephod robe was a long seamless garment. A hole in the neck for the head to pass through was bound so it did not tear. This was worn only by the High Priest so his sound could be heard in the Sanctuary.

   a. **All of Blue**
      Blue as we have seen is the color of heaven. It speaks of the Lord from heaven, the heavenly Man, our Lord Jesus Christ (1Cor.15:47). He came from heaven to earth to give His life a sacrifice and then

return to heaven, back to His Father (Jhn.16:27-28). The Epistle of Hebrews is the "Heavenly Epistle" and reveals Christ's heavenly ministry as our great High Priest. Note the use of the word "heavenly" in this Epistle (Heb.8:4-5; Heb.3:1; 4:14; 6:4; 7:26; 8:1; 8:5; 9:23; 11:16; 12:22 with Eph.1:3; 2:6; 3:10; Jhn.3:12; 1Cor.15:47-49). He is the heavenly Priest, the Lord from heaven, and the Second Man. He ministers in the heavenly Sanctuary.

Blue is the color of heaven, the color of Divine grace. It speaks of God coming to man, God taking the initiative, not man coming to God. The Gospel of John is also the heavenly man who came to earth. In the wilderness wanderings, the Ark of the Covenant was covered with the blue cloth (Num.4:1-12). And all Israelites had the hem of blue on their garments, reminding them that they were to keep His commandments (Num.15:38).

b. A Robe
The first use of "robe" in Scripture (KJV). Robe means "Mantle" (Young's Concordance). Lev.8:7; Ex.28:4, 31, 34; 29:5; 39:22-26.

Jonathan stripped himself of his princely robe to give to David (his mantle) – 1Sam.18:4. David was clothed with a robe (mantle) of fine linen (1Chr.15:27). He acted in priestly fashion. The robe is the mantle of righteousness. Judgment is as a mantle or robe and diadem (Job 29:14; Isa.61:10).

Jesus, at His judgment, was arrayed in a purple robe, or mantle (Jhn.19:2, 5; Lke.23:11). One may think of the best robe when the prodigal returned back to the father (Lke.15:11ff). Then there was the mantle of Elijah's double portion given to Elisha (2Kgs.2:8-14; 1Kgs.19:13, 19). Read also 1Sam.24:4; 2Chr.18:9, 29; Ezra 9:3-5; Job 1:20; Psa.109:29; Isa.22:21; 59:17; Ezek.26:16).

The robe speaks of Christ's distinctive qualities; of His character, His nature, His office, His dignity and ministry, even as such pointed all Israel to Aaron, their chosen and elected High Priest, by the Lord Himself. Nothing in time or eternity will ever change the fact that Jesus is the perfectly sinless Man, the Lord from heaven. He came down to our level to lift us up to His. We are ever under-priests. He alone is High Priest. A robe signifies dignity. Any person in official robes is to be respected in office and in ministry, be they King or Queen or Priest and Minister of God. So our Lord Jesus Christ commands that respect because of who He is before God and before His saints.

c. A Seamless Robe

The robe was made out of one piece of material, of woven work. It had, as it were, no beginning and end. So Jesus lives in the power of an endless life. His is eternity of being (Jhn.1:1-3, 14-18; Mic.5:1-2; Heb.7:1-4). He is without beginning of days nor end of life (Heb.13:8; Jhn.13:3-4).

Worthy to note that Jesus' personal robe was a "seamless robe" (Jhn.19:23). The BLUE robe marked Aaron out as High Priest from all other priests, even from his sons. Jesus also is the unique and the only begotten Son of God. He is eternally distinguished and distinguishable from the many sons He brings to glory (Heb.2:10). Nothing, not even redemption, alters the fact that He was the only begotten Son of God, born sinless and perfect. All others have been born in sin, shaped in iniquity and needed redemption. He alone has this robe of identification.

d. The Hole of the Habergeon

"With an opening in the center of the robe like the opening of a collar and a band around this opening so that it would not tear" (Ex.28:32 NIV). The habergeon belonged to a soldier's armor. This was actually a mesh of metal around the head of the armor. Its purpose was so that the garment could not be rent or torn or destroyed. It was the symbol of indestructibility. It was designed to prevent the tearing of the garment. It was a coat of mail that was not to be rent. The Aaronic Priesthood lineage carried through to the Messiahship of Jesus but ended there. Jesus was after the order of Melchizedek.

It is worthy to note several things that took place relative to the death of Christ, our sacrifice for sin, and His resurrection in the power of an endless life.

- The High priest, Caiaphas, 'rent' his priestly garment, which was forbidden by the Law, and in doing so, he disqualified himself as High Priest and in actuality pronounced the 'death', or the cessation of the Aaronic and Levitical Priesthood (Matt.26:65 with Lev.10:6; 21:10; Ex.28:32).
- When Jesus died on the cross, the Father God 'rent' the veil of the Temple, signifying that the sacrificial system was at an end, believers in Christ may now enter "within the veil" into the Holiest of All because of Jesus. It also pointed to the new priesthood, after the Order of Melchizedek (Matt.27:50, 51 with Heb.7:1-17).

- It also has significance that, when the soldiers gambled for Christ's garments, because it was a seamless robe, they did not 'tear it' but gambled for it by lot (Jhn.19:23-24). Surely the overall sovereignty of God. His garment was not 'rent' because His priesthood will be eternal. It will never ever pass to another.

e. **The Hem of the Robe**
It would appear that there was a double hem on the Robe of the Ephod. In Num.15:37-41, the children of Israel were commanded to have a **hem of blue** on their garments. The purpose of this was to remind them of the Commandments of the Lord and their identification with those commandments.

Here the robe of blue has a hem (or hems) on it also. With relation to Jesus, it points to the fact that HE perfectly kept all of the Father's commandments. Out of all of Adam's race He is the only One who did so. He is the Lord from heaven (Jn.8:26-29; 12:44-50).

It is significant that the sick sometimes would just "touch **the hem** of His garment" and be made whole (Matt.9:20; 14:36). Sickness came as a result of sin. Sin was the violation of the commandment of God in Eden. Jesus perfectly kept the commandments. We can touch Him, the perfect One (Heb.10:5-10, 11; Psa.40:7, 8), and be made whole.

By comparing Ex.28:33 and 39:24 it would appear that there was **a double hem** on this garment of blue. The word is "**hems**" (39:24 KJV). Apparently it had its own hem, and then also another hem of fine twined linen on which the bells and the pomegranates were placed. If this was so, it points to the double portion. It also points to the two great commandments: Love God and love your neighbor as yourself. On these two hang all the Law and the Prophets (Matt.22:34-40).

f. **The Golden Bells**
The golden bells are the symbol of that which is Divine; gold, the metal of Deity. As Aaron, the High Priest, ministered in the Holy Place, the bells would ring. There was that tinkling sound in the Sanctuary. There was movement of the High Priest from article to article. Each of the golden bells had a 'tongue' in it, so that as there was movement in the Sanctuary, then the sound of the High Priest was heard in ministry. The bells would give a musical sound, a tinkling sound.

We think of the coming of the Holy Spirit to the New Covenant Sanctuary, the Church, and they were filled with the Spirit and began to "speak in tongues" as the Spirit gave them the utterance (Acts 2:4). It was a joyful sound, a sound from heaven. This is the sound seen and heard in the Book of Acts as believers were baptized in the Spirit by the Lord Jesus Christ, THE Baptizer (Acts 10-11; Acts 19).

g. The Pomegranates

Then there were the pomegranates placed between the bells. So there was a bell and a pomegranate, a bell and a pomegranate, right around the hem of the garment of blue. If the golden bells speak of the GIFTS of the Spirit, then the pomegranates speak of the FRUIT of the Spirit. It is like 1Cor.12-13-14 where we see the GIFTS of the Spirit, and then 1Cor.13, the FRUIT of the Spirit, which is love. These chapters belong to each other. In the language of the symbol here, it is "the bell and the pomegranate, the bell and the pomegranate", the gifts and the fruit working together, the fruit and the gifts working with each other, not one without the other. Without the fruit of love, we become as sounding brass and tinkling cymbals.

The pomegranate is a fruit consisting of hundreds of blood-colored seeds; where the white and red seeds mingle together. It was the fruit of Canaan land (Num.13:23).

It was the fruit used in the ornamentation of Solomon's Temple and the two Pillars, Jachin and Boaz (1Kgs.7:18-20, 42; 2Chr.3:16; 4:13). It points to the blood-washed multitude and the fruit of the Spirit (Song 4:13).

But that was not all. The pomegranates were colored blue, purple and scarlet. It reminds us again of Christ, our High Priest (1Tim.2:5). He is the Heavenly Man (blue), the Royal King (purple) and the Sacrificial Mediator (scarlet). The Gospels present Him in all His glory. His 'sound' was heard as He moved about in Jerusalem and Judea. In Him "fruit and gifts" were in perfect manifestation and balance. He was moved with compassion (fruit) and healed all who were sick (gift) – Matt.9:35-38.

h. His Sound in the Sanctuary

Whenever Aaron ministered in the Sanctuary of the Lord, he wore the robe of blue and His sound was heard in the Tabernacle. It was the evidence that he was alive in the presence of the Lord, ministering on the behalf of his people Israel. Death and silence belong to each other. But the sound of the bells and pomegranate sounded to all that their High Priest Mediator was alive and well.

Much of all this truth is applicable to our Lord Jesus Christ, of whom Aaron was the imperfect type. It was the tongue that gave the bell the sound. Without the tongue, the golden bells would be silent. Jesus is alive in the heavenly Tabernacle; the heavenly Temple and His sound is heard throughout the earth. He lives in the power of an endless life.

5. The Ephod itself with Chains of Gold and Onyx Stones – Ex.28:4, 6-14; 39:1-5; Lev.8:7; 1Sam.30:7; Hos.3:4

There is a need to distinguish between the Ephod Robe of Blue and the Ephod itself. "And they shall make the ephod of gold, of blue, and of purple, and of scarlet and fine twined linen and with cunning work. It shall have the two shoulder pieces thereof joined at the two edges thereof; and so shall it be joined together." (Ex.28:6-7).

The Ephod was an outer garment, a sleeveless tunic, coming below the waist. There were two pieces, consisting of a front and back, fastened at the shoulders by the two onyx stones each of which had engraved the 12 names in all of the tribes of Israel. That is, six names on each of the stones.

a. Of Fine Twined Linen – ever the symbol of righteousness. All born of mankind are born in sin and born unrighteous. Pointing to Jesus, the fine linen confirms He is the Righteous One, the only perfect Man born of a woman.

b. The Colors – the same colors are repeated as in the girdle, the curtains and the veil, except there is the gold woven in this Ephod. The same truths are taught through the use of these words in Exodus.

- Gold – symbol of Deity, that which is Divine. It speaks of the Divine nature, character, words and deeds as in the Lord Jesus, our great High Priest. Gold was worked into the Ephod (Ex.39:3). Christ, the Divine Son and Priest. The gold was beaten into thin plates, cut into wires and needle-worked throughout the Ephod. This symbolizes the God-Man. This perspective of Christ is seen in the Gospel of John.
- Blue – Christ, the Heavenly Man. The Lord from heaven. Gospel of John. The Son of God.

- Purple – Christ, the Royal or Kingly One. Gospel of Matthew. The Son of David.
- Scarlet – Christ, the Sacrificial and Mediatorial One. Gospel of Mark. Son of Man.

c. **Cunning Work** – Speaks of the work of the Holy Spirit woven throughout the perfect humanity of the Lord Jesus Christ (Jhn.1:14-18; Matt.17:1-5; Heb.1:11-12). "Cunning" means "wise, skillful" (Young's Concordance). Through the Gospels we see the Deity and Humanity of our great High Priest, in all He was, all He said and all He did. As noted previously, these colors were evidenced in the garments related to His crucifixion as in the Gospels and repeated here.

- Scarlet – Matt.27:28
- His seamless robe and blue hem – Matt.27:31; Jhn.19:23
- They parted His garments among them – Matt.27:35
- The linen cloth for His body – Matt.27:59 (Note: In resurrection, the linen garment about His head was folded, but not the linen garments about His body!)
- His death associated with the rent veil – Matt.27:51
- The crown (like the mitre) of thorns – Matt.27:29
- Clothed in purple – Mrk.15:17-46
- A gorgeous robe – Lke.23:11
- His garment divided into four parts (Jhn.19:23) as the four colors here. They did not rent (tear) His seamless robe but cast lots for that. Thus, as Aaron's garments identified him with the veil, the door, the gate and the covering curtains, so also the same colors were identified relative to the death of Christ. That which was symbolic in Aaron became typical and prophetical and was fulfilled in our Lord Jesus Christ. All was "needle-worked" in Christ's life by the Holy Spirit's ministry.

d. **Shoulder Pieces Joined** – The government shall be upon His shoulders. The shoulders speak of government and speak of strength (Isa.9:6-7; 40:11; Lke.15:5; 1Pet.1:5). He bears the names, like Aaron, did, of His people on his shoulders.

e. **The Two Onyx Stones** – the two shoulders had the two onyx stones set in gold which acted as buttons for the shoulder pieces. These were set in pouches or "settings or foundations of gold". In these two stones were written the names of the 12 tribes of Israel, six names on each stone (Ex.28:9-12). Thus Aaron bore the names of Israel upon his shoulders. Christ bears, supports and upholds His people upon His government.

The stones were brought by the rulers of Israel (Ex.25:7; 35:9; 35:27). It was by the wisdom and Spirit of God the names were cut and engraved into these two stones (Ex.35:30-33). The two onyx stones are spoken of as "green beryl" stones. Also used in Solomon's Temple (1Chr.29:2). They were very precious stones. The names of the tribes of Israel were graven on them, six on each stone. There is significance in the meanings of these names also. The name in Scripture speaks of the nature and character of the persons involved. We note also that on one stone was JUDAH and on the other stone was JOSEPH. Judah represented the SCEPTRE and Joseph represented the BIRTHRIGHT House. Here are how the names were inscribed. The names were **according to their birth** (Gen.30 details this order, along with Gen.35:22-26).

Judah – the Scepter – Left shoulder	Joseph – the Birthright – Right Shoulder
1. Reuben – "Behold, a Son" 2. Simeon – "Hearing and Obeying" 3. Levi – "Joining or Cleaving to" 4. Judah – "Praise" 5. Dan – "Judge" 6. Naphtali – "Wrestler or Striver"	1. Gad – "A Company" 2. Asher – "Blessed" 3. Issachar – "Reward" 4. Zebulon – "Home or Dwelling Place" 5. Joseph – "Added or Addition" 6. Benjamin – "Son of Sorrow, Son of Right Hand"

Jesus Christ, our High Priest, fulfills all these spiritual significances in Himself. He is of the tribe of Judah (Gen.49:10), and He gives His people the birthright (Gen.48 with 1Chr.5:1-3). All His people are on His shoulders, governed by Him, supported and upheld by Him. The names were to be remembered by Aaron. All the names of the redeemed are remembered by our Lord.

Onyx stones are also mentioned in Gen.2:12; 1Chr.29:2; Job 28:16; Ezek.28:13; Ex.25:7; 28:9, 20; 35:9, 27; 39:6, 13). The names were engraved in these stones on Aaron's shoulder (Ex.39:6-7; Isa.49:16). Jesus promises the overcomer a "stone with a new name written on it" (Rev.2:17). Our names are written in His heart and mind. Our names are there according to our spiritual birth (Jhn.3:1-5; 1Pet.1:23).

f. Secured by Chains of Gold – it seems that, hanging from the two onyx stones were two wreathen (or golden ropes) chains of gold (Ex.28:14). To these two chains of gold, the top part of the Breastplate was joined by gold rings. One may think of a chain that is made up of many links. No link has strength on its own, but the strength of the chain lies in its many links, link after link. A chain is only as strong as the links in the chain. Unity is strength. Through the Scriptures, there are many links in the chains of Divine revelation. This is seen in the links in the chain of Covenants, Redemption, the Promises of God, the Messianic truths, the Nation of Israel in Old Testament times, and the New Testament Church. One may see these truths as links in "Bible Chain References" when brought together in the great Bible themes. Every Book in the Bible is "a link" in the chain of Divine revelation. "In the volume of the book, it is written of Me" (Psa.40:7-8; Heb.10:1-10; Lke.24:27, 44-46). So it is with the truth of Priesthood, linked from Genesis to Exodus to Leviticus and on to Hebrews and Revelation.

g. **As a Signet** (Ex.28:11, 21) – the word "signet" is "seal" (Young's Concordance). Gen.38:18; Ex.28:11, 21, 36; 39:6, 14, 30; Jer.22:24; Hag.2:23. It is the seal of God. The name is the seal or signet (Rev.7:1-7; 14:1-4). The names on the two onyx stones were the seal of God on the true and spiritual Israel.

h. **As a memorial** (Ex.28:29) – a memorial is a reminder and so the names on the onyx stones were a memorial, a reminder to Aaron of his ministry and responsibility to uphold the names of the 12 tribes before the Lord as he ministered in the Sanctuary of God. It is worthy to note that the names of the 12 tribes of THE Israel of God are found eternally in the New Jerusalem, the city of God (Rev.21-22).

What a wonderful picture of Christ, our High Priest, bearing the names of the true Israel of God upon His shoulders before the Father God!

6. **The Curious Girdle of the Ephod – Ex.28:8; 39:5**
Aaron, the High Priest, wore a curious girdle which was much more elaborate than the former girdle. This girdle had gold in it. The girdle, once again, speaks of service unto the Lord or to His people. It was skillfully made, and it is distinguished from the girdle of the embroidered coat by the needle-work of fine gold woven through out. It was made of exactly the same materials and colors as the Ephod and therefore teaches us the same spiritual lessons. This girdle acted as a belt and belonged to the Ephod.

- It was of fine linen – points to Christ, the Righteous One
- It was of blue – Christ the Heavenly One
- It was of purple – Christ, the Royal One
- It was of scarlet – Christ, the Sacrificed One, the Mediator
- It was of gold needle-work – Christ, the Divine Son.

As Aaron was a type of Christ, so all he did and all that was associated with him points to the work and ministry of Christ. In Rev.1:13, Christ, in His garments of glory and beauty, is girded with a golden girdle as He is about to minister to the seven Churches.

- Eliakim (The Hebrew means "the resurrection") was clothed with a robe and strengthened with a girdle (Isa.22:21).
- Righteousness and faithfulness are His girdle (Isa.11:5; Psa.18:39).

In Israel, some people wore an Ephod, and an Ephod could be used without the Breastplate of Judgment on it by those in the tribe of Levi. Examples are seen here.

- Samuel had an Ephod of linen on him (1Sam.2:18, 28)
- Priests had an Ephod (1Sam.14:3; 21:9; 22:18; 23:6,9; 30:7)
- David at one time wore a linen Ephod (2Sam.6:14. Note also Hos.3:4)
- Gideon made an Ephod which became a snare to Israel (Jud.8:27)
- Here it speaks of the Ephod of the priest (Jud.17:5; 18:14-20)

The reason it was called the "curious girdle" was that gold was interwoven in it, and it strictly belonged to Aaron's ephod. There was the counterfeit and there was the true. "Curious" also means "embroidered" girdle. The previous girdle points to Christ's humanity, but this with the gold woven throughout pointed to His Divinity! But in it all, Christ was the Divine Servant of His Father and serves His people – the Church!

7. The Breastplate of Judgment – Ex.28:15-30; 29:5; 39:8-21; Lev.8:8

The Lord provides much detail for the making of the Breastplate of Judgment, showing the significance and the importance of this part of the High Priest's garments of glory and beauty.

a. Description: the breastplate was made of the same material as the Ephod and curious girdle. It was interwoven with the gold, the blue, the purple and the scarlet. It was a four-square piece of cloth folded like a pocket, to hold the Urim and Thummim, and on it were the 12 stones of the 12 tribes of Israel, each with a tribal name inscribed. It was bound to the ephod by rings of gold just above the curious girdle.

b. The Breastplate (Ex.25:7) – this is the first use of the word in the Bible. The breast is the place of love and affection, the place of the heart (Lev.7:30-34; 8:29; 9:20-21; 10:14-15; Num.6:20; 18:18). "The shoulder" and "the breast" were connected in certain offerings and both are connected in the garments of the High Priest, in the two onyx stones (the shoulder) and the 12 stones in the breastplate (the heart). Read also Lke.18:13; Jhn.13:25; 21:20; Rev.15:6). As noted, the breastplate was literally "a bag, or covering over the breast" (Young's Concordance). For the Bride of Christ, it speaks of the "breastplate of faith and love" (1Thess.5:8).

c. **The Breastplate of Judgment** – the Hebrew thought is "ornament", the priestly investment. The Scriptures speak of different breastplates, worn according to the occasion.

- The Breastplate of Righteousness – Eph.6:14. For a soldier
- The Breastplate of Faith and Love – 1Thess.5:8. For the believer
- The Breastplate of Iron – Rev.9:9. For Satanic spirits
- Breastplate of Jacinth and Fire – Satanic spirits also – Rev.9:17
- The Breastplate of Judgment – Ex.28:15-30. For the High Priest, Aaron, who alone wore this garment of glory and beauty.
- This breastplate is also spoken of as "the Breastplate of Decisions" in some versions (e.g. NIV Ex.28:15) as it was used in decision making in the chosen nation of Israel. Although the breastplate is sometimes not mentioned, it was the normal means of consulting God, along with the Urim and Thummim (Ex.28:15; Deut.33:8; 1Sam.28:6; 1Kgs.3:11; Isa.30:18; Ezra 2:63). The Most Holy Place in Solomon's Temple was called "the oracle", which means "the speaking place of the voice of God". In the Septuagint (the Greek translation of the Old Testament) the word is "logeion". The "oracle" is where God spoke from the blood-stained Mercy-Seat of the Ark of the Covenant in the Holiest of All (1Kgs.6-7 chapters). We note the use of the word "oracle" in 2Sam.16:23; 1Kgs.6:5, 16-31; 7:49; 8:6-8; 2Chr.3:16; 4:20; Psa.28:2; Acts 7:38; Rom.3:2; Heb.5:12 and 1Pet.4:11. The Lord Jesus Christ, our great High Priest is indeed "God's speaking place" in these last days. God spoke by the Prophets, but in these last days HE has spoken to us in the person of His Son (Heb.1:1-2; Deut.18:17-22). God only speaks to us today through His Son and by the Holy Spirit. We are to "hear Him" (Matt.17:15). He is God's Oracle, even as was Aaron in Israel at that time.

As God once spoke to them from the oracle and through the Breastplate of Decisions, He now speaks to us through the person of Jesus Christ.

- The Breastplate of Judgment was God's means of dealing with decisions in the nation of Israel. This will be seen more fully in the use of the two mysterious stones in the Breastplate, the Urim and Thummim, in the section following here. It points to the truth that the

Father has committed all judgment to His Son (Jhn.5:22, 30). He is THE Judge in that day.

d. **Rings of Gold** (Ex.28:23) – the breastplate of judgment itself was fastened to the Ephod with rings of gold, like wreathen chains of gold. Gold is ever the symbol of that which is Divine. It speaks of God's everlasting covenant that was in the eternal counsels of the Godhead (Heb.13:20). There were chains of gold and here the rings of gold, all symbolize the same truths.

e. **The Four Colors** – the same four colors are to be seen in the breastplate of judgment, therefore telling the same truth symbolically as previously seen in the Ephod and the curious girdle.

- Linen – Christ, the Righteous One
- Blue – Christ, the Heavenly One
- Purple – Christ, the Royal One
- Scarlet – Christ, the Sacrificed One, the Mediator
- Gold – Christ, the Divine One. All are fulfilled in Jesus, of whom Aaron was the type and shadow.

f. **Of Cunning Work** (Ex.28:15) – that is, the intricate, wise and skillful work of the embroiderers pre-figures the intricate work of the Holy Spirit inter-woven throughout the life, ministry and person of the Lord Jesus Christ. It would be humanly impossible without the wisdom and the Spirit of God.

g. **Foursquare Breastplate** (Ex.28:16) – the breastplate was doubled and made like a bag in which the two precious stones – the Urim and Thummim – were kept. A span by a span, or a span of the hand. There were many 'four-squares' in the Tabernacle of the Lord. All point ultimately to the foursquare City of God, the New Jerusalem (Rev.21:16ff).

- The brazen altar was foursquare
- The golden altar was foursquare
- The Holiest of All was the same
- The Outer Court consisted of a double foursquare in its measurements
- All speak of the Gospel and the ministry of our High Priest reaching into the four corners of the earth, that is, worldwide in its effectiveness. The Gospel is to the whole world (Matt.28:18-20; Acts 1:8; Mrk.16:16-20). The redeemed come from every kindred, tongue, tribe and nation (Rev.5:9-10).

8. **The Twelve Stones – Ex.28:17-21**

   There were 12 stones set in gold attached to the breastplate. All were precious stones, each having their own particular glory and beauty as represented in the 12 tribes of Israel which names are found eternally in the foursquare City of God (Rev.21:12-13). This points to the true, the spiritual and eternal Israel of God. The 12 stones were placed in a different order to that of the two onyx stones on the High Priest's shoulders. There it was according to birth. Here it is according to the order of the tribes in camp. It will be noted that Reuben, who forfeited his birthright, is replaced by Judah as being first. Also the tribe of Levi is not named but represented in the Priesthood, and Joseph is seen represented in his two sons, Ephraim and Manasseh.

   The two stones on his shoulders and his breast speak of the names (i) Upon his shoulders – government, and (ii) Upon his heart – affection. The diagram illustrates what the order on the breastplate could have been.

First Row	Second Row	Third Row	Fourth Row
1. Sardius – Judah 2. Topaz – Issachar 3. Carbuncle - Zebulon	4. Emerald – Reuben 5. Sapphire – Simeon 6. Diamond - Gad	7. Ligure – Ephraim 8. Agate – Manasseh 9. Amethyst - Benjamin	10. Beryl – Dan 11. Onyx – Asher 12. Jasper - Naphtali

   Read also Isa.54:11-12; Zech.9:16; Mal.3:17.

   They were placed according to their positions in the camp. The tribes were positioned in four lots of three tribes around the Tabernacle of the Lord. Aaron bore the names **upon his heart**. Jesus bears our names **upon His heart**. The High Priest was decked as a bridegroom indeed (Isa.61:10).

   The number twelve is also the number of Divine Government. It is prominent in the Tabernacle of Moses as it is also prominent in the New Jerusalem, the City of God (Rev.21-22 chapters).

   - There were 12 loaves of showbread on the Table
   - There were 12 by 2/10ths deal of fine flour in each loaf of bread
   - There was the number 12 in the shaft of the ornamentation of the Golden Lamp Stand
   - Two sockets of silver represented 12,000 of the redeemed in Israel
   - In the 96 sockets of silver for the foundation of the Tabernacle boards, there was represented 576,000 souls, or 4 x 144,000 souls of Israel.

- The two onyx stones on the shoulders of the High Priest has the 12 names of Israel in them
- Here again on the breastplate there are the 12 names of Israel
- And in the ministry of Jesus, the number 12 is seen in prominence. He chose 12 apostles, called the 12 apostles of the Lamb. He sent these to the lost tribes of the House of Israel. There are 24 elders gathered around the throne of God and the Lamb, and there are many 12's to be seen in the City of God (Study carefully Rev. chapters 21-22 to obtain a complete list).

   a. Lace of Blue – blue, once again, speaking of that which is heavenly, the Heavenly Man, Christ Jesus. He came from heaven to earth, to redeem many from earth to take back to heaven in the appointed time. Aaron was fulfilling a heavenly ministry on earth as he made atonement for Israel and made intercession for the nation at the altar of incense.

   b. Judgment to the Son – all that Aaron was and did for Israel finds its fulfillment in the person and ministry of our Lord Jesus Christ. The Father has given all judgment to the Son (Jhn.5:22, 30). In Rev. chapters 1-2-3, we see Jesus standing as High Priest in the Sanctuary of God. He wears the garments of glory and beauty. Standing amidst the golden lamp-stands, He bears the breastplate of judgment because judgment is about to begin at the house of God (1Pet.4:17; 2:5-9).

There are many Scriptures that speak of judgment, the Lord discerning right from wrong as He judges His people. There is a "judgment unto restoration" and a "judgment unto condemnation" (1Cor.11:23-34). If we would judge ourselves, we would not be judged. Judgment of the Lord comes as a chastening from the Lord. Jesus will judge righteously and not after the sight of His eyes nor the hearing of His ears, because He sees the heart and the motives of His people. He will do that which is right (Gen.18:25; Ex.24:3; Lev.18:5, 26; Deut.16:18; 32:4; Isa.9:7; 11:1-4; 33:22; Jhn.7:24; 8:15, 16, 26, 50; 12:47, 48; 1Cor.2:15). There is no chance of deception. There is no chance of mistaken judgment with Him. This great picture of Aaron wearing the garments of glory and beauty with the Breastplate of Judgment points to Christ in many ways. These are just some of those many ways.

9. **The Urim and Thummim Stones – Ex.28:30; Lev.8:8**
   The most marvelous part of the garments was these two mysterious stones, placed in the pocket, or the foursquare-like bag of the Breastplate. By these the High Priest, Aaron, communicated with the Lord and

received Divine answers relative to the tribes, individuals and places. These were upon Aaron's heart as he went before the Lord.

Nothing is given to tell us how these stones worked, or how they operated. Undoubtedly, because of man's fallen and sinful nature, and because man is a great imitator of Divine things, it has pleased God to keep these things secret (Deut.29:29). If man had known, they would have been turned into some form of commercialized witchcraft, counterfeiting that which was of the Spirit.

a. The Place – these two stones were placed inside the bag or the pocket of the breastplate. They were unseen by human eyes and only the High Priest knew of their ability to communicate.

b. **Definition of Names** – "Urim" means "lights" and "Thummim" means "Perfections". The Sept. Version of the Scriptures writes, "Put in the manifestation (Urim) and the truth (Thummim) in the oracle." That is, the breastplate became "the oracle" – the speaking place of the voice of God, or Divine communications.

Strong's Concordance (S.224) defines Urim as "lights, the oracular brilliancy of the figures in the high priest's breastplate. "Thummim" (SC.8550) defined as "perfections", one of the epithets of the objects in the high priest's breastplate as an emblem of the complete Truth."

c. **Differing Views** – several different views are given as to how the Urim and Thummim worked, but, as has been said, all these are speculations of that which God has kept secret in His own counsels.

- Some suggest the stones were a black and white stone and by these the 'lots' would be drawn for apportioning out the land inheritances of Canaan (Num.26:55; 27:21; 34:17; Josh.17:4; 18:11; 19:1, 17 with Prov.16:33 and Acts 1:26). This was the casting of lots.
- Some suggest, as the Priest stood before the Ark of the Lord, there was the flashing of light on the various letters of the 12 names of the tribes of Israel. These together would identify the tribes or else spell out some kind of sentence or answer needed to a given situation. This was God's secret code language in the stones, and by the lighting up of names or letters, sentences were formed.
- Some suggest the prayer for guidance of Psa.43:3,4, "O send out Your **light and truth** (or Urim and Thummim), let them lead me" was done through these mysterious stones. According to some expositors, the same Hebrew word, translated "fires" or "light" is used in Isa.24:15;

31:9; 44:16; 47:14; 50:11; Ezek.5:2). Refer Strong's Concordance (SC.224) with Hebrew-Chaldee Concordance.

However, each of these views speculate things that God has kept in His own secret counsels!

d. Symbolic Truth – there is some symbolic truth to be seen in the High Priest and the Urim and Thummim which finds its real and spiritual fulfillment in the Godhead, as Father, Son and Holy Spirit.
- The Father – Urim, or Lights. God is the Father of Lights (Jas.1:17; 1Jhn.1:5). God IS Light. As such He is symbolized by this unseen or invisible stone. He is the source of revelation.
- The Son – the visible High Priest; made visible by the virgin birth, by the incarnation. Aaron's name means "very high", and God has highly exalted His Son above all as our Mediator and great High Priest (Phil.2:1-11). In Him is the Divine and human natures, HE is the seen One of the Godhead (Heb.3:1; 4:14).
- The Holy Spirit – Thummim or Perfections. All the perfections of the Holy Spirit are seen in the gifts and graces and fruit of the Holy Spirit, perfectly in Jesus and then manifested in the saints, members of the Body of Christ (1Cor.12:1-13; Gal.5:22, 23). He is symbolized in the unseen, the invisible One. HE is the Spirit of revelation.
- Thus two invisible and one – the High Priest – the visible Person of the Godhead.

e. Alpha and Omega – the word "Urim" begins with the letter Aleph, the first letter of the Hebrew alphabet. The word Thummim begins with Tau, the last letter of the Hebrew alphabet (see Psa.119 where all verses are arranged under the letters of the Hebrew alphabet). In Rev.1:8, 17 and 22:13, our Lord Jesus Christ, as our great High Priest, is declared to be the Alpha (Aleph) and Omega (Tau). In Him dwells all the fullness of the Godhead bodily. In Him are hidden all the treasures of wisdom and knowledge (Col.1:19; 2:3, 9). As our High Priest He has been declared both Lord and Christ (Acts 2:36). The Lights of the Father and the Perfections of the Holy Spirit are seen in Him.

f. References to Urim and Thummim – there are seven references in Scripture to these mysterious stones. A careful reading of these Scriptures supplies some interesting thoughts on the function of these stones. They were definitely used to ascertain the mind and will of the Lord and to receive Divine guidance.

- Num.27:18-23. Joshua is to stand before the Priest and ask counsel of the Lord by means of the Urim and Thummim. He was to receive the

word of the Lord to go or stay, and, no doubt, in the dividing of the land to the tribes for their inheritance. It is quite possible that this was the way in which Achan was found out because of his evils (Josh.7).
- 1Sam.14:3, 19. This latter reference, Saul enquired of the Lord through the Priest, but he just did not have the patience to hear from the Lord and told the Priest to "withdraw his hand."
- 1Sam.23:9-12; 30:7. David enquired of the Lord by the Urim and Thummim and the Lord answered him, delivering him from the enemy. David would say to the Priest, Abiathar, "Bring here the Ephod and enquire of the God of Israel", sometimes adding, "I beseech You, tell me Your servant", and he would receive an answer from the Lord.
- 1Sam.28:5-6. God refused to answer Saul by Urim and Thummim, dreams, visions or prophet because of constant resistance and rebellion against the Lord's word.
- 1Sam.30:7-8; 2Sam.2:1. David enquired of the Lord through the appointed Priest. He was willing to wait for guidance, unlike King Saul.
- Ezra 2:63 with Neh.7:64-65. Only those Priests who were holy could receive an answer by God through Urim and Thummim. This was after the Babylonian Captivity ended.
- Deut.33:8. The tribe of Levi was the chosen tribe to receive from the Lord answers by Urim and Thummim in the breastplate.
- Lev.8:8 with Ex.28:15-30. God would speak through the Urim and Thummim through His High Priest.

g. **Fulfilled in Christ Jesus by the Spirit** – seeing that Aaron was a type of Christ, all that was seen in him as the Mediator between God and man, finds its fulfillment in our Lord Jesus, the New Covenant Priest after the Order of Melchizedek. In Him the fulfillment of these two mysterious stones is seen.

- In Him the fullness of the Godhead dwells in bodily form (Col.1:19; 2:9).
- He is the Light of God, and in Him are the Perfections of God, symbolized in the Urim and Thummim. Note the word "perfect" in Hebrews, the Epistle of Christ's Priesthood (Heb.2:10; 5:9; 6:1; 9:11; 10:1, 14; 12:23 and also Matt.5:48). He is the Light of the world (Jhn.8:12).
- He is God's High Priest. We stand before the Father, and He communicates through Christ, His Son, the Living Word (Jhn.1:1-3, 14-18). God who is light and dwells in unapproachable light (1Tim.6:15-

16), speaks to us through His Son (Heb.1:1-3) and this by the power of the Holy Spirit.

- The Word and the Spirit agree. No longer do these mysterious stones exist – and all false religions who claim such are cultic – God speaks through the Word and the Spirit. These TWO agree and together, without contradiction, give us the mind of God. These are the "two stones" this side of the Cross.
- He is the Alpha and Omega. He replaces all of the Old Testament Priesthood and all that was fore-shadowed therein. No need to seek God through human channels. He is the one and only way to the Father, and only Mediator between God and man (Jhn.14:1-6; 1Tim.2:5-6).
- In Him was the fullness of the Father and the fullness of the Spirit. God the Father is light, and all light is in the Son (Jhn.1:1-14; 1Jhn.1:4-6). Jesus is the High Priest (Heb.4:14; Heb. ch.9-10), always associated with sacrificial blood He brings to us the perfections of the Holy Spirit (Heb.6:1; Matt.5:48; Isa.11:1, 2).
- He is God's Oracle, the speaking place of the voice of God. God has nothing to say to man apart from speaking through His Son. His eyes are as two flames of fire; searching, penetrating light, with insight and foresight. He sees all from light within, and perfect discernment (Rev.1, 2, 3).
- Guidance for all believers, this side of the Cross, is NOT through these two stones, but through THE WORD and THE SPIRIT; the Written Word and the Quickened Word (Rom.10:17). The peace of God should rule in our heart and our minds should be renewed as we present ourselves to do His good, acceptable and perfect will (Rom.12:1-2).
- Believers need to be warned against false prophets, or religions that claim they have access to these Old Testament stones, the Urim and Thummim, and the false writings that have been produced by demonic, religious spirits.

10. The Mitre/'Holy Crown' – Ex.28:4, 37-38; 29:6; 39:28

The final piece of the holy garments was the Mitre / 'Holy Crown' which was placed on the head of Aaron, the High Priest. The word 'mitre' means 'to roll or wrap around'. It was wrapped around the head of Aaron in folds and was like a turban.

   a. Material – made of fine twined linen, and as ever, the symbol of righteousness, both internally and externally (Rev.19:7, 8). In Christ's resurrection, the linen garments that had been about His head were wrapped in a place by itself, but not the grave-cloths on the body (Jhn.20:6-9). The 'Head' had touched death, burial and resurrection; the 'Body' was yet to reach that state.

b. The Holy Crown (Ex.39:30. NKJV). So Aaron was crowned as High Priest, all pointing to the crowning of Jesus as King and Priest after the Order of Melchizedek (Psa.110; Heb.7). Though man crowned Him with thorns, God crowned Him with glory and honor (Heb.2:9 with Rev.19:12). He returns with many crowns on His head. The 24 elders cast their crowns before Him (Rev.4:4-10). He is King and Priest (Zech.6:9-15).

11. **The Golden Plate – Ex.28:36-38**
Moses was to "make a plate of pure gold and grave on it, like the engravings of a signet, HOLINESS TO THE LORD …" This was to be put on the Mitre. It was to be on Aaron's forehead, that Aaron would bear the iniquity of the holy things, which the children of Israel would hallow in their gifts to the Lord. It was always to be on his forehead that the people of Israel would be accepted before the Lord.

   a. A Gold Plate – gold is ever the symbol of Deity, the Divine nature, that which pertains to God Himself.

   b. Holiness to the Lord – everything in the Tabernacle, the furnishings, the priesthood and the service, was to be holy to the Lord. The key word in Leviticus is "holy" and used numerous times (Lev.11:44, 45; 19:1; 20:7 with 1Pet.1:15, 16). Jesus is the Holy One of Israel. He was born absolutely sinless and was called "that holy thing" (Lke.1:35). Read also Psa.93:5; Isa.35:8; 1Cor.1:30; Heb.7:26; 12:10).

   c. On the Forehead – the golden plate on the mitre was to be placed on Aaron's forehead. The forehead is the seat of the mind, the reason, the intellect, the imaginations and understanding. Sin entered through the mind and the mind has to be totally cleansed by the holiness of the Lord (2Cor.11:1-3). It was to be on Aaron's forehead that **they** (the Israelites) may be accepted of the Lord. The spiritual Israel of God is only "accepted in the Beloved" (Eph.1:6; Lev.1:4; 22:27; 23:11).

   - Leprosy rose up in the forehead of King Uzziah when he presumed to be a king and priest (2Chr.26; Isa.6).
   - Leprosy in the forehead needed cleansing (Lev.13:42-46; Jhn.3:3).
   - Babylon's harlot system has blasphemous names in the forehead (Rev.17).
   - The name of the Godhead is in the forehead of the sealed ones (Rev.7:1-7; 13:16; 14:1-8; 20:4; 22:4).

- The mark of the Cross (Tau) is in the forehead of the intercessors in Israel also (Ezek.9:1-7). The name is the nature and the character of Him whose name it is.

d. **Aaron's Responsibility** – there was a three-fold responsibility laid upon Aaron, Israel's High Priest. All finds fulfillment in our Lord Jesus Christ. He was to bear:

- Upon the shoulders – the names of the twelve tribes, six on each of the onyx stones (Ex.28:12). The shoulders are the place of government and support and strength.
- Upon the heart – Ex.28:29-30. He bore the names of the 12 tribes, each name in a particular precious stone. The heart – the place of love and affection – the breastplate.
- Upon the forehead – the mitre – Ex.28:38. The forehead, the place of memory, reminder, imagination, thoughts and wisdom.
- So Christ bears His people, with all our weaknesses and infirmities, on His shoulders, on His heart and on His mind before the Father God.

e. **Three 'Appearances'** – Heb.9:24-27 speaks of the "three appearing's" of Christ in the presence of God for His people. Each was shadowed forth in the 'appearances' of Aaron in relation to the Sanctuary services.
- Aaron appeared in the Outer Court at the altar for the sacrifice of sin. So Christ appeared in the end of the Old Testament to put away sin by the sacrifice of Himself.
- Aaron appeared in the Holy Place at the articles of furniture there as he ministered for Israel's acceptance. So Christ appears in the presence of God for us, as intercessor.
- Aaron appeared in the Holiest of All, on the great Day of Atonement as he took the blood and sprinkled it on the Mercy-Seat - so Christ has entered into the Holiest of All with His own blood and from which He will return again the second time in His glory.

f. **Bearing Iniquities** – Aaron bore the iniquities of the children of Israel. All were to be accepted before God through their High Priest. So the Father God accepts the Church, the believers, in spite of frailties, imperfections through the mediatorial and intercessory ministry of Christ Jesus, our High Priest (Heb.7:25-28). All our prayers, praises and worship are passed through Him, with all their short-comings.

12. **The Ribbon of Blue**
    The golden plate with "Holiness to the Lord" inscribed on it, was tied to the turban (the High Priest's Mitre) with a lace of ribbon of blue. Blue, as always, is the color of the Lord from heaven, the Heavenly Man, and it is seen woven throughout the various garments telling the same truth (1Cor.15:46-49).

E. **The Garments of Aaron's Sons – Ex.29:8, 9; Lev.8:13**
    In concluding this chapter on the garments of Aaron and his sons, we note the following truths. In contrast to Aaron, as High Priest, the sons were entirely clothed in fine linen. This sets Aaron out as unique, distinct from, yet also identified with his sons. It points to Jesus. Believers are kings and priests unto God, the Father. But Jesus stands unique among all. He stands above all, and is clothed in garments of glory and beauty, such as the believers can never have. The reason: Because of WHO He is and WHAT He did before the Father. He is the unique and only begotten Son of God. He is the only perfectly sinless One ever born of the human race. He alone died to redeem fallen mankind. His body and blood stand unique in both time and eternity. Nothing, not even redemption, alters these truths. Aaron stood alone as High Priest. However, he was succeeded by reason of sin and death. Jesus lives now in the power of an endless life. He will never know succession by any other in time and eternity. In all things He has the pre-eminence (Col.1:14-20; Rom.8:26-30). He is the head of the Church, His Body. He is head over all things.

Aaron's Sons:
1. Linen breeches (or trousers)
2. Linen coats
3. Linen girdles
4. Linen bonnets (or head gear)

So believers are clothed in the white linen of faith-righteousness, as symbolized in the linen garments. It is the color of Christ, the saints and the angels in the Book of Revelation. The color "white" is mentioned some twenty times in the book. It always points to the righteousness of angels or saints, or the perfect righteousness of Jesus Himself (Note several of these references – Rev.1:14; 3:4, 5, 18; 4:4; 6:11; 7:9; 19:8).

Believers are kings and priests to God and His Christ (1Pet.1:2-9; Rev.1:6; 5:9-10).

CHAPTER 12 - PHYSICAL QUALIFICATIONS OF THE PRIESTS

Scripture: Lev.21:16-24; Ezek.44:9-23
Introductory:
The Lord was expressly concerned about the personal appearance (the garments) and the physical fitness of the Priests in ministry. The physical qualifications are spelt out in the above passage of Scripture. God set the physical standards for priestly ministry. This was given to Aaron and his sons, and for the priesthood of Levi, and it was told to all Israel. So the priests were taken from among men, ordained for men in things pertaining to God, His Tabernacle and the offerings (Heb.5:1-5). The people knew what the standard was and what they expected the priest to be. None dare alter the standard to get into priestly ministry. It was God Himself that set the standard.

Even the qualifications of the sacrifices and offerings to be presented to God follow almost the same standards as the physical qualifications of the priests (Lev.22:17-25). The Offeror must be of a similar standard to the Offering, the Priest like the Sacrifice.

God moves from the natural to the spiritual (1Cor.15:46). It may be questioned as to why God commanded such physical standards for the Old Testament priesthood. When one considers the physical work of the priest, the offering of the sacrifices, the heavy and hard work of the Altar of Burnt Offerings all done by the priest who had to be 30-50 years of age, then one may understand why he must be physically fit. That then would be the primary reason for God's physical standard for the ministry of the priests. The priestly ministry would be very difficult for anyone who was physically unfit.

On the other hand the natural points to the spiritual and within the physical qualifications, there would be – and there are – spiritual lessons to be discovered. This will be seen as this chapter works through the list of qualifications.

Of course over and beyond all is the fact that both Priest and Sacrifice pointed to our Lord Jesus Christ, who was **"the perfect One"** in His total being. God could only accept that which was perfect for ministry, service and His altar, **"It shall be perfect to be accepted"** (Read carefully, Lev.22:21 NKJV).

Of course, these things are not carried over in New Testament qualifications for believers, as many of God's people today do have some physical infirmities which would disqualify them in Old Testament times. God uses many of His people regardless of their physical problems, looking rather at the heart, the motives and those qualifications that qualify a person on the spiritual level. However, the spiritual truths may be applicable, and that is what is especially emphasized in this chapter. The physical or the natural brings us to that which is spiritual. The bottom line is that a believer-priest can better serve the Lord and His people IF they are fit both spiritually and physically, so all believers should aim for both. Throughout these qualifications, we move from the natural to the spiritual.

The Physical/Spiritual Qualifications

1. Must be without blemish – as the sacrifices were to be 'perfect' or 'complete' or 'without blemish'. Christ Himself is the LAMB and PRIEST without blemish. HE wants a Church, a Bride that is like Himself, that is "without spot or blemish" (Ex.12:5; Lev.22:17-25; Eph.5:26-27; 1Pet.1:19-20). It must be like sacrifice, like priest! No defect.

2. No blindness – one cannot lead others if blind. Can the blind lead the blind? Jesus charged the Pharisees with being blind religious leaders who fall into a ditch with the people they are leading. Blindness speaks of a film over the eyes where one cannot see straight or clearly. Jesus came to heal blind eyes. Blindness means lack of vision, no sight, no insight. Jhn.9-10 refers to the healing of the blind man, while the Pharisees who "saw" really were 'blind'. They could see naturally but were blind spiritually. They could not see the truth Jesus presented (Read also Deut.15:21; Isa.56:10; 61:1-4; Matt.15:14; 23:16, 17, 19, 24, 26; Lke.4:18; 2Pet.1:9; Rev.3:17-18).

    Without a vision, people perish (Prov.29:18; 1Sam.3:1). People stumble along in blindness.
    What a terrible thing it would be for an Israelite to come to a blind priest!

3. No lameness – one who is limping or stumbling along in their walk. Jesus came to heal the lame. When healed one can walk straight (Deut.15:21; 2Sam.4:4; 9:3; Prov.26:7; Isa.35:6; Mal,1:8, 13; Matt.11:5; 15:30-31; Acts 3:2; 8:7; Heb.12:12-13). It speaks of an uneven walking. A priest must have a clean and straight walk before the Lord (Heb.12:13).

4. No flat nose – not a marred face. A flat nose can be a lack of sense of smell, symbolically signifying a lack of discernment, unable to discern between good and evil (Heb.5:14; Song 7:4, 8; Isa.11:1-3).

5. Nothing superfluous – being deformed by excess of members of the body. Something that is in excess, more than the body needs (Heb.12:1; Lev.22:23).
6. Not broken-footed – refer to #3, lameness. A breach of the foot, slowing down one's walk. This may be a fracture, a bruise, a breach, or anything which affects one's walk naturally. Throws one out of balance in their walk (Isa.61:1).

7. Not broken-handed – a breach of the hand. Unable to handle things rightly because of the hand being broken. Not able to hold things in God's service (Isa.35:3). "Lift up the hands that hang down" is difficult with a broken hand.

8. No crooked back – having a weak back bone. Cannot stand upright. Hump-backed. Arched back (Lke.3:5; Isa.40:4).

9. Not a dwarf – Margin. Too slender, lean, thin, small. Speaks of immaturity, never grown up. Undeveloped physically, stunted (1Cor.3:1; Eph.4:13; Heb.5:12).

10. No blemish of the eye – refer #2. Blindness. A cataract, a film, not totally blind, but out of focus, blurry, lacking clear vision. Cf. Mrk.8:22-26. Blind man at first saw men "as trees walking". Needed another touch. Not clear, not perfect sight or insight (Matt.7:1-5; Jas.1:22-25; 2Pet.1:5-9).

11. No scurvy – an itch, scratching, a tormenting skin disease produce by entrance of a parasitic insect into the substance of the skin. Lack of balanced diet. Pain in the limbs, disease seen in various sizes in the flesh. Always got 'the itch' (Lev.22:22).

12. No scab – scabs cover blemishes, sores healed, leave unhealthy scabs, unhealthy condition. A 'scab' – speaks of a mean and low person. Incrustation over a sore or wound (Lev.13:2, 6-8; 14:56; 22:22; Isa.3:17).

13. No broken stones – or a testicle, unproductive, cannot reproduce himself, lack of fruitfulness, or a eunuch (Jhn.15:16; Col.1:10; 2Pet.1:5-8).

14. No defilement for the dead – Lev.21:1-4, 10, 11; Ezek.44:25-27, 31. Death and dead things defile. Ceremonial defilement pointed to spiritual defilement with the dead things of this world. Sardis had a name that it was alive but was dead, devoid of life and defiled believers' garments (Rev.3:1-6). A dead church defiles.

15. Not make the head bald – Lev.21:5, 10; Ezek.44:20. Hair given for a covering. Heathen custom of priesthood often to shave off hair. Hair styles identified with their gods.

16. Not shave the corners of beard – Lev.21:5; 19:27. Also heathen custom and identifies with heathen culture and gods (as #15).

17. Not to make cuttings in the flesh – Lev.21:5; 19:28. No markings, tattoo marks, cuttings in the flesh, all of which identify with heathen culture and customs, gods or idols of other nations.

18. Not to marry contrary to word – Lev.21:7, 10-15; Deut.24:1-4; Ezek.44:22. Not to marry a harlot, a whore, a widow, a divorced or profane person. Must marry a virgin of his own people. Marriage standard before the Lord. Marriage and ministry belong to each other.

19. Not to profane his office – Lev.21:4, 6, 7, 9, 12, 14, 15, 23. "Profane" used at least nine times here (KJV). "To speak lightly of sacred things" = profanity. Esau was a profane person, speaking lightly of his Divine birthright (Heb.12:16).

20. To be holy before the Lord – Lev.21:6, 7, 8, 15 and 23. Holiness involves sanctification, consecration and separation from evil unto the Lord for ministry as a priest to the Lord. Without holiness no one will see the Lord (Lev.11:44, 45; Heb.12:14; 1Pet.1:15-16).

21. Not a winebibber – Lev.10:1-7, 8-11; Ezek.44:21. Refer elders' qualifications (Titus1:5-9). Not given to drinking or drunkenness. Refer Strong's Concordance for dangers of the drunkard. Two sons of Aaron offered strange fire in drinking state. Death struck.

As noticed, the natural points to the spiritual. There are many spiritual lessons to be learnt from that which is natural. As noted, these things do not carry over into the priesthood of New Covenant believers, but they do have spiritual import. It is good that a person be fit physically as well as spiritually in order to serve the Lord and people to the best of their ability. But many, many are the believers who have had physical defects and yet have been mightily used of the Lord in the Body of Christ. Such are too many to mention and all believers would know some in such a state. But the lessons arising out of the physical are seen above and bring a challenge to all believers.

CHAPTER 13 - THE CONSECRATION OFFERINGS and ORDER

Scripture: - Ex.29:1-46. Outline of Chapter and Comments

A. **Order of Consecration** – Ex.29:1-9
   1. **The Offerings** – vs.1-3
      - One young bullock
      - Two rams without blemish
      - Unleavened Bread
      - Unleavened Cakes mixed with Oil
      - Unleavened wafers anointed with Oil – of wheat flour
      - All the bread in one basket and bring them with the bullock and the two rams. These were the specified offerings by the Lord to be brought in the consecration or sanctification of Aaron and his sons to the Priestly Office.

   2. **The Washing** – vs.4
   Aaron and his sons are wholly washed with water at the door of the Tabernacle (cf. Ex.30:18; Lev.8:6). They are not washed as sinners but redeemed people for the service of the Lord in His Tabernacle. It points to the washing of water by the Word for priestly function (Psa.119:9, Jhn.15:3; Eph.5:26).

   The ministry of the witness of the water is always evident in Israel's history (1Jhn.5:7-8; Lev.6:27; 13:34, 54, 58; 14:8, 9, 47; 15:5;27; 16:26, 28; 17:15-16; Num.19:8-10, 19-21). There were the waters of separation and purification in the ceremony of the ashes of the red heifer (Num.19:8-10, 19-21). It was the washing of purification (Lev.13:58; Psa.51:2, 7; Jer.4:14; Ruth 3:3).

   There was the molten sea for priestly washings in the Temple of Solomon (2Chr.4:6).

   In Jhn.13, Jesus washes the feet of His disciples. They had been wholly washed (Grk. 'louo', or bathed). All they needed was to wash their hands or feet (Grk. 'nipto'). Jhn.13:5, 6, 8, 19, 12-14; 1Tim.5:10.

   So Moses gave the initial bath to Aaron and his sons. In New Testament language, this points to the 'washing of regeneration' (Titus 3:5; Jhn.3:5). After that, Aaron and his sons needed to wash their hands and feet at the Brazen Laver of water. This equates to the already regenerated Christian being continually washed by the Word

(Eph.5:26). Then they could minister in the Sanctuary. Such were the 'divers washings' (Heb.9:10; 10:22; Rev.1:5; Acts 22:16; 1Cor.6:11). The washing of water by THE WORD and the daily application of that Word is the truth foreshadowed in "the water" cleansing here.

3. **The Clothing** – vs.5, 6
    After the washing came the clothing. The garments, as noted in a previous chapter, were then put on Aaron and his sons. The special garments of glory and beauty were but for Aaron the High Priest only. He put on the coat, the robe of the ephod, the ephod itself, the curious (or intricately woven) girdle, the mitre (turban) on his head, and the holy crown on the mitre.

    In Old Testament times, the Hebrew thought in a number of places was, "the Spirit of the Lord **clothed Himself** or clothed a person for service" (Jud.6:34; 1Chr.12:18; 2Chr.24:20). The New Testament speaks of believers being "endued" or "clothed with power from on high" (Lke.24:49). That speaks of the baptism of the Holy Spirit and His clothing believers with Himself (Acts 2:1-4).

    Jesus was "clothed with the Holy Spirit" at the River Jordan and began ministry after that (Matt.3:16-18; Jhn.3:33, 34). The members of His Body were clothed at Pentecost and began preaching the Gospel to all nations after that occasion. First it is Christ the Head, and then His Body, the Church.

    The reader is referred to the chapter on Aaron's Garments as to the significance of garments in the Word; being clothed for the occasion (Read additional references in 1Chr.15:27; Psa.93:1; 104:1; 132:16-18; Isa.22:21-24; 61:10; Dan.12:5-7; Zech.3:4, 5; Rev.19:7, 8). As the sick touched the garments of Jesus, they were healed (Mrk.5:28-30). The clothing of Aaron for priestly service pointed to the clothing of the Holy Spirit from on high.

4. **The Anointing** – vs.7
    After the washing came the clothing, and after the clothing came the anointing. Aaron was anointed first and then his sons (Lev.8:1, 2). Christ must be the pre-eminent One in all things, and then the Church (Col.1:17-19; 2:9). The Holy Spirit is "the anointing" (Grk. 'the chrisma', or the oil). The Holy Spirit is 'the unction' on both Christ and the Church (1Jhn.2:20, 27; 2Cor.1:21; Lke.4:18; Isa.10:27 KJV; 61:1-3). It was the Holy Spirit on the believers that made them truly 'Christians' or 'anointed ones' (Acts 11:26). The Church is the Body of CHRIST; that is, the Body of the Anointed One. It is not "the body

of Jesus" because His physical body is in heaven. But it is the Body of CHRIST, along with all the significance which that name or designation entails.

That same anointing had to be upon all the vessels of the Sanctuary before being used in the service of the Lord.

In the name of "Christ" we have the Godhead involved, as Father, Son and Holy Spirit.

The Father is the Anointer (Grk. 'Chrio') – Lke.4:8; Isa.61:1-3; Acts 10:38
The Son is the Anointed (Grk. 'Christos') – 1Cor.12:10-13. Christ and His Church
The Holy Spirit is the Anointing (Grk. 'Chrisma', Oil) – 1Jhn.2:20, 27

5. **Aaron's Sons** – vs.8, 9
After Aaron (the High Priest, the head of the Priesthood) was anointed, then Aaron's sons were clothed with coats (tunics), girdles, bonnets (hats) and thus consecrated to the Priesthood. They were also anointed (Ex.29:21). The sons were clothed entirely in linen, NOT in the garments of glory and beauty, which was entirely distinctive for Aaron, as for Jesus, our great High Priest. Believers are clothed in the white linen of faith-righteousness. Only Jesus is clothed in the garments of glory and beauty, because of WHO He is and WHAT He alone has done!

B. The Sin Offering – Ex.29:10-14 with Lev.4
The sin offering involved:
- The young bull for a sin offering
- Aaron and his sons were to lay hands on the head of the bullock
- The bullock was killed before the Lord, by the Tabernacle door
- Some of its blood was sprinkled on the horns of the Brazen Altar
- The rest was poured out at the base of the altar
- All the inward parts were burnt on the altar
- The body of flesh and offal was burnt with fire outside the camp of Israel
- This was the sin offering (Lev.4; 8:14-17).

If it were not for the New Testament, we would not have any clues as to the meaning and significance of these actions. One wonders how many of the Israelites had any insight into these things!

In the laying on of hands, there was identification, impartation and substitution as the animal was sinless and innocent. This is a SIN offering and sin must be dealt with first, before priestly service can begin. Death must take place, because the wages of sin is death. The animal must die (Gen.2:16, 17; Rom.5:12-21; Rom.6:23).

Jesus was our "sin offering" and He suffered outside the camp of Israel, outside the gate of the city (Heb.13:10-13). God was particular as to what happened to His BODY and His BLOOD (Matt.26:26-28). Jesus supersedes all animal sacrifices because He is the God-Man, the perfect sinless sacrifice (human nature) and priest (Divine nature). He is both sacrifice and priest in the one person. He is both Offeror and Offering, Priest and Sacrifice, God and Man, Deity and Humanity (Heb.5:1-5; 4:14-16; 8:1-5).

The sin question has been dealt with at Calvary. On the basis of His shed blood, the blood can be applied to our hearts and lives (Ex.29:21; Lev.8:14-17; 17:11; 1Jhn.1:5-7; Rev.12:11). He is our sin offering; He was made sin for us so that we could be the righteousness of God in Christ (2Cor.5:15-21; Isa.53). "When I see the blood, I will pass-over you" (Ex.12).

C. The Ram of the Burnt Offering – Ex.29:15-18 with Lev.1
The burnt offering involved:

- One of the two rams is taken
- Aaron and his sons lay hands on the head of the ram
- The ram must be killed
- The blood sprinkled around and on the Brazen Altar
- The ram cut in pieces and pieces arranged together
- The whole ram burnt on the altar
- It is a burnt offering, and a sweet savor or offering to the Lord

Basically the same truths are seen in this offering: the laying on of hands; death must take place, the blood must be sprinkled, the whole ram burnt on the altar. The differences between the SIN offering and the BURNT offering are seen in the following. The burnt offering was wholly burnt on the altar of brass. The sin offering was taken outside the camp. The burnt offering was a sweet sacrifice to the Lord. There was nothing 'sweet' about the SIN offering.

The burnt offering of Jesus as a perfect substitute for us. He perfectly fulfilled the will of the Father (Heb.10; Psa.40). "I delight to do Your will O God, Your law is within My heart." In the Sin Offering, sin is dealt with. In the Burnt Offering, the will of God is done completely and perfectly. The very essence of sin is self-will. Jesus did the Father's will perfectly, and there was no sin in Him.

D. The Ram of Consecration – Ex.29:19-28; Lev.8:22-24, 30
The things involved in this offering were:

- The other ram is taken
- Aaron and his sons lay hands on the head
- The ram must be killed
- The blood is now applied to Aaron and put on his right ear, his right thumb and his right toe
- The blood is sprinkled on the Altar of Brass
- Some of the blood is sprinkled on Aaron and his garments
- Some of the blood is sprinkled on Aaron's sons and their garments
- The blood hallowed (made holy) the garments of Aaron and his sons

Some of the same truths are evident in the laying on of hands and the death of the victim. It is worthy to note that hands are laid on the HEAD of the animal in each case. SIN entered the mind of man in the Fall (2Cor.11:1-3; Rom.5:12-21).

In the Fall, the three members of the body were defiled by sin. The ear listened to Satanic temptations, the hand partook of the forbidden fruit, and the walk to the tree was against the commandment of the Lord. These three were defiled and corrupted by sin (Gen.3:1-6). Each need to be cleansed by the blood in order to be used in the service of the Lord; to hear His voice, serve Him faithfully and walk in His ways.

E. The Wave Offering – Ex.29:22-25
The things involved in this offering were:

- The inward parts, the fat, the kidneys and the thigh of the ram of consecration
- One loaf of bread, one cake made with oil and one wafer from the basket
- These were put into the hands of Aaron and sons and they were to be a wave offering before the Lord
- After this all were to be given back to Moses and burnt on the Brazen Altar as a sweet savor to the Lord
- This wave offering was an offering made by fire (continued next part)

F. The Heave Offering – Ex.29:27-28 KJV

- In the heave offering, the thigh of the sacrifice was given to the priest, to Aaron and his sons
- The thigh was then offered as a heave offering to the Lord
- This was counted as a Peace Offering – Lev.3. These offerings from the people belonged to Aaron and his sons.

In the wave and the heave offering, we discover the following truths. The average Israelite probably never did understand the significance of these symbolic acts. The "**wave**" offering means "to wave to and fro". This was done with the breast of the animal, and the breast speaks of love and affection.

The "**heave**" offering means "to go up and down". This was done with the shoulder, the place of strength, support and government. It may be remembered that the garments of Aaron involved both the shoulder (onyx stones) and the breast (the 12 stones in the breastplate of judgment). It speaks of the government of God and His love for His people.

It is also worth noting that when the Priest performed the "wave and heave" offering, he actually made the sign of the cross: "To and fro" and "up and down". This was only ever done with the Peace Offering. Jesus made peace through the blood of His cross (Col.1:20; Eph.2:12-17).

G. Aaron's Garments – Ex.29:29-30

- Aaron's High Priestly garments were to be passed on to his sons
- They were to be anointed in them
- They were to be consecrated in them
- The inheritor son was to wear them for seven days in the Tabernacle when he ministered in the Holy Place

This would be symbolic of the passing on of Aaron's mantle of Priesthood to the son, even as Elijah passed his mantle on to his successor, Elisha (2Kgs.2). Christ will never be succeeded in His Priesthood. He lives forever in the power of an endless life (Heb.7).

H. The Meal of Aaron and Sons – Ex.29:31-34

- The flesh of the ram of consecration to be boiled in the Holy Place
- Aaron and his sons to eat it with the bread in the basket by the door of the Tabernacle
- No outsider (stranger) was to eat of it. It was holy.

- Anything left over until morning of the flesh or bread was to be burnt in the fire and not be eaten as all was holy to the Lord

This was the priestly food. They fed upon the consecration offerings. They fed on what they were to minister. It was their communion service even as we feed on the "body and blood of the Lord" in the communion table (1Cor.11:23-34; Jhn.6). It is our life. The priests handled these offerings and fed upon the portion given to them (1Jhn.1:1-3). For us, it is Christ crucified, Christ unleavened, Christ anointed, Christ incarnate (Heb.7:24-28). As Moses consecrated Aaron and his sons, God has consecrated Christ and His Church to minister as kings and priests unto Him.

The meaning of the word "consecration" has several thoughts in the Hebrew:

1. "To fill the hand" – Young's Concordance (Ex.28:41; 29:9, 29, 33, 35; Lev.16:32; 21:10)
2. "To set apart" – Young's (Ex.28:3; 30:30)
3. "Fillings in or up" – Young's (2Chr.26:18; Ex.29:22, 26, 27, 31, 34; Lev.7:37; 8:22, 28, 29-33).
4. "Separation" – Young's (Num.6:7, 9, 12)
5. "Act of setting apart from a common to a sacred use", "to devote, hallow or make sacred" – Collins Dictionary
6. "To hallow, to set apart" – Young's (Ex.29:1, 21)

So Christ and His Church are set apart to God for His service and will. "As He is, so are we in this world" (1Jhn.4:17).

I. The Seven Days Consecration – Ex.29:35-37; Lev.8:33-36

This was for the Priests (vs.29-30, 35) and for the Altar (vs.36, 37). Seven is the number of fullness, that which is complete, the Divine number. It is the number of consummation, the number of the Book of Revelation. We are kings and priests unto God and His Christ (Rev.1:6; 5:9, 10; 1Pet.2:5-9). Both He who sanctifies and those who are sanctified are all one (Heb.2:9-11).

- The consecration was to take place over seven days
- A bullock was offered every day as an atonement, a sin offering
- The altar was cleansed by sacrificial blood
- It was anointed
- It was sanctified
- It was most holy
- Whatever touched it must also be holy

Note the importance of the words used relative to this chapter on consecration:
1. Atonement – vs.33, 36, 37. The reconciliation, the appeasement, the covering
2. Consecrate – vs.33, 34, 35. To fill the hand
3. Hallow or make holy – vs.1
4. Cleanse – vs.36. To make clean, to purify
5. Anoint – vs.36
6. Sanctify – vs.33, 36, 37. To set apart from and set apart unto the Lord.

J. The Daily Offerings – Ex.29:38-46

The daily offerings were as follows, and this was the priestly ministry:

- Daily offerings were two lambs of the first year
- One lamb offered in the morning, the other at evening
- One lamb with $1/10^{th}$ of a measure of flour mingled with oil, plus wine for a drink offering in the morning
- Same with the evening lamb – a sweet savor offering
- God will meet and speak at the Tabernacle door
- The priests will minister in the Tabernacle, at the Brass Altar
- God will dwell among His people, and be their God
- They will know He brought them out of Egypt as He dwells among them as the Lord their God

The congregation of Israel witnessed this consecration (Lev.8:3-5). On the eighth day, the glory of the Lord in fire appeared. The people shouted. They worshipped prostrate before the Lord. This was God's seal on His chosen priesthood, that of Aaron and his sons. The glory of the Lord is to fill all the earth in the appointed day (Num.14:20; Isa.6:1-6; Psa.63). Moses saw the glory of the Lord (Ex.33-34).

CHAPTER 14 - THE LEVITICAL OFFERINGS

Introductory:
The Book of Hebrews clearly shows that, if there is a Covenant, there must be a Sanctuary. And if there is a Sanctuary, there must be a ministering Priesthood. And if there is a Priesthood, then there must be of necessity the offering of Sacrifice and Oblation. Priesthood demands Sacrifice. One cannot be a Priest without an Offering to the Lord. Read carefully Heb.8:1-6 where these things are confirmed.

A. Old Testament Sacrifices

The truth of the introductory comments finds its origin right from the beginning of time, from the very fall of Adam and Eve into sin. God required the body and blood of sacrificial victims. It may be asked 'Why?' The reason is, God created man in His own image, as a triune being (Gen.1:26-28; 1Thess.5:23). Man is spirit, soul and body. The life of the body is in the blood (Gen.9:4; Lev.17:11). Man's physical life is body and blood. The death penalty, in due time, would touch man's physical being (Gen.2:16, 17). When Adam and his wife sinned, the truth of substitutionary redemption was initiated by God in His grace. So an innocent, sinless animal – a victim – was killed. The body and the blood of the animal were taken instead of the body and blood of Adam and his wife at that time.

Adam and Eve witnessed the first substitutionary death. They understood the animal was dying in their stead; the innocent for the guilty, the sinless for the sinful. God clothed Adam and his wife in the coats of skin, provided by the death of the victim (Gen.3:1-24). Without doubt, Adam would pass on the truth to his sons, Cain and Abel. By faith Abel accepted that the one and only way of approach to God was through sacrifice, the body and blood of the victim (Heb.11:4). Cain rejected the blood of atonement and brought his own bloodless sacrifice, the fruit of the cursed earth and the product of his works (1Jhn.3:10-12).

Thus, sacrifice was established by God Himself at the very fall of man. Those who are of faith continued this way of approach to God for over 2000 years. It was under the Levitical Law that a fuller revelation and greater detail was given as to the sacrificial system. Shadows of the atonement are seen in the time of the patriarchs.

1. The coats of skin provided for Adam and Eve (Gen.3:21)
2. Abel's sacrifice of faith (Gen.4 with Heb.11:4)
3. Noah's altar of sacrifice (Gen.8)
4. Abraham's five sacrifices as commanded by the Lord (Gen.15)

5. Abraham's typical sacrifice of his only son Isaac (Gen.22 with Heb.11:16-21)
6. The altars of Isaac and Jacob (Gen.35)

All pointed to the fuller revelation that would be given under the Levitical system in time.

B. The Levitical Offerings

It was under the Law Covenant and the Aaronic and Levitical Priesthood that we find a fully developed, detailed and intricate sacrificial system. To the unregenerate mind (and often to the regenerate mind?), the details of these sacrifices are boring and meaningless. But to the soul who sees that **God had Christ in mind**, nothing is boring. All the details and intricacies pass to and/or through the cross and find fulfillment in our Lord Jesus Christ as to truth and/or actuality. The Christ of the cross is the key to understanding these things.

1. The Five Offerings – Lev.1-7

These five offerings are a detailed study in themselves. Such is not the purpose of this text. The reader is referred to the Bibliography for recommended reading of text pertaining to the same. However, these five offerings become the foundation for all other offerings. All other offerings point back to these foundational five, being in themselves one or the other of these. All offerings point to the multiple aspects of Christ's once-for-all sacrifice, as the New Testament clearly confirms (Heb.9-10 chapters).

In summary of these five offerings we note:

- The Burnt Offering – Lev.1:1-17; 6:8-13
  Points to Christ's voluntary and willing sacrifice on the cross completely to the Father's will.
- The Meal Offering – Lev.2:1-16; 6:14-23
  Points to Christ's sacrifice as the corn of wheat, who died and rose again to be the Bread of Life to His own.
- The Peace Offering – Lev.3:1-17; 7:11-21
  Points to Christ's sacrifice to bring about peace and reconciliation between both God and mankind.
- The Sin Offering – Lev.4:1-35; 6:24-30
  Points to Christ's compulsory offering, when He was made sin for us that we might become the righteousness of God in Him.
- The Trespass Offering – Lev.5:1-19; 6:1-7; 7:1-10
  Points to Christ's sacrifice for all our trespasses and violations of relational laws between both God and our fellow-man.

2. **The Day of Atonement Offerings** – Lev.16
      The Day of Atonement offerings also pointed to Christ's sacrifice which made possible the cleansing of all sin in both heaven and earth, thus providing access "within the veil" into the immediate presence of God. This Day was the most important and significant day of the year for Israel and in the Feasts of the Lord.

   3. **The Sacrifice of the Red Heifer** – Num.19
      Points to Christ's once-for-all sacrifice and the constantly available "washing of water by the Word" cleansing in order to live a purified life before the Lord (Eph.5:26; Titus 3:5).

C. **Ordained without Pleasure**
   There are various Scripture references that tell us that, even though God Himself ordained animal sacrifices and oblations, He was never really pleased with such. The following references confirm the truth of these things.

   1. Psa.40:6-8 with Heb.10:5-10. The Psalmist plainly tells us that sacrifice and offering God did not require. God had opened his ears. Burnt offerings and sin offerings God did not want.

   2. Isa.1:11-17. The passage here shows that, although the Lord ordained sacrifices, offerings, the details concerning the fat and the blood, the oblations, the incense, the new moons and Sabbaths, as also the Feasts, God Himself became fed up with the hypocrisy of it all. It was internal cleansing of the heart He required, not merely that which pertained to the external ceremonial cleansing.

   3. Isa.66:3. The Prophet Isaiah foretold the time would come when sacrificing a bullock, or a lamb of oblation, and the burning of incense would become an abomination to the very God who ordained these things. Once the sacrifice of Messiah (Isa.53) had been offered, then these things became an abomination or a detestable thing to the Lord.

   4. Psa.51:1-15, especially verses 16, 17 clearly say: "For You desire not sacrifice or I would give it. You delight not in burnt offerings. The sacrifices of God are a broken spirit, a broken and contrite heart, O God, You will not despise." David knew the truth of this Psalm he wrote.

5. Micah 6:6-8. The Prophet Micah asks: How shall we approach the Lord God? Does God want burnt offerings, calves and rams and oil? Will He accept the sacrifice of the firstborn for sin and transgression? The answer is evident. He desires justice, mercy and humility. Jesus confirms the same (Matt.23:23). These things were the weightier matters of the Law.

D. The Lamb of God

Although God ordained animal sacrifice and oblation, He was never pleased with it. He was pleased with His Son. All Old Testament sacrifice and oblation pointed to Christ and His redemptive work.

In Gen.22, Isaac (the only begotten son of the Old Testament) asks his father, Abraham: "…where is the lamb for a burnt offering?" Abraham said, "God will provide Himself a lamb for a burnt offering." Some 2000 years later, John the Baptist answers Isaac's question as he sees Jesus (the only begotten Son of the New Testament) coming to the River Jordan, "Behold, the Lamb of God who takes away the sin of the world" (Jhn.1:29, 36).

HE is the fulfillment of all Old Testament sacrifice and oblation. At the cross, He caused "the sacrifice and oblation to cease" by His own one sinless human sacrifice, the presentation of His own body and blood (Heb.9-10 chapters with 1Pet.1:18-20). When John made the announcement, the Father spoke from heaven and said, "THIS is My beloved Son, **in whom I am well pleased**" (Matt.3:16, 17). Although He was never pleased with all that He ordained in Old Testament times, He was "well pleased" with His only Son. All pointed firstly to Christ's supreme sacrifice, and then secondarily to the "spiritual sacrifices" of the Church, the believers as the Body of Christ and the New Covenant Priesthood (1Pet.2:4-9).

CHAPTER 15 - PRIESTLY MINISTRY IN MOSES' TABERNACLE

The Ministry of the Priest (or Priests) varied in the Tabernacle of Moses. All finds its spiritual fulfillment in the New Testament Church. Paul tells us that all these things happened to them for types and examples and they are written for our admonition upon whom the ends of the ages have come. Old Testament truths, whether in type or symbol or prophecy, were written for our instruction and learning (1Cor.10:6, 11; Rom.15:4). Though the external forms have passed away, the knowledge and the truth that was hidden in the external form remains (Rom.2:20).

A. **The Ministry of the Priest**
    The basic ministry of the Priest was threefold in reality:

    1. Ministry to the Lord was first and foremost – Ex.28:1-5. "That he may minister unto Me" was the repeated phrase when God spoke to Moses about Aaron's calling (1Sam.2:11, 18; 3:1 with Acts 13:1-4).

    2. Ministry to the Sanctuary, or the Tabernacle, the House of the Lord. Refer Ezek.44:11-19, 27.

    3. Ministry to Israel, the people of God – Ezek.44:11-19, 27.

B. **The Ministry of the Priesthood**
    The ministry of the priests was wide and varied. The books of Exodus, Leviticus, Numbers and Deuteronomy through to Chronicles and Nehemiah provide a broad spectrum of priestly ministry. The following outline gives us an idea of the ministry of the priesthood.

    1. To read the Book of the Law in the Feast of Tabernacles every seventh year, in the Year of Release (Deut.31:9-13).
    2. To minister in the priest's office (Ex.29:1, 44; 30:30; 31:10; 35:19; Lev.7:35; 16:32; Num.3:3-4).
    3. The Tribe of Levi was to teach the people of Israel the Laws of the Lord and to burn incense before the Lord (2Chr.29:11). The High Priest was custodian of the Urim and Thummim and from him the people would know the mind of the Lord (Deut.33:8-11). This was the prophecy of Moses over the Tribe of Levi. Note the "teaching seminars" that Godly King Jehoshaphat conducted by the Levites scattered in the cities of Judah (2Chr.17:1-6, 7-10 with 2Chr.15:1-6, especially verse 3). See also Deut.24:8; 31:9-13; 2Chr.34:14-18).
    4. To bless the people in the Name of the Lord (Num.6:24-27 with 2Chr.30:27).

5. To encourage the people of Israel when they went to battle. Note the seven priests with the Ark of God when they conquered the city of Jericho (Josh.3-6 chapters).
6. To bless in the Name of the Lord (Deut.10:8).
7. To minister in the Name of the Lord (Deut.18:5-7).
8. To give thanks to the Lord and to praise His Name (2Chr.31:2-4).
9. To officiate at the Brazen Altar of sacrifice and the Golden Altar of Incense (Ex.28-30 chapters).
10. To receive the priestly portions of the various sacrifices and offerings (Lev.1-7 chapters). Read also Deut.18:3-8; 26:1-11).
11. To make atonement for the Israelites (Lev.12). Especially the great Day of Atonement under the ministry of the High Priest (Lev.16).
12. To officiate in the Feasts of the Lord (Lev.23).
13. They could partake of the Table of Showbread (Matt.12:4).
14. They were to discern in the Laws of leprosy, whether in a person, a garment or in a house (Lev.13-14 with Matt.8:1-4).
15. To see people cleansed from ceremonial defilement (Lev.15).
16. To administer the waters of separation and purification (Num.19).
17. To receive of the people's tithes and/or offerings (Num.18).
18. The priests also helped the Judges in certain cases of judgment (Deut.17:9-18; 21:1-15).
19. To keep their eyes on the Cloud, to blow the trumpets and tell the people God was moving (Num.10:1-10).
20. The Levite has no inheritance in the land. They were given cattle and some cities as cities of refuge, priestly cities (Deut.18:1, 2).
21. To wait on their office (Num.3:10; 18:7 with 2Chr.7:6, 7; 31:15).
22. Phinehas was given the "covenant of an everlasting priesthood" (Num.25:13). This could only be possible through the Priesthood of Jesus Christ, made a High Priest forever after the Order of Melchizedek (Psa.110 with Heb.7). Read also Neh.13:29; Ex.29:9; 40:15). The Aaronic and Levitical Priesthood was abolished at the cross of Jesus.

As noted previously, all the external forms and ceremony are passed away, but the knowledge and truth hidden in the external form remains. It passes through the filter of the cross into the spiritual priesthood of all believers, functioning as members in the Body of Christ, the New Covenant Priesthood (1Pet.2:5-9; Rev.1:6; 5:9, 10). All believers are now "kings and priests unto God and His Christ" and minister in their place accordingly. There are many spiritual lessons to be learned from the Ministry of the Priests in the Tabernacle of Moses.

CHAPTER 16 - PRIESTLY MINISTRY IN DAVID'S TABERNACLE

Introductory:
In 1Chr.17:5 we are told how the Lord said, "For I have not dwelt in a house since the day that I brought up Israel unto this day; but I have gone from **tent to tent, and from one tabernacle to another**." And so it was. God moved from the tent of Moses to the Tabernacle of the Lord that Moses built at Sinai. And God kept moving "from tent to tent" and "from one tabernacle to another tabernacle".

In due time God moved from the Tabernacle of Moses on into the Tabernacle of David, and finally into the Temple of Solomon. Each of these habitations of God were called after the names of the builders. There was a distinct order of approach to God in the Tabernacle of Moses and there was a different approach to the Lord in the Tabernacle of David. The order of David's Tabernacle was carried forward into the Temple of Solomon, along with the order of the Tabernacle of Moses. The following brief history explains.

For a short time in history during the reign of David and through to the early years of Solomon's reign, Scripture shows that there were **two Tabernacles** in existence at the same time. The reader is referred again to the Bibliography and the associated textbooks which deal fully with each of these structures. However, for the purpose of this chapter, we note a brief outline of these two Tabernacles along with their attendant priests of Levi and the orders of service.

That the two Tabernacles existed at the same time is plainly seen in the following passages of Scripture.

1. 1Chr.15:1 and 16:1-38 recount the setting of the Ark of the Covenant in the tent or Tabernacle which David had prepared for it. Also 1Chr.16:39-42 shows that, at the same time, the Tabernacle of Moses was still functioning.

2. A careful reading of 2Chr.1:3, 4 confirms the same truth as above.

A. Comparison of the Two Tabernacles
Each of these Tabernacles had an attendant company of priests to minister to God but the similarity ends there.

1. The two tents (or tabernacles) were on two different hills. Moses' Tabernacle was on Mt Gibeon (1Chr.16:39), about 8km northwest of Jerusalem. David's Tabernacle was on Mt Zion in Jerusalem

(1Kgs.8:1; 2Chr.5:2). Mt Zion is the eastern most of the ridges or hills upon which Jerusalem is built.

2. The priesthood serving at the Tabernacle of Moses continued on with the order of service as given by God to Moses. This was largely characterized by animal sacrifice and a limited ministry of music and song (1Chr.16:40-42; 2Chr.1:3-6). The priesthood serving at the Tabernacle of David held an initial commissioning service with animal sacrifices (1Chr.16:1, 2) and from then onwards *continually* (vs.6) offered up spiritual sacrifices of joy, thanksgiving, prayer, praise, worship and adoration in music and song.

3. Moses' Tabernacle had an Outer Court, the Holy Place, the veil and the original articles of furniture, BUT there was no Ark of the Covenant in the Holy of Holies. The Ark, which was the speaking place of God (Ex.25:10-22), which the Israelites understood to be the presence and glory of God (1Sam.4:21, 22) was no longer there. It was gone. By way of contrast, David's Tabernacle had no Outer Court, no veil, no furniture but the Ark of the Lord God of Israel.

4. To approach God in Moses' Tabernacle, one had to come by way of the Outer Court, the Holy Place – which only the priests could enter – and the veil before the Holy of Holies – which only the High Priest could enter on the Day of Atonement. To approach God in David's Tabernacle, there was no veil to separate the people from God. One simply had to be a worshipper with a clean heart. Everyone could come without discrimination between Israelite, priest or proselyte. The Holiest of All, in that sense, had been transferred. There was access before God and the Ark of His Presence.

5. The central *human* figure in the Tabernacle at Gibeon would be the Prophet and Priest, Moses, the great leader who led them out of Egypt and had received and given them the Law.

   The central *human* figure in the Tabernacle at Mt Zion was King David. He was the only Old Testament King to have performed any priestly duties and escaped unscathed by the Lord (2Sam.6:12-19; 1Chr.16:1-3). One can compare, for instance, King Jeroboam who was about to do priestly service and was smitten by God (1Kgs.13:1ff). Also think of King Saul and King Uzziah (1Sam.13:7ff with 2Chr.26:14ff).

6. David wore the priestly garment – the ephod (1Chr.15:27; 2Sam.6:14). He also ate of the Bread of the Presence (1Sam.21:1-6)

which was not lawful for any but the priests to eat (Lev.24:5-9; Lke.6:1-4). He also gave it to the people who accompanied him. In the matter of the pestilence sent by God upon Israel (1Chr.21:14ff), David built an altar and offered sacrifices (vs.24-27). Even though David was a King, God permitted him to perform priestly functions just as Aaron performed priestly functions and staved off the plague on the people (Num.16:44-50).

7. Although David was not a King-Priest, he certainly was a King who touched Priestly functions. In Gen.14:17ff, Melchizedek (melchi=king, tzedek=righteousness), King of Salem (peace) was seen by Abraham. This man, who was King of Righteousness and also King of Peace, was the priest of the Most High God (vs.18) – a King and a Priest.

The Lord Jesus Christ is the true King of Righteousness and King of Peace (Heb.5:5-10; Heb.7). David wrote of the priests in the Tabernacle of Moses (Psa.133). and he also wrote of the revelation he had of Melchizedek, the King-Priest (Psa.110).

8. Melchizedek and David point to Jesus both in type and prophecy. Both also point to the New Testament Church, a multitudinous company of "kings and priests" unto God. They would be both kings and priests unto God and His Christ who would reign on this earth (Rev.1:6; 5:9, 10; 20:6).

B. Order of Worship Contrasted

The contrast of the orders at these two Tabernacles comes to sharper focus when we consider the two orders established there until the building of the Temple of the Lord, the Temple built by Solomon. Whether the priests understood the significance of these things or not, we do not know, but it is evident that David saw something in the Spirit. He received the pattern of the Temple, the house of the Lord, where both orders were established until the coming of Christ, David's greater Son.

It was a glorious foreshadowing of the New Testament Church Age, as seen in the final comments in this chapter.

This may be seen in the comparison on the next page:

Tabernacle of David Order Mt Zion	Tabernacle of Moses Order Mt Gibeon
1. Singers and Singing – 1Chr.15; 16:2-7; Col.3:16	1. None (Mt Gibeon – a few). 1Chr.16:37-43
2. Instruments of Music – 1Chr.23:5; 25:1-7; Eph.5:18, 19	2. None
3. Levites minister before Ark – 1Chr.16:37; Heb.6:19, 20; 10:19-21	3. High Priest only
4. Recording – 1Chr.16:4; Psa.80:1 (title); Rev.1:10, 11	4. None
5. Thanking – 1Chr.16:4, 8; 1Thess.5:18	5. None
6. Praise – 1Chr.16:4, 36; Heb.13:15	6. None
7. Psalm Singing – 1Chr.16:7; Eph.5:18, 19; 1Cor.14:26; Jas.5:13	7. None (Psa.90 only)
8. Rejoicing and joy – 1Chr.16:10, 27, 31; Acts 13:52	8. Commanded
9. Clapping – Psa.47:1	9. None
10. Shouting – 1Chr.15:28; 1Thess.4:16	10. None (Except Jericho – Josh.6)
11. Dancing – 1Chr.15:29; Psa.149:3; Lke.15:25	11. None (Except Ex.15)
12. Lifting Hands – Psa.134; 1Tim.2:8	12. None
13. Worship-Bowing – 1Chr.16:29; Jhn.4:20-24	13. Worship – Afar off
14. Seeking the Lord – 1Chr.16:10, 11; Acts 15:17	14. Sought the Tabernacle
15. Spiritual Sacrifices – Psa.27:6; 116:17; 1Pet.2:3-5	15. Animal Sacrifices and Oblations
16. Amen (in blessing) – 1Chr.16:36; 1Cor.14:16	16. Amen (To Curses – Deut.27:15-26)

Such is the contrast and comparison between the two Tabernacles and the two companies of Priests ministering in each according to God's order. Surely the Law Age and the New Covenant were being shadowed forth in the two Tabernacles.

C. New Covenant Realities

The Prophet Amos prophesies of a restoration of the Tabernacle of David (Amos 9:11). This prophetic word must have been a puzzle to many of that time as it has in subsequent times.

In Acts 15 we read of the Council at Jerusalem. The apostles and elders are trying to unravel the issue about whether the Gentiles coming to Christ need to keep the Law of Moses and be circumcised. After much debate, James receives a word of wisdom from the Lord. The very fact that God visited the Gentiles and they had received the same Holy Spirit as the Jewish believers settled the issue. Both James and the rest of the brothers understood the visitation and God's acceptance of the Gentiles, apart from the Law and outside the Covenants, that this was a fulfillment of the prophecy of Amos to "rebuild the Tabernacle of David" (Acts 15:12-21).

How do we understand these things? As directed by James, we understand David's Tabernacle to be a type or a prophetic picture of the New Testament Church Age. The same typical truths are seen in David acting as a King-Priest under that order.

From the very beginning, God has had in His mind a select company of mankind, a royal priesthood, who would be His unique people on this earth. He sought to have this in Ex.19 with Israel as a "kingdom of priests" but settled for the lower level of the Aaronic and Levitical Priesthood. But still, in the mind of God, there remained the mysterious priesthood of whom Melchizedek was but the forerunner. God wanted a "kingdom of priests."

Centuries later, after a long period of the Law and animal sacrifices, King David came and he prophetically pictured in himself a Kingdom that was to come. David was under the Law Age, but the Tabernacle he built, and his manner of prayer, praise and worship foreshadowed something that would transcend the Law of Moses. There would come a time when one initial sacrifice would be offered, and then no more blood sacrifice would be needed. There would be sacrifices of joy, praise, worship and thanksgiving, characterized by music, singing and dancing and freedom from Mosaic regulations.

There would be no Outer Court, no Holy Place, no veil to restrict access into the Holiest of All and the very presence of God. All that would be done away; fulfilled and abolished by fulfillment. There would be no restrictions on who could come. Jews and Gentiles. All would be welcomed into His Presence.

When Jesus died on the cross, the veil of the Temple was torn from top to bottom. It signified the end of approaching God by the Law. It was a new day. It demanded a new order of priests – a new order of ministers who could stand before the Ark – "the Presence" – and worship the Father in spirit and in truth (Jhn.4:20-24).

The New Testament leaves no doubt about the identity of this company of priests. It is the Church, the Body of Christ and the members of that priestly company. The service of David and the Tabernacle of David prefigures that royal priesthood "after the order of Melchizedek" – kings and priests unto God and His Christ (Rev.1:6; 1Pet.2:1-10; Rev.5:9, 10; 20:6).

CHAPTER 17 - PRIESTLY MINISTRY IN SOLOMON'S TEMPLE

In the previous two chapters, we have seen the function and ministry of the Priests in both the Tabernacle of Moses and the Tabernacle of David. As noted, in David's time the two Tabernacles existed and functioned together at one and the same time, one on Mt Gibeon and the other on Mt Zion. This lasted for some 30 years, before the Temple of the Lord was built. But now, under King Solomon, with the building of the temple, the House of the Lord, the order of BOTH these Tabernacles, with their respective Priesthood, are merged into one in the order of the Temple.

The sacrificial order and system of Moses' Tabernacle is continued on in the Temple. The order of the singers and musicians from David's Tabernacle is also continued on in the Temple. The details of this are to be found in 1Kings 5-9 chapters along with 2Chronicles 1-8 chapters. These together provide us the intricate details of the building of the Temple of the Lord.

A. The Tabernacle of Moses Order

As seen in the above comments, BOTH of the orders of the Tabernacle of Moses and the Tabernacle of David were incorporated into the Temple order. In the larger picture of things, both shadowed forth and typified the Dispensation of the Law (Moses) and the Dispensation of Grace (David).

The Tabernacle of Moses typified the way of approach to God by way of sacrificial atonement, through the blood. The Tabernacle of David typified the way of approach (on the basis of blood) in worship and praise, by way of singers and musicians. In the dedication of the Temple, we see the order of Moses and the order of David together in that glorious day.

In the Tabernacle of Moses order, there were numerous sacrifices offered to God according to the Law that God gave Moses.

The Dedicatory Sacrifices – 1Kgs.8:62-64; 2Chr.7:4-5
With the glory of the Lord filling the house, the fire of God burning on the altar, Solomon and the people of Israel offered to the Lord numerous sacrifices on this same day. In all there were 22,000 oxen, 120,000 sheep making a total of some 142,000 offerings to God. These were burnt offerings and peace offerings with their particular meal offerings. These were voluntary offerings.

The sin and trespass offerings are not mentioned. These would have been offered by the priests and not by King Solomon, for he was a King, not a King and Priest!

All pointed to Christ our great High Priest, who offered Himself to God as our sin and trespass offering at Calvary. In the building, the Church, believers offer themselves as voluntary offerings in the day of Messiah's power (Psa.110 with 1Pet.2:5-10). Solomon, as will be seen, offered himself as a "living sacrifice", representing the thousands of sacrifices offered by Israel to the Lord.

All point to the fact that Christ would give Himself as a living sacrifice and a voluntary one-for-all sacrifice for sin (Dan.9:24-27 with Heb.9-10). But none of the untold thousands of animal sacrifices could compare with the glory of Christ's divine-human sacrifice, both sinless and perfect (Eph.5:2; Isa.53). No animal sacrifice could compare with His. Believers also present themselves as "living sacrifices" (Rom.12:1-2) as their priestly service to God, and also offer "spiritual sacrifices to the Lord" as a Royal Priesthood (Read 1Pet.2:5-9; Rev.1:6; 5:9, 10).

B. The Tabernacle of David Order

Fuller details have been dealt with in other textbooks (the reader is referred to Bibliography) so a brief outline is noted here only. At the dedication of the Temple, we find the David order of singers and musicians functioning. There are numerous lessons for the New Testament Church.

1. Davidic Order

In the Tabernacle of David, 30 years beforehand, the orders of singers and musicians was established there. Here again that order is seen in Solomon's Temple.

2. White Linen

The singers and musicians were arrayed in white linen. These were of the Levites and of the three chief singers, of Asaph, Heman and Jeduthun. They had instruments of cymbals, psalteries and harps as well as the trumpets, all spoken of as musical instruments of David (2Chr.7:6). White linen is ever the symbol of righteousness and purity. The worshipping priests of the Lord were clothed in the righteousness of faith in the coming Christ (Rev.19:8).

3. East end of the Altar

The priests stood at the east end of the altar. It was at the east end of the altar that the ashes were kept and then carried outside the camp in time. Ashes spoke of a finished work, the finished sacrifice (Lev.1:16; 6:11; Heb.13:11-13). So these priests, as it were, presented themselves as a living sacrifice as they stood at the east end of the sacrificial altar.

4. **The 120 Trumpeters** (2 Chr.5:12)
   There were 120 trumpeters at this dedication. The number is significant of the "end of flesh and the beginning of life in the Spirit". In the days of Noah the Spirit was striving with mankind before God made an end of ungodly flesh by the Flood (Gen.6:1-13). On the Day of Pentecost, there were 120 disciples waiting for the Spirit to come on them as they began life in the Spirit in a new way (Acts 1:15).

5. **One Accord** (2 Chr.5:13)
   The singers and musicians were of one accord, in one place, making one sound. It was unnatural. It was super-natural. They were one in praising and thanking the Lord along with the instruments of music. The choir sang, "For the Lord is good and His mercy endures forever." With such unity, the Lord commanded the blessing (Psa.133). It was so much like the 120 on the Day of Pentecost, being in one place, of one accord (Acts 1:15; 2:1-4). It was after this that 3000 souls turned to the Lord Jesus Christ.

C. The Dedication of the Temple

The dedication day of the Temple of the Lord was a wonderful day. Details may be read in 1Kgs.8:1-66 and 2Chr.7:1-21. In summary we note:

1. The sacrifices of the Law, according to the order of Moses' Tabernacle – founded on blood sacrifice.

2. The Temple itself was dedicated in the Feast of Tabernacles, the Feast of the seventh month, also called the "Feast of Booths" (2Chr.5:3). It was not dedicated in the Feast of Passover or the Feast of Pentecost. Israel kept this Feast in the Promised Land. The Restored Temple, built after the Babylonian Captivity, was also dedicated in this month (Neh.8:17; Ezra 3; Hag.2:1-9). Christ taught significant truths in this Feast also (Jhn.7:37-39). It has typical and prophetic significance for the Church in the end of the age also. (Refer "Feasts of Israel" text – Bibliography).

3. The Ark of God was brought from the Tabernacle of David in Mt Zion and placed in the Most Holy Place (or "Holiest of All") under the wings of the great Cherubim (2Chr.5:2-10). The poles were withdrawn and placed in their position between the Holy Place and the Most Holy (1Kgs.8:1-9; 2Chr.5:1-10). The Wilderness journeyings and the traveling days were over. God would rest in His House.

4. Only the Ten Commandments on the Table of Stone were in the Ark of God.

5. The Priests were sanctified and came out of the Holiest of All, and the other Priests stood at the east end of the altar, singing and praising the Lord, the trumpeters being of one accord. Such unity! (2Chr.5:11-14).

6. It came to pass when the 120 trumpeters and the singers were making one sound in praising and thanking the Lord for His mercy and goodness, the Shekinah Glory-Cloud filled the house (1Kgs.8:10, 11; 2Chr.5:14; 7:1-3). The result was that none of the Priests could minister by reason of the Glory of God. That Cloud had led Israel from the Red Sea to Canaan Land (Ex.13:21-22; Acts 7:38). It had provided shadow in the daytime and light at night. It was on Mt Sinai and then came to the Tabernacle of Moses (Num.7:89; Lev.16:1-2). It had directed Israel's wanderings in the Wilderness over the years (Num.9:15-23; 10:1-36; Deut.1:33; Neh.9:19; Psa.78:14). And now, it came to dwell in the Most Holy Place with God's nation Israel. It all pointed to the ultimate dwelling place of God in the New Jerusalem, the City of God, where God and the Lamb are the light and temple of that eternal habitation (Rev.21-22).

7. The Glory-Fire – 2Chr.7:1-3
Not only was there the Glory of the Lord in the cloud, the FIRE of God came out from the Glory. It was so similar to the descent of the Lord at the dedication of the Tabernacle of Moses. Fire and glory belong to the Lord (Ex.40:34-38; Lev.9:22-24; 10:1-3). Israel's history shows that God is a "consuming fire". He is the God who answers by fire. The theme of glory and fire is woven throughout these Scriptures (1Chr.21:26; 1Kgs.18 and 19; Ex.13). And on the Day of Pentecost, the disciples were baptized with the Holy Spirit FIRE (Acts 2:1-4). The end result was that the people shouted, fell on their faces and worshipped God.

D. Solomon – "the Living Sacrifice" – 2Chr.6:12-13
One other thing in the dedication day of the Temple was Solomon's symbolic personal dedication to the Lord. What a tragedy that he did not live all his life in the truth of his symbolic action.

Solomon set a brazen (bronze) scaffold in the middle of the great court, stood upon it, and then knelt before the Lord and the people as he made this great dedicatory prayer to the Lord. Here was the King of Israel praying to the King of kings and Lord of lords. We note several significant truths in this act of Solomon with its attendant truths.

1. **A Brazen Scaffold**
   Brass, as always, is symbolic of judgment against sin and self. Here Solomon allows sin and self to be dealt with in symbolic manner.

2. **Measurements of the Scaffold**
   When one reads Ex.27:1-8, the brazen altar measured 5 cubits long by 5 cubits broad and 3 cubits high. It was also four-square. The bronze scaffold that Solomon built was the very same measurements. He is presenting himself as a "living sacrifice" on a similar 'altar' as he prayed to the Lord. What a picture!

3. **Position of Scaffold**
   The scaffold was positioned in the middle of the court which had been hallowed for the numerous animal sacrifices (1Kgs.8:64; 2Chr.7:7). While the animals went as unwilling sacrifices offered to the Lord, although voluntarily offered by the Priests, Solomon was presenting himself willingly and humbly before the Lord. The sacrifices of God are a broken and contrite spirit. The external pointed to the internal.

4. **Solomon's Position**
   Solomon stood on the scaffold first of all, and then, with outstretched hands, knelt before the Lord and made his great prayer of dedication (1Kgs.8:54-55; 2Chr.6:12-13). Standing, kneeling, lifting his hands – all speak of total surrender to the Lord of Glory. As noted, if only he had maintained this attitude through his whole life, the record would have been written differently.

5. **Solomon's Prayer**
   Solomon's prayer is the most amazing and comprehensive prayer in the Bible regarding the Kings of Israel and Judah (Read 1Kgs.8:12-61; 2Chr.6:1-42). The prayer covers every area of personal and national life. God's house was to be a house of prayer for all nations, not just for the nation of Israel.

   - Solomon prays for God's constant care
   - Prayer in defeat
   - Prayer in time of drought
   - Prayer in famine or pestilence
   - Prayer of the foreigner
   - Prayer in time of warfare
   - Prayer when in captivity

Godly kings were men of prayer: Jehoshaphat – 2Chr.17; Hezekiah – 2Kgs.18; Isa.37:1; 2Chr.29-30; Solomon – 1Kgs.8; 2Chr.6.

E. The Twenty-Four Courses and Temple Orders

Solomon built all according to the pattern the Lord gave to his father, David. The Priestly Courses were established once the Temple was dedicated to the Lord. The details of the priestly courses are to be found in 1Chr.23, 24, 25, 26, 27 chapters.

For details, the reader is directed to the textbook, ***"The Temple of Solomon."***

- The Courses of the Levites – 1Chr.23:1-32
- The Division of the Sons of Aaron – 1Chr.24:1-19
- The Courses of the Singers and Musicians – 1Chr.25:1-31
- The Courses of the Porters – 1Chr.26:1-32
- The Officers and Judges – 1Chr.26:29-32
- The Twelve Princes of Israel – 1Chr.27:1-34

Everything was done according to Divine order, including their allotted place in the House of the Lord as priests unto God.

All point to the Church, and the members of the Body of Christ as being "kings and priests" unto God, functioning in their proper place and gifting in the Body of Christ, which is the New Testament Temple, the House of the Lord (Eph.2:19-22; 1Cor.12).

The dedicatory service is replete with lessons for the Church. The Church is now God's Temple, God's House. The Holy Spirit is the Shekinah Glory in the midst of His people. In His Church, the Name of the Lord, His Law, the presence and glory of the Lord abide. The believers offer spiritual sacrifices to the Lord as a New Covenant Priesthood, a Royal Priesthood (1Pet.2:5-9; 1Tim.3:15-16; 1Cor.3:16). We are His Temple. His House is to be a House of Prayer!

PART FIVE - AN OVERVIEW OF PRIESTLY GENEALOGY

Chapter 18   The Genealogy of the Order of Aaron

CHAPTER 18 - THE GENEALOGY OF THE ORDER OF AARON

Introductory:
As noted previously, Aaron was chosen by the Lord to be Israel's first High Priest. Other Gentile nations also had their Priesthood orders, but they were corrupt, immoral and politically powerful. We see this in Egypt and Midian as examples (Gen.41:41-50; 46:20; Ex.2:16; 3:1; 18:1).

Aaron was Divinely appointed (Heb.5:1-5). None could assume or presume into this high office unless they were of the line of Aaron. Any usurpation would be met by Divine judgment.

A. The Genealogy of Aaron

The genealogy of Aaron, the High Priestly family, is primarily found in 1Chr.6:1-15 along with Ezra 7:1-7, given after the return from the Babylonian Captivity. The account in Chronicles seems to lend itself to some significant sections, which are outlined here.

1. **Section One** – The sons of Levi, the third son of Jacob, and of the tribe chosen to be the priestly tribe, are listed, through to Aaron and Moses (vs.1-3).

2. **Section Two** – The genealogy from Aaron to Azariah, the High Priest in the Temple of Solomon is listed (vs.4-10). We list the names accordingly:

    - Aaron and his four sons = Nadab, Abihu, Eleazar and Ithamar. Nadab and Abihu were struck dead by the Lord for their sin of presumption (Lev.10:1-2).
    Then from Eleazar we have the genealogy through to the High Priest, Azariah, of the Temple of Solomon.
    - Phinehas
    - Abishua
    - Bukki
    - Uzzi
    - Zerahiah
    - Meraioth
    - Amariah
    - Ahitub
    - Zadok
    - Ahimaaz
    - Azariah

- Johanan
- Azariah – High priest in the Temple that Solomon built.

3. **Section Three** – Then we have the list of priests through to Jehozadak, who went with the House of Judah into the Babylonian Captivity, when the Temple was destroyed under King Nebuchadnezzar, in approximately B.C.604-606.

    - Amariah
    - Ahitub
    - Zadok
    - Shallum (or Meshallum)
    - Hilkiah
    - Azariah
    - Seraiah
    - Jehozadak – Priest into Babylonian Captivity

4. **Section Four** – In vss.21 and 22 we have the sons of Levi: Gershon, Kohath and Merari, who were in David's Tabernacle until the Temple was built, and then they continued their ministry in the Temple of Solomon. "Now these are the men whom David appointed over the service of song in the house of the Lord, after the Ark came to rest. They were ministering with music before the dwelling place of the tent of meeting, until Solomon had built the house of the Lord in Jerusalem, and they served in their office according to their order."

5. **Section Five** – Sons of the son's lineage listed here as they minister in the house of God (vs.33-48).

6. **Section Six** – Aaron's sons to minister at the brazen altar of sacrifice, the golden altar of incense and the work of atonement in the Most Holy Place (vs.49). The sons of Aaron came through Eleazar, after the firstborn two sons, Nadab and Abihu died before the Lord (vs. 50-53). Names are listed to the tenth generation, from Eleazar to Ahimaaz (Refer Section Two).

7. **Section Seven** – Cities and suburbs given to Aaron's sons and the Levites out of and from the other tribes as their inheritance (vs.54-81).

Ref. Neh.8:1-18 with Neh.12-13 chapters and Ezra 2:36-42, 61-70. After the Babylonian Captivity ended, we see the priests and the Levites and the singers, after checking their genealogy, ministered in the rebuilt house of the Lord (Ezra 7:1-13). Ezra himself was a priest and a scribe (Neh.8:1-2, 9). Eliashib was the High Priest at that time (Neh.3:1, 20). And when it came to the time of the prophets Haggai and Zechariah, in the restoration period, Joshua was the High Priest (Hag.1:14; 2:1, 2 with Zech.3:1-10; 6:11-13 and Ezra 3:2; 5:2; Neh.12:26).

B. Character Studies

A cursory glance over the list of names from Aaron and his four sons (refer Strong's Concordance) show that a number of them do not record any significant events taking place in their lifetime.

Like the Kings of the House of Israel and the House of Judah, having both good and evil rulers, so it was with the Priests in the genealogy of the Priestly Tribe of Levi. There were good priests and also corrupt priests over the years. We see the tragic end of this in Christ's time when the Priesthood of His era clamored for His death by crucifixion. To a certain degree, many of them were ignorant of the Lord of Glory!

A careful reading of the Scriptures reveals that often Kings and Priests worked together in the affairs of the chosen nation of Israel. In due time, God raised up great and mighty Prophets, who spoke the word of the Lord, a word of rebuke or encouragement, to both Kings and Priests. The Prophets became the dominant ministry in Old Testament times until John the Baptist and the Messiah came.

However from the list of High Priests in the line of Aaron's succession, there are a number of Priests where notable events are recorded under the inspiration of the Holy Spirit. Some are good and some are evil. As it was with the Kings of Judah and Israel, so it was with the Priests of Levi. It is by these character studies that we, as believer "kings and priests" unto God and His Christ *may learn what to do and what NOT to do!*

The lives and events of the Priests of Aaron's line provide us with great character studies from which we as New Testament priests may learn many lessons. In the following chapters we consider some of these priests.

PART SIX - CHARACTER STUDIES OF SIGNIFICANT PRIESTS

Chapter 19   Aaron, Israel's First High Priest
Chapter 20   Nadab and Abihu – Priests of Presumption
Chapter 21   Eleazar – The Priest without Fault
Chapter 22   Phinehas – The Priest with Divine Zeal
Chapter 23   Priests of History
Chapter 24   Zadok, The Priest who Maintained Loyalty

CHAPTER 19 – AARON: ISRAEL'S FIRST HIGH PRIEST

It is fitting that we consider Aaron, as Israel's first High Priest (Ex.28:1-3; 6:20; 1Chr.6:3-15, 49-53). Aaron is the elder brother, and Moses his younger brother, and then his older sister was Miriam.

Aaron's name means "A Mountain of Strength" or "Enlightened". His father and mother were Amram and Jochebed, of the family of Kohath, who was the second son of Levi. Aaron married Elisheba, daughter of Amminadab and sister of Naashon, and by her he had four sons – Nadab, Abihu, Eleazar and Ithamar (Ex.6:16-23).

Aaron was first called a Prophet (Ex.7:1) and became the spokesman for Moses (Ex.4:10-17, 27-31). After the revelation of the Tabernacle was Given, Aaron was chosen by the Lord to be Israel's first High Priest and his sons were to be his successors in the appointed time.

It should be kept in mind that in all believers, whether in Old or New Testament times, there is that which is of the human side and also that of the Divine side. This is worked out in their personalities. Sometimes there is something of the Satanic because of human, fallen and sinful nature (e.g. Judas, the fallen apostle). This, for example, may be seen in saints like Noah, Abraham, Isaac and Jacob, Moses, David and many other heroes of faith (Heb.11).

It is true also of the High Priests of Aaron's line. It is true of Aaron himself. We consider here that which is of the human side and that which pertains to the Divine side, or that which worked in him the characteristics and qualities necessary for him to become a suitable type of Christ (Heb.5:1-5).

A. On the Human Side

Aaron's greatest weakness is seen in his major part in the golden calf idolatry. In spite of his high calling, Aaron yielded to the murmurings of the people (Ex.16:2; 32:1-2) and thus made the golden calf for them to worship. He even said these were the gods that led the people out of Egypt (Ex.32).

His greatest punishment was, like Moses, he was not allowed to enter the Promised Land, the very land he and Moses wanted to bring the people into (Num.20:12). He died at the age of 123 years on Mount Hor, in the land of Edom, and was buried there. His successor was his son, Eleazar (Num.20). Aaron was penitent as a leader and God permitted him to fulfill his role as being High Priest ministering in the Tabernacle of the Lord.

B. On the Divine Side

On the Divine side, or that which was Divinely inwrought in him, Aaron becomes an imperfect, yet a wonderful type of our Lord Jesus Christ in His Priesthood (Heb.5:1-5). His sons become the type of the Church, the believing Priesthood.

W.W. Patterson provides a good picture of Aaron as being a type of Christ, our Great High Priest. He writes: A Priest brings God to man and man to God. He is the Mediator between God and man. In the Book of Genesis, the word 'priest' is found in Gen.14:18-20. Melchizedek is priest of the Most High God. This Priesthood finds its fulfillment in Christ as our great High Priest (Psa.110:4; Heb.6:20; 7:28). Note that Abel (Gen.4:3, 4) and Noah (Gen.8:20), Abraham (Gen.15:9, 10), Isaac and Jacob act as priests unto the Lord. In the Tabernacle in the wilderness, Aaron was the High Priest and his sons served as priests (Ex.28:1).

The High Priest had to be a man of sympathy and compassion, ready and willing to minister. He had to have heartfelt concern for the people (Heb.2:17, 18; 5:2). This was fulfilled in Christ as the Son of Man, the Perfect Man – the one and only Mediator between God and man, the Man Christ Jesus (1Tim.2:5; Heb.3:1; 4:14-16).

	Aaron the High Priest		**Christ Jesus as our High Priest**
1.	Called and chosen by God (Ex.28:1). From the Tribe of Levi.	1.	Called and chosen by God (Heb.5:4-10; 7:20, 21 and 28). By an oath. From the Tribe of Judah (Heb.7:14; Rev.5:5)
2.	Clothed in proper garments (Ex.28). For glory and beauty (Ex.28:2).	2.	Clothed in sinless flesh (Jhn.1:14; Rom.8:3; Heb.7:26). Glorious and beautiful
3.	Cleansed (Ex.29:4; 40:12; Lev.8:6). By the washing of water.	3.	The holy One of God (Heb.7:26). Baptized in water (Matt.3:13-17).
4.	Consecrated – anointed (Ex.29:7; Lev.4:3, 5, 16; 6:20; 8:12, 30; 21:10; Num. 35:25; Psa.133:2).	4.	Consecrated – anointed with the Holy Spirit (Matt.3:16; Acts 10:38; Heb.1:9)
5.	To serve in a God appointed place – the Tabernacle (Ex.25:8; 40:34-38). The Temple – 1Kgs.5:5; 8:10, 11; 2Chr.2:1-5; 5:13, 14; 7:1,2.	5.	To serve in a God-appointed place. On earth – at and outside Jerusalem (Heb.13:12, 13). In the Church (Rev.1-3). In heaven (Heb.9:23, 24).
6.	To have a God-ordained ministry a. Reconciliation – to offer sacrifice for the people openly at the brazen altar b. Intercession – to intercede for the people within the veil c. Benediction – to bless the people by coming forth (Num.6:22-27)	6.	To have a God-ordained ministry a. Reconciliation – to atone. The cross (Jhn.1:29; 2Cor.5:19-21; Heb.2:17; 7:27; 9:12, 28a; 10:12). b. Intercession – to pray. The Ascension and Glorification (Jhn.17; 1Jhn.2:1; Rom.8:34; Heb.4:14-16; 7:25; 9:24) c. Benediction – to bless at Pentecost, throughout the Church Age and in His Second Coming)Acts 2:33, 38; Heb.9:28b)
7.	To have a proper bride. He shall take a virgin of his own people to wife (Lev. 21:10-15).	7.	To have a proper bride. The Church is the Bride, the Lamb's wife (Rev.19:5-9; Eph.5:22-33). For I have espoused you to one husband, that I may present you as a chaste virgin to Christ (2Cor.11:2).

So Aaron and his sons point to Christ and His Church. We also are called to be kings and priests unto God. We are to be clothed in His righteousness; cleansed by His blood, washed in the water of the Word, the waters of baptism and anointed with the holy oil, the Holy Spirit of God. We are to serve God and minister in His sanctuary, the Church in earth, and then eternally in heaven.

CHAPTER 20 - NADAB & ABIHU: PRIESTS OF PRESUMPTION

Nadab and Abihu were the first two sons of Aaron. Nadab being the firstborn, to whom the birthright would go and then Abihu, the second son in line if Nadab failed to receive the birthright.

A careful study of the following passages of Scripture provides the content of this brief chapter (Lev.9:22-24; 10:1-3; Num.3:4).

The context tells how the Glory of the Lord appeared in the Tabernacle of the Lord. Divine fire came out from the Glory and consumed the sacrifices on the brazen altar: the Sin Offering, the Burnt Offering and the Peace Offering, and all the truths that were symbolized in those offerings.

When the people of Israel saw it, they shouted, fell on their faces to worship the God of Glory and Fire. In the midst of this amazing scene, these two sons of Aaron – Nadab and Abihu – take their censers, put incense on them and "strange fire" (profane fire), and presumed to rush into the Presence of God.

God used fire to fight fire. These two sons were both struck dead. They violated the proper approach to a holy God and His manifest Presence and Glory (1Chr.24:1, 2).

Aaron's uncle's sons (relatives) buried them outside the camp. The brothers – Eleazar and Ithamar – were forbidden to mourn for them, Aaron also. Only the Israelites were allowed to mourn for these presumptuous sons. Nadab and Abihu had no children. The anointing oil had been placed on them (Lev.10:4-7).

A careful reading on Lev.10:8-22 shows that it was possible that these sons had been drinking and this became the cause of their sin of presumption which led to their deaths. As noted, either of these sons could have been successor to their father's High Priestly ministry in due time.

What lesson may be learned from these two sons? Beware of the sin of presumption. David writes of it in this manner in Psalm 19.

> "Who can understand his **errors**?
> Cleanse me from **secret faults**.
> Keep back Your servant also from **presumptuous sins**.
> Let them not have dominion over me.
> Then I shall be blameless
> And innocent of the **great transgression**" (Psa. 19:12, 13)

So is every religion that presumes to offer strange fire to the Lord God and presume to enter into His presence apart from His one and only Mediator between God and man, the Man Christ Jesus (1Tim.2:5, 6). It is also an example to all believer-priests not to become guilty of "errors, secret faults, presumptuous sins, and the great transgression" – which becomes the unpardonable sin. Judas is an example of such, as were the two sons of Aaron.

Perhaps an example is also seen in Acts 5:1-11. Two believer-priests, Ananias and his wife, Sapphira, in the midst of the Glory of God in the early Church offered "strange fire" before the Lord and were both struck with death. The lied to the Holy Spirit. They were guilty of errors, secret faults discussed in their house, presumptuous sins and the great transgression. Only eternity will reveal their final state. But it was a sin unto death (1Jhn.5:16, 17). These are the lessons we may learn from this tragic account.

CHAPTER 21 – ELEAZAR: THE PRIEST WITHOUT FAULT

Introductory:
With the death of Nadab and Abihi, Aaron's third and fourth sons Eleazar and Ithamar now take their place and minister in the priestly office. Eleazar is the subject of this chapter.

"Eleazar" means "God is helper". He would serve the people of Israel under both Moses and his successor Joshua. He served Moses in the wilderness and then Joshua in the promised land. His name is mentioned about 60 times in Scripture. He is the third son of Aaron and father of Phinehas (Ex.6:23-25; 28:1). He is chief of the Levites (Num.3:32). Read also Num.3:1-4; 1Chr.24:1-2). Though not a perfect man, his record of service to his generation is without fault.

His life falls into two parts: time with Moses and time with Joshua.

A. Eleazar with Moses

1. Moses reproves both Aaron's sons Eleazar and Ithamar for not partaking of the sin offering in the Holy Place. Moses accepts their reason as being the sudden death of their two brothers for their presumptuous offering and strange fire (Lev.10:1-20; Num.3:1-4).

2. The appointed duty of Eleazar was the oil for the light, the incense, the daily grain offering, the anointing oil and the general oversight of the Tabernacle and its furnishings (Num.4:16). This was a great responsibility.

3. With the rebellion of Korah and his company and the subsequent divine judgment, Moses commands Eleazar to collect the censers of brass of these "sinners against their own souls" and hammer them into plates. These plates were used to cover the brazen altar. It would be a sign and a reminder to all Israel that no one was to presume the priestly office as did Korah and the 250 men with him (Num.16:1-50, espec. vss36-40). It was a warning against the sin of presumption (Num.15:30; Deut.1:43; 17:12-13; Psa.19:13; 2Pet.2:10).

4. Eleazar also took the responsibility of the intricate details of the laws of purification by means of the ashes of the red heifer (Num.19:1-22, espec. vss.3-4).

5. In Num.20:1-20 both Moses and Aaron were guilty of disobedience to the word of the Lord. Divine punishment was laid on them. Their punishment was to not enter the very promised land they were leading the people of Israel into. Both were to die. At this point the Lord spoke to Moses about Aaron's successor as Israel's high priest. It was to be Aaron's son Eleazar. Moses was called to take both Aaron and Eleazar up to Mt Hor. There on the mount Moses was to strip Aaron of his high priestly garments – the garments of glory and beauty – and put them on Eleazar. It was in that sense the passing on of Aaron's mantle and ministry. Moses did so and then both Moses and Eleazar came back down the mount. Israel mourned the death of Aaron for thirty days (Num.22:29). Eleazar became Aaron's successor as high priest in Israel. Read also Num.27:12-14 with Psa.106:32-33.

6. Eleazar's son Phinehas must have picked up or learnt some of the good qualities of his father. The Lord commended him through a prophetic word that he would have an "everlasting priesthood" for his zeal in killing an Israelite in blatant adultery with a Midianite woman (Num.25:1-17, espec. vss.7-10).

7. Moses and Eleazar work together in taking the census of the new generation which would enter Canaan land. The previous census had been taken by Moses and Aaron. Because of unbelief that earlier generation would die in the wilderness (Num.26.1-62, 63-65).

8. Moses and Eleazar together settle the inheritances of the daughters of Zelophehad before the Lord (Num.27:1-15). Moses is also told of his coming death as was Aaron (vss.12-14).

9. The Lord shows Moses that Joshua is to be his successor. Joshua is to stand before Eleazar the high priest and receive counsel by means of the Urim and Thummim. Eleazar is to lay hands on Joshua and inaugurate him before all Israel. Moses did as the Lord commanded him (Num.27:15-23).

10. Moses and Eleazar choose the men of war to go out against the Midianites for their evil in Israel (cf Num.25). The Lord gave Moses and Eleazar the laws concerning the spoils; what the men could keep and what had to be dedicated to the service of the Lord in the Tabernacle of the Lord (Num.31:1-54).

11. Moses and Eleazar together settle on which tribes would stay on the east side of Jordan for their inheritance (Num.32:1-42, espec. 2 and 28).

B. Eleazar with Joshua
1. Eleazar the high priest with Joshua the captain were to divide the land to the tribes according to the word of the Lord by Moses (Num.34:1-29, espec vs.17).

2. Eleazar and Joshua accordingly divide the land to the tribes for their inheritance (Josh.14:1; 17:4; 19:51; 21:1).

3. Eleazar the son and successor of his father Aaron, died and was buried in the inheritance of his son and successor, Phinehas (Num.24:33; Jud.20:27-29).

Eleazar, like all humans, was not perfect. But as we consider his life we find no real fault recorded against him. He was a good high priest who served the Lord God, Moses the servant of the Lord and also Joshua and the people of Israel all the days of his life. Without doubt he learned what NOT to do from the death of his two brothers Nadab and Abihu. No doubt he also learned from the rebellion of Korah and the 250 rebel leaders. He learned what to do under the leadership of the prophet Moses and his own father Aaron as high priest. Such are the lessons available to all believers called to be "kings and priests" unto God and the Lord Jesus Christ.

CHAPTER 22 – PHINEHAS: THE PRIEST WITH DIVINE ZEAL

As noted in the previous chapter, Eleazar passes on from this life and his son, Phinehas, becomes his successor as Israel's new High Priest.

His name, Phinehas, means "Face of Trust" or "Mouth of a Serpent." He was the third of Israel's High Priests and was zealous and faithful for the years he served the Lord and the people of Israel (Ex.6:25; Num.25:10-15).

When Israel fell into idolatry and immorality with the women of Moab, the Lord's anger was stirred against them. The plague of judgment fell on the offenders. One brazen Israelite by the name of Zimri (a leader of the tribe of Simeon), and the woman of Midian (whose name was Cozbi, also a leader of Midian), were caught in the very act of adultery, and this in the sight of the other Israelites.

Phinehas, the son of Eleazar, saw it. His zeal for the Lord and His holiness, caused him to take a small javelin (small sword or dagger) and thrust the man and the woman through the belly and kill them. The plague of God's judgment was stopped. Some 24,000 men died in this plague (Num.25:1-6, 7-18; Ex.40:15 with Psa.106:30; 1Cor.10:8 – says 23,000).

Because of his zeal for the Lord, God gave Moses a prophetic word for Phinehas. God gave him a covenant of peace to him and his descendants. God also gave him the covenant of an "everlasting priesthood". A study of the Scriptures clearly tells us that the only "everlasting priesthood" is that "after the order of Melchizedek" (Psa.110 with Heb.7). The Aaronic and Levitical Priesthood was fulfilled and abolished at the cross of Jesus on Calvary.

Therefore, the only way this prophetic word could be fulfilled to Phinehas was through the order of Melchizedek, the "everlasting priesthood", as the Lord promised, and NOT through the temporary and transitional priesthood of Aaron and Levi. What a great promise the Lord gave Phinehas for his zeal of holiness of a holy God. The promise is fulfilled through the New Covenant and that peace that is brought to light by the blood of Jesus' cross (Col.1:20).

For other references to Phinehas, the reader is referred to Num.31:6; Josh.22:13, 30-32; 24:33; Jud.20:28; 1Chr.6:4, 50; Ezra 7:5). The strong characteristic of Phinehas is his stand against immorality. This is seen in the case of the Midianites and also the immorality of the Benjaminites (Details in Jud. chapters 19, 20, 21. Note especially Jud.20:27-28 where Phinehas enquires of the Lord as to the battle).

What do we learn from Phinehas as a Priest to the Lord? We learn that believers should have the quality of zeal in the things of God. Phinehas was zealous for the sake of the Lord (Num.25:10), zealous for the things of God (Num.25:13). Zeal is a characteristic of God (Isa.9:7; 37:32; 59:17) and He requires it of us.

Paul was zealous towards God (Acts 22:3; Gal 1:14). We are to be zealous for spiritual gifts (1Cor.14:12). We are to be zealous of good works (Titus 2:14; Rev.3:19). Jesus was zealous for the house of His Father (Psa.69:9; Jhn.2:13-17).

It is possible to have a misguided and misplaced zeal (Rom.10:2. Phil.3:6; Acts 21:20). For the zeal that Phinehas had, the Lord gave him the promise of being an everlasting priest in the order of Melchizedek. So believers are called according to that order (Rev.1:6; 5:9, 10; 1Pet.2:5-9) and should be zealous for the things of God.

CHAPTER 23 - PRIESTS OF HISTORY

Introductory:
The next seven High Priests in the line from Phinehas do not apparently have any outstanding events recorded by inspiration of the Holy Spirit. They are mentioned here as "Priests of History" because they are listed in the genealogy of Aaron, the first High Priest of Israel.

1. Abishua – "Father of Safety or Salvation". Son of Phinehas and grandson of Aaron (1Chr.6:4, 5, 50; Ezra 7:5).

2. Bukki – "Mouth of Jehovah" or "Devastation sent by Jehovah". Son of Abishua and father of Uzzi, the fifth in descent from Aaron in the line of high priests through Phinehas (1Chr.6:5, 51).

3. Uzzi – "The Might of Jehovah". Son of Bukki and father of Zerahiah, descendant of Aaron (1Chr.6:5, 6, 51; Ezra 7:4). His name mentioned about 11 times.

4. Zerahiah – "The Lord is Risen" or "Jehovah is Appearing". A priest, being the son of Uzzi (1Chr.6:6, 51; Ezra 7:4). His name mentioned five times.

5. Meraioth – "Revelations" or "Rebellions". Son of Zerahiah, and ancestor of Azariah in the time of Solomon (1Chr.6:6, 7, 52; Ezra 7:3).

6. Amariah – "Jehovah has said or Promised". A son of Meraioth, a priest descended from Phinehas (1Chr.6:7, 52).

7. Ahitub – "Brother of Benevolence" or "Father of Goodness". Son of Amariah and father of High Priest Zadok (1Chr.6:11, 12).

This brings us now to Zadok, the Priest in both David's time and then on into the reign of King Solomon, another good character study in the High Priest's lineage.

CHAPTER 24 – ZADOK: THE LOYAL PRIEST

Introductory:
Zadok was a good and loyal High Priest. He served through David's time and on into the time of Solomon and was given ministry in Solomon's Temple.

It should be remembered that in David's time there were two High Priests – Abiathar and Zadok (2Sam.20:25). A separate chapter is given over to the study of Abiathar (Refer Chapter Thirty). Also, Zadok became quite a popular name. In all, there are some eight Zadoks referred to in Scripture. There were at least two Zadoks from the line of Aaron and on through Phinehas. The Zadok here is the Zadok of David's time who continued on in ministry in the Temple under King Solomon's time.

For some Bibliography, these Scriptures should be read (2Sam.8:17; 15:24-36; 17:15; 18:19-27; 19:11; 20:25).

Under David's time, as King over Israel, Abiathar was Priest at the Tabernacle of David on Mt Zion and Zadok was Priest at the Tabernacle of Moses on Mt Gibeon (1Chr.16:16, 37-40; 21:29; 2Chr.1:3-4).

A. Abiathar and Zadok

It is important to note that these two priests were together for some time serving in their particular place. Both of them went through three major tests. One failed in the third test, the other succeeded in these same tests. Zadok triumphed. Abiathar failed. One was promoted and the other was deposed. Zadok was promoted by Solomon to service in the Temple of the Lord.

As these three tests are dealt with more fully in Chapter Thirty, they are noted in brief here relative to Abiathar and Zadok.

1. **The Wilderness Test with David.**
   David experienced great trials under King Saul during the wilderness years. Abiathar, as priest, was of great help to David in these times (Read 1Sam.21:1-9; Mrk.2:29; 1Sam.22:9-23).

   When David became King, Abiathar and Zadok shared in the joys of bringing the Ark of God into David's Tabernacle (1Chr.15:11; 16:39-42; 24:3, 6, 31; 27:17).

2. **The Absalom Test under David**
   Under the rebellious era of Absalom, both Abiathar and Zadok, as priests, helped David on a number of occasions in the difficult times (Read 2Sam.15:1-18, 24-30; 17:15, 16; 18:19-32). After Absalom's

death, David sent to Abiathar and Zadok asking them both to call the elders together and bring him back to his throne (2Sam.19:11).

3. **The Adonijah Test under David**
Adonijah, son of David, endeavored to usurp the throne of David when David was old and about to die. Abiathar sided with Adonijah, the usurper. Zadok stood with David and was part of the anointing of King Solomon. Abiathar failed in this third test and was deposed from the Priesthood by Solomon. Zadok took his place and was promoted to service in the newly built Temple of the Lord (1Kgs.1:1-10, 11-27, 28-31 and 32-40).

Abiathar and Zadok had been together over these difficult years, but here the sad separation took place when it came to the matter of true loyalty. (Again, the reader is referred to Abiathar, Chapter Thirty).

B. Zadok, the Loyal Priest

1. Zadok's name means "Just", "Justified" or "Righteous". He was the son of Ahitub, of the line of Eleazar, one of Aaron's sons (1Chr.6:3-8, 53).

2. As a young man, he was a mighty man of valor (1Chr.12:27, 28).

3. He was loyal to David, along with Abiathar, in the time of Absalom's rebellion (2Sam.15:24-29).

4. He was a true friend to David, even though Abiathar deserted to Adonijah, in David's dying days (1Kgs.1:7-8).

5. Zadok had the joy of anointing the new king, King Solomon, the pouring out of the holy oil on the man of God's choice, the chosen son of David (1Kgs.1:39-40).

6. For this strong quality of loyalty to David, King Solomon promoted him to service in the Temple of the Lord. He held this office until the time of his death (1Kgs.2:26-27 and 35 with 1Kgs.1:7, 8). Abiathar's loyalty to Adonijah was misplaced and misguided.

7. Zadok became the founder of an important branch of the Priesthood, and from the time of Solomon his descendants constituted the most prominent family among the order of the Priesthood (Refer Ezek.44).

C. Zadok – an 'Everlasting Priesthood'

It is through Zadok that the promised word of the Lord to Phinehas finds fulfillment. We noted earlier that the Lord promised Phinehas, because of his zeal for God's holiness and the purity of His people, an "everlasting priesthood" (Num.25:6-13). As seen, this could only be through the Priesthood of Melchizedek. Phinehas was the son of Eleazar, who was the son of Aaron. Zadok comes of the line of Phinehas (Read again Num.25:12, 13 with Ex.40:15).

Years later, through the Prophet Ezekiel, the Lord speaks of two companies of Priests: the Priests of Levi and the Priests of Zadok. Both have particular areas of ministry given to them, but the privileges of the Zadok house are the greater. For brevity's sake, we note these things in outline form.

1. **The Priestly Ministry of the Levites** – Ezek.44:9-14
   This company of priests was chosen for the following:
   a. To be ministers in the Sanctuary
   b. To have charge of the gates of the House of the Lord
   c. To minister to the house
   d. To offer the sacrifices for the people in the Outer Court
   e. To minister to the people
   f. They were not to come near in the office of the Priest
   g. They were limited in function because of iniquity, idolatry and uncircumcised hearts and because of other abominations when the Lord God had called them to Priestly ministry

   This company of priests would serve the Lord and His House but would not be able to enter the Holiest of All as priests because of their sins. They limited themselves in the service of God. This is in great contrast to the Zadok Priesthood.

2. **The Priestly Ministry of the Sons of Zadok** – Ezek44:15-16, 17:31
   The seed of Zadok, the sons of Levi, was chosen by the Lord for the following:
   a. To come near unto the Lord
   b. To minister unto the Lord
   c. To stand before the Lord
   d. To offer the fat and the blood to the Lord, the highest and best of the offerings
   e. To enter the Sanctuary, into the Holiest of All, or the Most Holy Place
   f. To come near to His Table
   g. To minister unto the Lord and keep His Charge

All this service above was because they had kept their priestly charge and did not go astray when Israel strayed away from the Lord (Read also Ezek.40:46; 43:19; 48:11).

There are other repeated instructions given concerning their conduct, apparel, grooming, marriage, judgments and the gifts of the people, and their inheritance in the Lord. Much of this is as given under the original instructions for the Priesthood in the time of Moses receiving the Law (Read Ezek.44:17-31).

In Summary:
Surely there are great spiritual lessons which may be learned from these things for believers today. These things were written for types and examples to us, and they are written for our admonition, instruction and comfort (1Cor.10:6, 11; Rom.15:4).

All believers are called to be "kings and priests" unto God (Rev.1:6; 5:9, 10; 1Pet.2:5-9). All are called to stand before Him, serve Him, minister unto Him, in the priestly office (2Chr.29:11). All are called to a life of holiness before the Lord (1Pet.1:15, 16). The New Testament epistles call us all to a life of holiness.

But how many believers will follow in the way of Abiathar? Or of Zadok? How many will fail to cleanse themselves of iniquity and idolatry or other abominations (Gal.5:19-21; 1Cor.6:9-11). If so, they limit themselves in priestly ministry and service to the Lord. It is not that God is a respecter of persons, but believers determine how far they want to go in the things of God.

The greatest and highest service is that which is exemplified in Zadok in the times of King David and King Solomon and ultimately, in the service of our Lord Jesus Christ, as spoken of in Ezekiel.

Some will be like Abiathar, and fall because of disloyalty, unfaithfulness or involvement in the spirit of rebellion in the last days (Gal.5:21; 1Cor.6:10). But some will be like Zadok and his seed and will enjoy the blessings of an everlasting Priesthood, in Christ Jesus, after the Order of Melchizedek. Such will enter into the heavenly Sanctuary, within the veil and this forever (Heb.6:19-20; 10:19-22; Rev.5:9, 10).

Such are some of the lessons we learn from the Priesthood of Zadok, the Loyal Priest, true loyalty to our Lord and Savior, Jesus Christ.

PART SEVEN - PRIESTS OF ITHAMAR'S LINE

Chapter 25	Eli, The Priest that God By-Passed and Why
Chapter 26	Hophni and Phinehas, Priests of Presumption
Chapter 27	Ichabod, the Sign-Child of a Dead Priest
Chapter 28	Ahimelech, The Priest who died for David's Sake
Chapter 29	Ahiah, The Priest of an Impatient King
Chapter 30	Abiathar, The Priest who failed the Third Test

CHAPTER 25 – ELI: THE PRIEST THAT GOD BY-PASSED

Introductory:
In these next several chapters, we consider some of the High Priests of the line of Ithamar, the fourth son of Aaron and Elisheba (Ex.6:23; 1Chr.6:3; 24:1). By way of introduction, we note some significant things relative to Ithamar.

1. Ithamar means "Palm Coast" or "Palm Tree"
2. He is the fourth and youngest son of Aaron and Elisheba
3. Ithamar, along with his brother, Eleazar, is consecrated to the Priesthood (Ex.28-29; Num.3:4; 1Chr.24:2). They were priests together (1Chr.24:1-2).
4. When Nadab and Abihu died before the Lord, both Eleazar and Ithamar are forbidden to mourn for them (Lev.10:1-6).
5. Both sons are forbidden to leave the Tent of Meeting (Lev.10:7) in pain of death.
6. Both sons are blessed with portions of the offerings given to the Lord (Lev.10:12-15).
7. Both sons are reproved by Moses for failing to eat of the Sin Offering (Lev.10:16-20).
8. Ithamar is set over the inventory of the Tabernacle of Moses and sanctuary service. The Gershonites and the Merarites are "under the authority of Ithamar" (Ex.38:21; Num.4:21-33, especially vs.28, 33 with Num.7:7, 8 NKJV).
9. It appears that he was an ancestor of Eli (1Kgs.2:27; 1Chr.24:3, 6).
10. Zadok was of the sons of Eleazar while Ahimelech was of the sons of Ithamar (1Chr.24:3).
11. The family of Ithamar was only half the size of Eleazar's in the time of David (Read 1Chr.24:4-6).
12. The family of Ithamar is represented among the exiles returning from Babylon (Ezra 8:1, 2).
13. The genealogy of Ithamar seems to be as follows:
    - Ithamar and then on to
    - Eli and his sons, Hophni and Phinehas
    - Ahitub and Ichabod, born of the wife of Phinehas
    - Ahimelech and Ahiah, the Priests in Saul's time
    - Abiathar (put out of the Priesthood by Solomon)

    Note: There are difficulties in following the genealogy of Ithamar exactly.

A. **Eli – The Priest that God by-passed and Why**

There are many lessons for believer-priests that may be learnt from Priest Eli and his sons in our character studies. The reader should become acquainted with the chapters in 1 Samuel 1-4 for the comments given here.

1. Eli's name means "Jehovah is High" or "My God". His name is used some 35 times. He is of Ithamar's line, who was the fourth some of Aaron (1Chr.6:3-15).

2. He served as Judge and High Priest in Israel for about 40 years.

3. He had two sons, Hophni and Phinehas, who served with their father in the Tabernacle at Shiloh (1Sam.1:3). (Note: Phinehas, not to be confused with the godly Phinehas of Eleazar's line. Num.25).

4. We first find Eli sitting on a seat by the doorpost of the Tabernacle at Shiloh, probably waiting as worshippers came out of the tribes to Shiloh.

5. First impression is that he is a man without spiritual insight. Hannah is praying to the Lord in her grief at being barren. Her lips only moved in prayer. Eli mistakenly thought she was drinking and did not discern she was praying! However, when this came to his attention, he pronounced blessing on her that her prayer would be answered. Hannah took this word of the Priest as a confirmation that her prayer had been heard by the Lord.

6. Hannah conceived and as a result, Samuel was born. Samuel means "Asked of the Lord". Samuel was presented to the Lord as a young child and stayed at the Tabernacle in Shiloh. He ministered before the Lord and Eli, the priest (1Sam.1:1-28 with 1Sam.2:11).

7. Eli's sons, however, were corrupt (Sons of Belial – KJV). They were priests in the Tabernacle but sons of the devil at the Tent door. They did not personally know the Lord though 'preacher's kids'.

    a. When the people offered their offerings before the Lord, these wicked sons, Hophni and Phinehas, would take by force what they wanted first, and then gave the rest on the altar to the Lord. This was a great sin before the Lord, and people despised the offerings of the Lord because of their behavior (1Sam.2:12-17).

b. Eli was an old man. He knew all the evil his sons did, as well as their immoral acts with the women who assembled at Shiloh but there was no discipline.

c. He had a poor father image. He should have removed his sons from the Priesthood. Instead, he mildly reproved them but failed as a good father to discipline them. They took no notice of their father's mild reproofs (1Sam.2:22-26).

8. A man of God came to Eli with a strong word from God (1Sam.2:27-36). It involved such words as:

   a. A reminder how the Lord chose the tribe of Levi to offer on the altar of God,
   b. Wear the linen ephod, and
   c. Be a priest unto God.
   d. Eli's sons had 'kicked' at God's sacrifice at Shiloh.
   e. Eli honored his sons more than the Lord as they helped themselves to the best of the offering.

9. The prophetic word continued with a strong rebuke and warning of the things that would come on Eli's household because of the dishonoring and despising of the Lord.

   a. God would cut them off
   b. An enemy would come into God's habitation
   c. There would not be an old man of Eli's house
   d. There would be grief and death
   e. All would die in the best years of their lives (1Sam.2:27-33).

10. God gave Eli a sign that all this would come to pass:

    a. In one day, both of his sons, Hophni and Phinehas would die
    b. The reason for this was that he failed to discipline his priestly sons, so God would discipline them.
    c. God would raise up a faithful priest who would do according to His heart and mind. This one would have a sure house and walk before the Lord's anointed (Messiah) forever (1Sam.2:34, 35).
    d. Some would come and beg for silver, for bread and for a place in the priestly office just so they could survive (1Sam.2:36).

11. Several generations later this prophetic word was partially fulfilled by the removal of Abiathar, of Eli's lineage, from the priestly office (Read 1Kgs.2:26, 27).

12. In 1Sam.3:1-21, we read of the call of God to Samuel to be the beginning of the Prophets. The condition in Israel at that time was that "there was no open vision" or "no widespread revelation" (NKJV).

13. Eli's physical condition was also symbolic of his spiritual condition. It was actually a physical/symbolic picture.

    a. Eli lay down to sleep. He was spiritually asleep.
    b. His eyes were growing dim and he could not see. Both naturally and also spiritually.
    c. The lamp of God was going out in the Tabernacle of Shiloh where the Ark of God was placed.
    b. In similar fashion the light of God had nearly stopped shining on the nation and its priesthood. But – before the lamp went out, God called Samuel!

14. God called Samuel. Samuel, young, sensitive and responsive ran to Eli, saying, "You called me." What was Eli's response?

    a. Eli said, "I did not call you. Go back to sleep."
    b. Samuel did not yet know the Lord.
    c. The word of the Lord had not yet been revealed to him.
    d. Three times the Lord called Samuel. He ran to Eli.
    e. The third time, suddenly Eli realized God was calling.

    One wonders if Eli, the old priest, realized that the Lord was by-passing him for the boy Samuel. Eli and Samuel were both in the same Tabernacle. One heard the voice and the call of God. The other heard nothing! What a sad scene! Eli told Samuel if the voice called again, he was to say, "Speak Lord, Your servant is listening!"

15. The Lord came the fourth time and called as at other times. What wonderful grace and patience the Lord has toward the sensitive and willing hearted. Samuel responded. The Lord spoke, confirming the word of the man of God previously spoken in judgment upon the house of Eli.

    a. Eli's house would be judged forever.
    b. And this because of the iniquity of his sons and their immorality.
    c. And because Eli failed as a good father to restrain them.
    d. Their sins would not be atoned for ever.

16. No doubt Samuel had a restless night, pondering the word of the Lord spoken to him.

17. In the morning he opened the doors of God's House. He feared to tell Eli the vision until Eli pressed him to do so. Samuel told him everything. Eli recognized and acknowledged that it was the word of the Lord who spoke to Samuel, thus confirming the very word He had also spoken by the man of God. Eli accepted the judgment.

18. Samuel grew in grace and knowledge (2Pet.3:18).

    a. The Lord was with him.
    b. None of his words (from the Lord) fell to the ground.
    c. All Israel came to know that Samuel was established to be a Prophet of the Lord.
    d. There was fresh vision in Shiloh.
    e. God revealed Himself to Samuel in Shiloh by the Word of the Lord.

19. In 1Sam 4 we have the tragic end of a Priest of God and his family of undisciplined sons.

    a. The Philistines gather to battle against Israel (vs.1-3a).
    b. Some 4000 people were killed in battle.
    c. The elders question why the defeat.
    d. They unthinkingly suggested getting the Ark of God from the Tabernacle in Shiloh (vs.3b, 4). Note: the Ark becomes "it" to them, and not "HIM!" They evidenced their superstition in an article of furniture and not the God of the Ark! The Ark once carried the Glory and Presence of the holy God.

20. They send to Shiloh for the Ark of God.

    a. Hophni and Phinehas were with the Ark of the Lord.
    b. The Israelites shouted as the Ark of God came into the battle. But it was an empty shout, devoid of the presence of God.
    c. Hophni and Phinehas did not worry about Divine order in handling the Ark of the Lord.
    d. The Philistines shouted as they were superstitiously afraid of "the gods" of Israel. They remembered the stories of the plagues on Egypt by these "gods".
    e. They fought bravely against Israel and 30,000 foot soldiers were slaughtered in the battle (vs.5-10).

21. But there were other more terrible things that happened that same day:

    a. The Ark of God was captured by the Philistines.
    b. The two sons of Eli, Hophni and Phinehas, died.

    c. A man of Benjamin ran to Shiloh and told Eli what had happened in the battle.
    d. When Eli heard that the Ark of God was taken and his two sons were dead, as well as the great slaughter, he fell off his seat backwards (surely another physical/symbolic truth), broke his neck and died. He was an old man and heavy.

22. To add to all that, Eli's daughter-in-law, the wife of Phinehas, hearing the news of her husband's death, and her father-in-law's death, was struck with birth pangs. A son was born. She named the child "Ichabod" = "The Glory of the Lord has departed from Israel" because of the captured Ark of God by the Philistines. Such a thing had never ever happened in the whole history of Israel (vs.11-22).

What a tragedy! Death prevailed! The judgment of God is manifest.

    a. Some 30,000 soldiers died in battle.
    b. Hophni and Phinehas, the Lord's Priests died.
    c. Eli died.
    d. The Ark of God was captured and now in the hands of the enemy Philistines.
    e. Phinehas' wife bore a child and called him Ichabod – "The Glory has departed from Israel".

23. No wonder the Lord tells the House of Judah in the days of Jeremiah, "But go to My place which was in Shiloh, where I set My Name at the first, and see what I did to it because of the wickedness of My people Israel" (Read the whole passage – Jer.7:12, with vs.1-20). The Lord did to the Temple the same as He did at Shiloh. Such is the lesson we may learn from the history of Israel, God's chosen nation.

What lessons may we learn from the Priest Eli?

1. Eli's greatest fault. He failed to exercise authority and discipline as a parent over his own two sons, Hophni and Phinehas.
2. His reproofs were too soft, and his sons failed to take any heed, as priests of the Lord. He did not restrain them for their presumption and immorality.
3. They should have been dismissed from ministry.
4. Eli honored his sons above that honor which belonged to the Lord.
5. Twice he was warned of coming judgment on his house but did not really take heed.

6. As an old man, almost 90 years of age, almost blind and deaf, naturally and spiritually, his sons brought him down to the grave in sorrow (cf. Gen.42:38; 44:29, 31).
7. He died of a broken neck as he fell backwards, and also a broken heart.
8. As with Eli, sadly, so it is today when God by-passes older ministries who fail to hear the voice of God and lose vision. Sometimes God goes to and calls the younger generation.

As believer-priests unto the Lord, our families need to be guarded with loving discipline or be disciplined by God Himself. The New Testament Church, "the House of the Lord" must be cleansed and all priestly ministries must be a testimony to the holiness and grace of God. Such are the many lessons we learn from Eli and his household. "Be clean, you that bear the vessels of the Lord" (Isa.52:11-12). There are seasons when unrepentant believer-priests should step down from ministry. None should be "church saints" and "house devils".

CHAPTER 26 - HOPHNI & PHINEHAS: PRESUMPTIOUS PRIESTS

Introductory:
It has been truly said, "The only thing we learn from history is that we don't learn from history!"

This is true of Hophni and Phinehas, the two sons of the Priest Eli. They are the subject of this brief chapter which continues on from our previous study of Eli.

Hophni – his name means "Strong" or "Fighter".
Phinehas – his name means "Face of Trust" or "Mouth of a Serpent"

Both of these sons were true to their names, but in the sense of evil and not for the good. They were Priests of the Lord, sons of Eli and brothers together in priestly ministry.

The reader is encouraged once again to read afresh the Scripture account of these two sons of Eli (1Sam. ch.1-4). From this we can learn the following lessons. These sons did not learn from the history of the two sons of Aaron, Nadab and Abihu, who also died for their sin of presumption. Familiarizing oneself with the inspired record we learn the following lessons:

1. Hophni and Phinehas did not personally know the Lord though they were sons of Eli, their father being Priest at that period of time.

2. They were both selfish and sacrilegious in their behavior at the altar of the Lord and His offerings. This caused the worshippers to despise God's altar and sacrifices.

3. They were guilty of gross immorality with the women who assembled at the Tabernacle of the Lord in Shiloh.

4. They were "priests at God's altar" and "sons of Belial" (lawless) at the Tent door.

5. They rejected their father's mild reproofs for their evil behavior.

6. They were selfish, self-centered and spoilt young men.

7. Both were presumptuous in taking the Ark of God to battle which was duly captured by the Philistines. Did they fulfill any laws about the blood of atonement on the Ark of God, and the appointed coverings on

the Ark in its journeyings? Without doubt, they totally failed in this (Num.3-4) and fell into the great sin of presumption.

8. This caused the death of their father, Eli, when he heard the Ark of God had been taken.

9. This also precipitated the premature birth of Phinehas' child Ichabod, who was named, "The Glory is departed from Israel", or "Where is the Glory?"

10. Hophni and Phinehas never learnt from the history of Aaron's two sons and their sin of presumption.

11. Both knew a premature death under Divine discipline, and both died in the same day, according to the word of the Lord to Eli, by the mouth of both the Man of God and the young man, Samuel (1Sam.2:27-36; 3:10-18). The curse came on them. The curse does not come without a cause (Prov.26:2b).

12. They brought judgment on future generations (1Kgs.2:26, 27).

13. Both were evil examples to the boy Samuel in their behavior as Priests unto the Lord. God preserved Samuel from following in their steps and their evil ways.

14. They were a total disgrace on the ministry of Priesthood by their evil behavior.

All these things are written as examples to us and for our instruction and admonition as "kings and priests" unto God (1Cor.10:6, 11; Rom.15:4).

Believers should be examples to other believers, let alone unbelievers. How many times "preacher's kids" have caused others (both saved and unsaved) to despise the things of the Lord and His Church by the lifestyle they lived. Such has been a great stumbling block to those who know not the Lord (Psa.1). Unbelievers have a higher standard in their mind of what a true Christian should be! If there is failure in Church discipline, then sometimes God steps in and there is Divine discipline. If we would judge ourselves, we would not be judged (1Cor.11:23-34).

David's Psalm bears repetition:

> "Who can understand his **errors**?
> Cleanse me from **secret faults**.

> Keep back Your servant also from **presumptuous sins**,
> Let them not have dominion over me.
> Then shall I be blameless
> And I shall be innocent of **the great transgression**" (Psa.19:12, 13).

So Hophni and Phinehas were guilty of errors, secret faults, presumptuous sins and the great transgression that brought about death, not only themselves, but others also. None of us live to ourselves alone.

There was sacrificial pardon for "sins of ignorance" but NOT for the "sins of presumption" (Num.15:22-29, 30-31 with Heb.10:26-31).

CHAPTER 27 – ICHABOD: SIGN-CHILD OF A DEAD PRIEST

This chapter continues on from the previous as it relates to the posthumous son of Phinehas, and grandson of Eli (posthumous = "born after the death of its father, occurring after death"). Ichabod – his name means, "The Glory is not", or "The Glory is Departed" or "Inglorious". His father was Phinehas, killed in battle with the Philistines, along with his presumptuous brother, Hophni.

The shock of her husband's death, and her father-in-law's death (Eli), along with the capture of the Ark of God, precipitated the birth-pangs coming on the wife of Phinehas, the mother of Ichabod. She died in child-birth. The midwives tried to comfort her that a son had been born. She, however, because of shock, could not respond, but before she died, she named the baby "Ichabod", or "The Glory is Departed from Israel."

It was a tragic day for Israel. Never ever in the history of the nation, and all the warfare the nation had been through, had any enemy been able to touch the Ark of God let alone capture it.

Ichabod never saw his father or mother. He was brought up without his parents, having both died within the same period of time. He was an orphaned child and with that, all the accompanying trauma of childhood. But he became "**a sign-child**". There was a message in his name. One may refer to Isaiah's children. "Behold I and the children the Lord has given me are for **signs and wonders ...**" (Isa.8:1, 2, 18). Everywhere Ichabod went, as he grew up, the message was in his name, "The Glory is Departed", "There is no Glory".

His name is used only twice in Scripture. Surely no one would want to call any of their sons "Ichabod!" (1Sam.4:19-22 with 14:3). His name has become a kind of by-word for when a church or denomination loses the presence of God. They are spoken of as "Ichabod", as a sign written over the door! Many years later, two Major Prophets illustrate the truth of Ichabod's name in the "departing Glory" from the nation of Israel.

1. Jeremiah speaks of God's judgment on the Tabernacle in Shiloh, prophesying that this was about to happen again to the Temple in Jerusalem. The Lord speaks through Jeremiah: "Go back to Shiloh and see what I did for the wickedness of My people Israel!" What happened at Shiloh? The Glory of God departed when the Ark of the Lord was taken. So "Ichabod" happened to the Temple in Jeremiah's time under the King of Babylon, King Nebuchadnezzar. The Ark disappeared and

has never been seen since that time. Jer.3:8, 9 is the last mention ever in the Old Testament of the Ark of God.

2. Ezekiel also has a vision of the steps of the reluctant, departing Glory from the Temple of the Lord. It corresponds with the prophecies of Jeremiah of the same truth. The abominations in the Temple caused the Glory to depart. The Temple became "Ichabod" – "There is no Glory", or "Where is the Glory?"

3. The final picture is when the Messiah Jesus came. He ministered in the material Temple over some 3 ½ years. But that Temple rejected His cleansings and He prophesied of its desolation. "YOUR House (no longer the Father's House) is left unto you desolate", and in AD.70, the Temple was destroyed by the Romans. Christ, who was "THE Glory of God" personified departed from that Temple and Jewry has been desolate ever since. It became Ichabod! (Matt.23:37-39; 24:1-3).

What then is the lesson we learn from this son of a Priest? This can happen to any denomination or church once abominations are allowed into God's House. Church History is replete with examples where, spiritually, "Ichabod" is written over the door! The Glory is departed from how that place was born in revival fires, and then became desolate!

CHAPTER 28 – AHIMELECH: HE DIED FOR DAVID'S SAKE

Introductory:
It would be profitable to read the Bibliography of Scripture as it pertains to Ahimelech to become more acquainted with this Priest (Read 1 Sam.21:1-8; 22:9-20; 23:6; 30:7; 2 Sam.8:17 along with Psalm 52 with its super-inscription).

In these passages we read of Jonathan's final visit to David as David goes to the city of Nob. Nob is a Priestly City. David goes to the city to find Ahimelech. Ahimelech questions David as to why he is alone, but David actually lied to the Priest to protect himself from King Saul who is out hunting his life with some 3000 soldiers.

David asked for bread and, because all his company was ceremonially clean, he was given the "showbread", the food of the Priests. David also asked for a spear or a sword. Ahimelech gave him the treasured sword of Goliath that was wrapped up in a cloth. David took the sword and then fled to Achish, King of Gath. He feigned madness and afterwards escaped to the Cave of Adullum. His family and many others came to David, numbering about four hundred people.

King Saul heard of David's activities and whereabouts, with his family and the prophetic word that David received from the prophet Gad. As Saul is venting his anger on the men about him, charging someone as being in a conspiracy against him, Doeg, who was over Saul's servants, told how he saw David going to Nob, to Ahimelech, the son of Ahitub. Doeg said that Ahimelech had enquired of the Lord on behalf of David, had also given him bread and the sword of Goliath.

King Saul sent for Ahimelech and his father's house. All came to the king, for he was still king. Saul challenges them all as to their helping David. Ahimelech testifies of David's faithfulness to Saul as well as his own personal faithfulness to the king. But the king would not hear it.

The tragic end is that King Saul puts Priest Ahimelech to death and this by the hand of Doeg, the Edomite. Edom was established by Esau who along with his twin brother Jacob/Israel came from Isaac. Thus we have Esau and Jacob and the ensuing enmity between the resultant nations. Along with Ahimelech's death, 85 other priests who wore the linen ephod were slaughtered. The Priestly city of Nob was destroyed; men, women and children and even the infants, along with all of the animals of the city. All were destroyed by King Saul. He was not afraid to touch "the Lord's anointed" priests in his blind anger and hate for David.

In the mercy and providence of God, one of the sons of Ahimelech, grandson of Ahitub, escaped the sword and fled to David. He told David all that had happened under King Saul. David felt the guilt of it, taking the blame of it all, as he remembered Doeg the Edomite being there the same day he came to the city of Nob. The young priest's name was Abiathar. David assured him that he would be safe under his custody and that of his men.

What a noble priest Ahimelech was. He was loyal to David and died for it, as well as the other 85 priests and the senseless destruction of the Priestly city of Nob.

It is no wonder that God has nothing further to say to King Saul either by prophets, or dreams or through His priests (1Sam.28:15-19). Ahimelech, along with the 85 other priests, became martyrs for the Davidic cause in that time.

One may think of the thousands of believers (as "king-priests to the Lord") who have become martyrs for the cause of Christ, the greater Son of David under the 'Saul's' of today!

Note: Psalm 52 was one of the Psalms of David written about Doeg, the Edomite.

CHAPTER 29 – AHIAH: THE PRIEST OF AN IMPATIENT KING

Ahiah (or Ahijah – NKJV/NIV) means "Jehovah is my Brother". He was the son of Ahitub and grandson of Phinehas, son of Eli (1Sam.14:3, 18). He seems to be a priest under the reign of Saul.

King Saul is introduced to us as sitting under a pomegranate tree near Gilboa. He had with him 600 men, including Ahiah (Ahijah), the son of Ichabod's brother Ahitub, the son of Phinehas, the son of Eli, who was the Lord's Priest in Shiloh. Ahijah was wearing a priestly ephod (1Sam.14:2, 3).

Jonathan and his armor-bearer had won a great victory from the Lord against the Philistines. King Saul called the roll to find out who was missing and found that Jonathan, his own son, and Jonathan's armor-bearer were not there.

Saul calls for the Ark of God along with Ahiah. The Ark of God was still with Israel at that time. As Saul talked with the Priest, the noise in the camp of the Philistines increased. King Saul, restless and impatient, told the Priest, "Withdraw your hand". He and his army wanted to get into the battle and capitalize on the victory God had brought about that day through Jonathan (1Sam.14:1-23).

King Saul was ready to put his own son, Jonathan, to death, to save face and to show his authority as King. It was only the people that saved Jonathan from death by the hand of his father. The whole trouble was caused by King Saul's stupid curse he had put on the army, that none were to eat food in the day of battle. He expected his army to fight on an empty stomach (1Sam.14:24-34, 35-52).

In vs.35 Saul built his first altar to the Lord. And before going into battle, he asks counsel of the Lord. The Priest said, "Let us draw near to God." However, the Lord did not answer Saul that day through His Priest. But Saul, though appearing religious, was impatient. He just could not wait for the Lord to speak His mind.

It is worthy to note that:

1. This is the only altar that Saul ever built to the Lord (vs.35, 36).
2. This is the only specific mention of the ark of God in the time of Saul (vs.18).
3. This is the only specific time Saul sought counsel of the Lord through His appointed priest, as should have been done (vs.18-19 with vs.36-

37). This is in great contrast to David who always "enquired of the Lord" as to His mind and that through His Priest.
4. Ahiah had to deal with an impatient king but never seemed to have any good influence on the king because of his pride and stubbornness.
5. Saul failed to respond to the voice of the Lord through any of His Priests:
   - He was impatient with Ahiah
   - He killed Ahimelech
   - He slaughtered 85 other Priests of the Lord
   - It was the mercy of God that Ahimelech's son, Abiathar, escaped to be with David and give him some counsel from the Lord

In New Testament times, believers enquire of the Father God, through our Lord Jesus Christ, the one and only Mediator between God and man and our great High Priest after the Order of Melchizedek (Rev.1:6; 5:9, 10; 1Tim.2:5, 6). The only way of approach to God, even for Christians, is through our Lord Jesus (Jhn.14:1, 6). If people refuse to listen to God through Christ, they end up like King Saul. God has nothing to say to them.

CHAPTER 30 – ABIATHAR: THE PRIEST WHO FAILED THE TEST

In a previous chapter, we saw how Zadok and Abiathar were joint Priests together under David, the king-to-be (2Sam.20:25). David placed Abiathar in the Tabernacle of David on Mt Zion. Zadok was placed in the Tabernacle of Moses on Mt Gibeon (1Chr.16:37-40; 21:29; 2Chr.1:3-4). Zadok was from Eleazar (1Chr.6:4-8, 53). Abiathar was from Ithamar (1Kgs.2:27), Abiathar is from Eli's line (1Chr.24:6), Ahimelech is from Abiathar (1Chr.24:3); Ahimelech is from Ithamar. So the genealogy, with many gaps, is … Aaron, Ithamar, Eli, Ahimelech, Abiathar).

The reader is encouraged to refresh themselves with the chapter concerning Zadok (Chapter 24). The reader will bear with some repetition.

Abiathar's name means "Father of Pre-eminence" or "Excellent Father". He was the son of Ahimelech and High Priest in succession from Eli. For further Scriptures, see 1Sam.22:20-22; 23:6, 9.

He was High Priest in descent from Eli, or the line of Ithamar, the youngest son of Aaron. His name is referred to some 31 times in the inspired record. He and Zadok were together for some years under David. As already noted, after his father Ahimelech and 85 other priests had been killed, he escaped in the mercy of god to be with David and provide counsel to him under the hand of God. He, as Zadok, experienced three tests in his time with David, but sadly failed in the third and final test.

1. **The Wilderness Test – Abiathar and David**

    Abiathar fled to David at Keilah in his period of rejection under King Saul's reign and David asked him to be with him promising to be his safeguard (1Sam.22:20-23). As far as David was concerned, it was the blessing of the Lord to have the priest Abiathar with him in the wilderness times.

    When Abiathar escaped from the city of Nob, he had with him the priestly ephod and David was thus able to enquire of God through the priest and receive Divine communication. Through this means he was able to escape King Saul on several occasions (cf.Ex.28 with 1Sam.23:6, 7-13).

    In the conflict at Ziklag, David enquired of God through Priest Abiathar and the Lord showed him that he would recover all that had been lost in the battle (1Sam.30:6-8). Abiathar was in touch with God and could minister to David, the king-to-be, in due time.

In due time, Saul died, and David came to the throne. The Tabernacle of David was established in Mt Zion. Abiathar, along with Zadok, shared in the bringing up of the Ark of God into the Tabernacle of David (1Chr.15:11-14). He was also involved in the priestly courses established by David (1Chr.24:6; 27:34). Both of these priests had the glorious privilege of being amongst David's counselors in his kingdom. Abiathar had been a faithful and loyal priest in the sufferings of David in the wilderness and now he was honored in David's reigning period.

"If we suffer with Him, we shall also reign with Him" is the lesson applicable here (2Sam.8:17; 2Tim.2:12).

2. **The Rebellion Test – Abiathar and Absalom**
After about 20 years glorious reign, evil days befell King David because of his sin. David's rebellious son Absalom coveted the throne of his father. He stole the hearts of the people (2Sam.15:1-18). King David fled from Jerusalem out into the wilderness again even as he had previously fled from King Saul.

Zadok and Abiathar and other Levites accompanied David, bringing with them the Ark of God out of the Tabernacle of David on Zion. David asked these two priests to return to Jerusalem with the Ark of God and to keep in touch with him in the wilderness, letting him know just what events were transpiring there (2Sam.15:24-30).

Hushai the Archite desired to go with David also. However, David suggested that he also go to Jerusalem with Abiathar and Zadok and watch Absalom's doings. Zadok's son, Ahimaaz, and Abiathar's son, Jonathan, would be able to act as messengers to David in the wilderness (2Sam.15:32-37). On several occasions these priests and their sons were able to deliver messages to David (2Sam.17:15-16; 18:19-32).

In time, the usurper king, Absalom, was slain. David sent a message to Zadok and Abiathar to encourage them to encourage the elders to bring him back to his throne and his house (2Sam.19:11-15).

Thus, Abiathar, along with Zadok, proved loyal to David in spite of the spirit of lawlessness and rebellion manifest in Absalom and his men.

3. **The Usurper King Test – Abiathar and Adonijah**
However, there remained one further and final test for Abiathar. This was to take place under another rebellious son of David, Adonijah. The story is recounted for us in the Book of Kings.

King David was old and stricken in years. Death was soon to come. Adonijah, the son of Haggith, who was Absalom's brother, exalted himself to be king, seeking to gain his father's throne. He called a conference with Joab, the King's commander in chief and also Abiathar the High Priest. Together these men agreed to help him obtain the throne. Zadok, however, was not involved in this conspiracy (1Kgs.1:1-10).

The prophet Nathan told Solomon's mother, Bathsheba, of the plot and the coming usurpation of David's throne. Nathan and Bathsheba went to David and told him of the plot and how even Abiathar the High Priest had joined forces with Adonijah (1Kgs.1:11-27). David assured Bathsheba that Solomon was the son that the Lord had ordained to take his throne and that he assuredly would be king (1Kgs.1:28-31).

After this, David called for Zadok the priest, and Nathan the prophet, and Solomon his son. They took the horn of oil out of the Tabernacle and anointed Solomon to be the new king amidst great joy and rejoicing (1Kgs.1:32-40).

The tragic end of this story is that Abiathar made himself worthy of death in his identification with the rebel Adonijah. He was deceived in this third and final test. Solomon spared him from death because of two things:

1. He had been faithful to David in all the wilderness afflictions he had been through.
2. He had been faithful to David under the rebellious times of Absalom.

But sadly he failed and was deceived under the Adonijah test.

Abiathar was deposed from his priestly office and ministry to the Lord. This was also the fulfillment of the prophetic word against the house of Eli, spoken some years previously in Shiloh (1Kgs.2:26-27 and 35 with 1Sam.2:27-36).

Abiathar had been tested three times. He had proved faithful in the wilderness tests, staying with David the anointed yet rejected king. He stood the tests under King Saul and Jonathan. He also overcame in the test under Absalom when he took the throne, and through all the internal strife and trouble, stood with David. He had been true to God's anointed king.

But here, under the third test with Adonijah, he got caught in the spirit of deception and rebellion, in the mystery of iniquity that was at work in the kingdom and he failed. After all he had been through, willing to suffer with David, after all the joys of the Tabernacle of David, he failed in David's dying days and forfeited his priestly office.

The spiritual lessons are evident. They may truly be applied to New Testament believer-priests. All will experience similar tests and trials. One can enjoy the Tabernacle of David, and yet fail in the end by allowing oneself to be caught up in the mystery of lawlessness, and thus forfeit one's priestly ministry and service to the Lord.

There are so many "Abiathars" in our generation. May we learn what to do and what NOT to do from this High Priest, Abiathar. Zadok took his place.

Will we take our place among the "Abiathars" or the "Zadoks"?

It is our choice!

PART EIGHT - JEHOZADAK TO THE BABYLONIAN CAPTIVITY

Chapter 31   Jehozadak to the Babylonian Captivity

CHAPTER 31 - PRIESTS TO BABYLONIAN CAPTIVITY

Introductory:

As noted in Chapter 23, so there is a similar vein here. Apparently there are no particular outstanding events recorded under inspiration of the Holy Spirit. We have twelve Priests in the line from Zadok to Jehozadak and the Babylonian Captivity. They are mentioned here as "Priests of History", taking us to the total decline of Israel and on into the Babylonian Captivity.

1. Ahimaaz – "A Rascal" or "Powerful Brother" or, "My Brother is Counsellor". He was the son of Zadok, and, along with Jonathan (son of Abiathar) kept David informed of Absalom's activities. When pursued by Absalom's men, both Ahimaaz and Jonathan were hidden in a well for protection until it was safe to warn David of Ahithophel's evil counsels (2Sam.15:27-36; 17:15-22). When Absalom was killed, Ahimaaz ran without a message, having heard a lot of noise but did not know what it was all about (2Sam.18:19-33, especially vs.29, 30).

2. Azariah – "Jehovah is Keeper", or "Jehovah has Helped". He was the son of Ahimaaz (1Chr.6:9). This name was quite common among the Hebrews. There were several 'Azariahs' in the line of Eleazar, making it more difficult to identify who is who, unless they can be located in the time period of a particular king of Israel or Judah.

3. Johanan – "Jehovah is Gracious". A grandson or Ahimaaz, and father of Azariah, a Levite (1Chr.6:9, 10). Some suppose he is the Jehoiada of 2Kgs.11-12 with 2Chr.23-24).

4. Azariah – "Jehovah is Keeper" (As for #2). His father was Johanan. It is suggested he was the Priest who withstood King Uzziah as he presumed to burn incense on the altar of God in the Temple. The King was also withstood by some 80 other priests (See also 1Chr.6:10, 11 with 2Chr.26:17-20).

5. Amariah – "Jehovah has said" (1Chr.6:11). Son of Azariah.

6. Ahitub – "Brother of Benevolence" or "Father of Goodness" (1Chr.6:11, 12). A Priest about seven generations later than a previous 'Ahitub' in the priestly line.

7. Zadok – "Righteous". Son of Ahitub and father of Shallum (1Chr.6:12, 13; 9:11; Ezra 7:2).

8. Shallum/Meshullam – "Portion of Jehovah" or "Jehovah is Protection". Father of Hilkiah (1Chr.6:12, 13; Ezra 7:2). Called Meshullum in 1Chr.9:11).

9. Hilkiah – "Jehovah is Protection" or "Jehovah is my Portion". Possibly High Priest under King Josiah's reign (2Chr.24:9; 2Kgs.22:4). Son of Shallum (1Chr.6:13).

10. Azariah – as #2 and #4 above (1Chr.9:10, 11; 2Chr.31:10). Son of Hilkiah (1Chr.6:13).

11. Seraiah – "Jehovah is Prince" or "The Lord is my Prince" or "Soldier of the Lord". Son of Azariah and Chief Priest in Jerusalem when Nebuchadnezzar, King of Babylon, took the city. This Priest, along with other captives, was apparently put to death at Riblah (1Chr.6:14; Ezra 7:1; Jer.52:24-27).

12. Jehozadak – "Jehovah is Just". Son of Seraiah (1Chr.6:14, 15). It appears that Jehozadak was taken into Babylonian Captivity for the 70 years. He was the father of Jeshua (Joshua) the High Priest of the return from exile (Ezra 3:2; 5:2 with Hag.1:12-14; 2:2-4; Zech.3:1-6).

As already mentioned, several of these names are repeated in different generations, making it somewhat difficult to distinguish who is who among the Priests. Several of these Priests were ministering in the time period of either the Kings of Israel or more particularly the Kings of Judah. The House of Israel went into Assyrian Captivity about BC.721 and the House of Judah into Babylonian Captivity about BC.604. These things need to be kept in mind in endeavoring to follow the ministry of the different Priests of the line of Aaron, Israel's first High Priest.

PART NINE – MESSIAH'S RESTORATION TIMES

Chapter 32   Joshua, the Priest of Restoration Times
Chapter 33   Ezra, the Teaching Priest
Chapter 34   The Priesthood in Messiah's Times
Chapter 35   The End of the Aaronic-Levitical Priesthood

CHAPTER 32 – JOSHUA: THE PRIEST OF RESTORATION

Introductory:
With the 70 years in Babylonian Captivity coming to an end, a faithful remnant returned to the land of Palestine. They came to rebuild the temple, the city of Jerusalem, its walls and gates. The historical books of Ezra and Nehemiah deal with the details.

The High Priest of this time was Joshua (Hag.1:1), the son of Jehozadak who is mentioned in 1Chr.6:14-15. Joshua's name means "Jehovah is Salvation" or "Savior". His name is mentioned in Ezra 3:1-2; 5:2; Neh.12:26; Hag.1:1, 12-14; 2:1-5; Zech.3:1-10; 6:9-15).

Through His prophets, the Lord speaks a word to both people and priests, reproving them for their hypocritical fasts over the various months. They really had not fasted to the Lord (Zech.7:1-10). Their fasts had become a farce! The real fast the Lord wanted was obedience to the word of the Lord through His Prophets. Read also the true fast of which Isaiah speaks (Isa.58).

A. The Vision of Joshua, the High Priest – Zech.3
The scene before us in vs.1-7 is actually a Court scene in heaven. With the restoration of the temple, there is of necessity the cleansing of the High Priest and the priesthood for ministry in the House of the Lord.

There are a number of spiritual lessons that may be gleaned from the vision of Joshua, the High Priest of these restoration times. These things were written, not just for their times, but for all times and believer-priests may learn from them (1Cor.10:6, 11; Rom.15:4). These are noted in outline form.

1. **Joshua Challenged** – vs.1, 2
   In the vision, Joshua is seen standing before the Angel of the Lord. Satan is standing at his right hand to resist him, to oppose him or to be his adversary (Hag.1:1; Rev.12:9-10; Gen.3:1-2. Note also Job 1-2 as he accuses Job before God). It is a Satanic challenge to his ministry as High Priest of Judah. It is spiritual warfare. Satan hates both Christ and the Church, His Body.

   Satan is standing at Joshua's right hand (Psa.109:6; Lke.1:11) as this is the place of the accuser. Satan is resisting the work of restoration of the temple, Jerusalem and the priesthood (1Chr.21:1; Matt.4:16-23). He resisted Christ. He resists the Church.

2. **Joshua Condemned** – vs.2, 3
    Satan stands on the ground of accusation and condemnation. Why? Because Joshua, as High Priest is clothed in filthy garments. He stands condemned. He should have been like Aaron, clothed in the garments of glory and beauty (Ex.28:1-4). He should have been clothed in the garments of white linen. Note these scriptures on clothing and garments (Gen.3:21; Psa.45; Isa.52:1, 2; 61:1-3, 10; 63:1-4; Rev.19:8, 9).

    In Persian Courts, the accused were clothed in filthy garments. So Joshua has come out of Babylon. He is representative of the nation or people of Judah. They have been defiled by Babylonian traditions, and the spirit of Babylon, which means "confusion". Jude tells us to hate the garments spotted by the flesh (Jude 23 with Rev.3:4, 5; 16:15). The filthy garments speak of self-righteousness and leprous garments (Lev.13:47-50 with Prov.30:12; Isa.4:4; 64:5, 6; Rom.3:22; Phil.3:1-9).

3. **Joshua Cleansed** – vs.4
    The word came, "Take away the filthy garments". Joshua is stripped of the old and filthy garments and clothed in new garments. The priests are to be clothed in the garments of righteousness and salvation (Psa.132:9, 16 with Isa.61:6, 19).

    There are those who have washed their robes white in the blood of the Lamb (Rev.7:14). The fine linen is the righteousness of the saints (Rev.19:7, 8; 3:4, 5). He gives the garment of praise for the spirit of heaviness (Isa.61:3). The ground of condemnation is taken away. Joshua can stand there cleansed to minister to the Lord on behalf of the people of Judah. His iniquity was caused to pass from him. This was as on the Day of Atonement in Israel (Lev.16). He is acquitted.

    The Lord spoke to the Lord as Father to Son (see Psa.110:1, 2). The Lord rebuked Satan (Gen.19:24). The Angel of the Lord was probably a Christophany, a manifestation of the Lord Jesus Christ prior to His incarnation (Read Gen.16:7-10; 31:11-13; 32:25-31; Ex.3:2-4; 23:20-23; 32:34; Jud.6:11-22).

4. **Joshua Clothed** – vs.4
    Joshua was clothed with a change of raiment, a raiment of rich apparel (Isa.43:25; 52:1; Ezek.36:25; Matt.7:18, 19). He was as a brand plucked from the fires of Hades (Amos 4:11; Rom.8:33;

11:5; Jude 9, 23). As a worm saved from the fire. As the three Hebrew youths were saved from the fire of the furnace (Dan.3).

5. **Joshua Crowned** – vs.5
Then Joshua had a fair MITRE (turban) placed on his head. Refer to Ex.28:36-38. This was the linen turban with the gold plate, inscribed with "Holiness to the Lord" on it, laced with the ribbon of blue. On the forehead was the gold plate. "Holiness to the Lord", for "without holiness, none can see the Lord" (Heb.12:14). We are to worship the Lord in the beauty of holiness (Psa.29:1-2).

The forehead = the seat of the mind, the reason, the imaginations, the understanding, the intellect. Sin entered through the mind (2Cor.11:1-3). Repentance means a change of mind. Believers are to be transformed by the renewing of the mind (Rom.12:1, 2). The enemy battles for the mind of man (2Cor.10:1-5). Later on, Joshua is crowned as King-Priest (Zech.6:9-15).

6. **Joshua Charged** – vs.6, 7
The Messiah = Angel solemnly protested (that is, solemnly and earnestly protested and affirmed, giving him a charge. Amp. OT). Note how the Lord laid a charge on His leaders (Num.27:23; Deut.31:23; 1Tim.5:21; 6:13; 2Tim.4:1). So the charge is laid on the people of God. Note how this charge is spelt out:

   a. If you will walk in My ways – note 'walk' in Eph.2:1-3, 10; 4:1, 17; 5:1-2, 8, 15. It points to the believer's walk before the Lord.
   b. My ways – Psa.95:10; 103:7
   c. My Charge – Num.3:28-38; Josh 1:7-9; 1Kgs.2:3; Ezek.44:6-8
   d. My House (the Temple) - as High Priest (Lev.10:10; Ezek.44:23; Mal.2:7; Hos.8:1; Deut.17:9).
   e. My Courts – Psa.100:1-4. The Outer Courts of the Lord. Access into My Presence (Amp. OT).
   f. Among those who stand by i.e., the angelic messengers.

7. **Joshua commissioned** – vs.7
Now that Joshua was cleansed and clothed and crowned and charged, he could fulfill the commission laid upon the Priesthood. Worship, intercession and reconciliation were the things involved in the ministry of the High Priest along with the rest of the priesthood.

B. The Order of Melchizedek – Zech.6:9-15

In this passage we have a remarkable prophetic picture of the coming of our Lord Jesus Christ, who is our perfect and sinless 'Joshua', our Lord and Savior. We note this symbolic act with relation to Joshua of the Old Testament times.

1. The Prophet Zechariah is told, by the Lord, to take silver and gold from those men of the Captivity (6:10-11a).
2. He is to make an elaborate crown with the silver and gold (6:11b).
3. He is to set it on the head of Joshua, the High Priest (6:11c).
4. He is to speak a prophetic word about "the Man whose name is the Branch" (6:12ff), pointing to our Lord Jesus Christ.
   - This Man is to branch out from His place.
   - He is to build the Temple of the Lord (the Church).
   - He is to bear the glory.
   - He is to sit and rule upon His throne (as a King-Priest).
   - He is to be Priest on His throne.
   - The council of peace shall be between both of these offices, the King and the Priest.
5. Those that are afar off (i.e., the Gentiles) shall come and build in the Temple of the Lord (6:15).
6. This will happen upon diligent obedience to the voice of the Lord (6:15).

This prophecy first found fulfillment in Joshua of the Restoration times, but it pointed prophetically to the Lord Jesus Christ in His Church. This would be the Order of Melchizedek, where the offices of King and Priest would be combined and reconciled in the one person. It would also find its fulfillment in the Church, the Body of Christ, as all believers are called to be "kings and priests" unto God and His Christ (Rev.1:6; 5:9, 10; 1Pet.2:5-9). All points to the New Testament Church, the New Covenant Temple of the Lord (Eph.2:19-22).

In this wonderful vision, we can see a picture of the Church, the believer-priests of the Lord. The Church must respond to the call to "Come out of Babylon" and all that causes spiritual confusion. The Church, in its ministry of worship, intercession and reconciliation, is challenged and resisted by Satan and his hosts. The Church needs to be cleansed, clothed, crowned, charged and commissioned to fulfill the purposes of God in the earth. This will be the Order of Melchizedek!

Jesus could say, "The prince, the evil genius of this world cometh, and there is no ground in Me on which to work, there is nothing in Me that belongs to him, I have nothing in common with him and he has no power over Me."

(Jhn.14:30, 31. Amp. NT, with 1Jhn.5:18). This is God's purpose for the Church and for all believer-priests!

That which was local becomes typical and prophetic of the New Testament Church.

1. Joshua challenged – vs.1, 2
2. Joshua condemned – vs.2, 3
3. Joshua cleansed – vs.4
4. Joshua clothed – vs.4
5. Joshua crowned – vs.5
6. Joshua charged – vs.6-7
7. Joshua commissioned – vs.7

CHAPTER 33 – EZRA: THE TEACHING PRIEST

Introductory:
Although Ezra was not counted among the High Priests, yet he was a Priest, and he was descended from Hilkiah, from Zadok and Phinehas (Ezra 7:1-25, especially vs.1-6). He was the son of Seraiah, the High Priest who was slain after the King of Babylon, Nebuchadnezzar, took Jerusalem (2Kgs.25:18, 21). The Vulgate speaks of him as Esdras.

Ezra means "Help" or "My Helper" (Psa.121. "The Lord is my Helper in time of need" is illustrative of his name).

As a Priest, much is attributed to him in the restoration period. There was a time in Judah's history when "For a long time, Israel had been:

1. Without the true God
2. Without a teaching priest and
3. Without Law" (2Chr.15:3).

In the restoration period following the Babylonian Captivity, Ezra became a "teaching priest" for the people of Judah. He was a great man of God. Following we note some of the remarkable things about this great teaching-priest.

A. Ezra – the Scribe-Priest

1. Ezra was a famous priest (2Chr.34:14; Ezra 7:11-12; 10:10-16; Neh.8:2-9; 12:26).

2. Ezra was also a Scribe (Ezra 7:6, 11, 12; Neh.12:26).
   As a Scribe he was a theologian and hermeneutician of the Sacred Scriptures. He fulfilled 2Chr.15:3. He taught the people about the true God, he was a teaching priest, and he taught the people about the Law of the Lord. It should be remembered that the House of Judah had been in Babylon for some 70 years.

3. Ezra was also a student of the Law (Ezra 7:10). "For Ezra had prepared his heart to seek the law of the Lord, and to do it, and to teach statutes and ordinances in Israel."

4. Ezra was an excellent interpreter and teacher of the Word of God. He taught what he had learnt from his study of the Scriptures (the Torah). The different Levites helped the people to understand the law. They read the Scriptures distinctly, gave their sense and understanding.

The remnant that came out of Babylon was totally ignorant of things in the Divine book (Neh.8:2-18).

5. Ezra was willing to leave the comforts of Babylon, and to accept the message of Restoration. He was the leader of the good company willing to leave Babylon for Jerusalem, and the hard work involved in the restoration (Ezra 7:1-28).

6. Ezra was also thankful to God for His sovereignty and His mercy as pertaining to the House of the Lord. He was encouraged as he saw the hand of God upon him as a leader willing to take responsibility under God (Ezra 7:27, 28; 8:18, 22, 31).

7. Ezra was a Priest periodically given to prayer and fasting (Ezra 8:23; 9:5-15; 10:1-6).

8. Ezra evidenced much sorrow and grief of heart over the sins of the people and the mixed marriages among them (Ezra 9:1-15; 10:1-6).

9. Ezra was a trustworthy person. He could be trusted with the finance and the offerings for the altar of God (Ezra 7:13-21).

10. Ezra used all his skills to bring about genuine repentance in the former exiles in his endeavor to keep the "holy seed" unto the Lord and the coming Messiah (Ezra 9). He saw the great danger of mixture of the seed of the chosen race with the seed of the surrounding nations.

11. Ezra helped the people to enter into the great Feast of the Seventh Month, the Feast of Tabernacles, also called the Feast of Booths (Neh.8:13-18).

12. A study of his book shows the great reformation that was brought to the people of Judah under his time, along with Nehemiah, Joshua the High Priest and the prophets of God, Zechariah and Haggai. The Reformation was seen in:

- Purity of worship
- Rebuilding the Altar of God – Ezra 3
- Restoring the House of God, His Temple – Ezra 3:10-13
- Keeping the Feast of Tabernacles, none like it since the days of Joshua – Neh.8
- Cleansing the people from Babylonian idolatry and mixed marriages – Neh.9-10

- Sanctifying the Sabbath of the Lord – Neh.9:14; 10:31; 13:15-32 with Psa.92, which bears the title, A Psalm for the Sabbath.

B. Traditions Attributed to Ezra

There are certain traditions attributed to the times of Ezra, the teaching priest, as in the following list:

- The formation of the Great Synagogue
- Settlement of the Canon into the Law, the Psalms and the Prophets
- Writing of the Scriptures from old Hebrew into Assyrian characters
- Compilation of the Books of 1 and 2 Chronicles, Ezra and Nehemiah
- Institution of the Local Synagogues
- Psalm 119 is attributed to him as "The WORD Psalm". One may note the various designations of "the Word" in the Psalm and see the use of the same in the Book of Ezra.

Conclusion:

Although Ezra was not a High Priest, he was an excellent Scribe and Priest. His greatest honor is being a "teacher-priest" for his generation and generations to come in the giving of the Scriptures in much of its present compilation.

He sets an example to all New Testament believer-priests to be sound in theology, sound in hermeneutics (principles of interpreting the Scriptures) and to be a good communicator of the Word of God.

God always preserves a faithful remnant who are willing to "come out of Babylon" (religious confusion) and accept the message of Restoration of the House of the Lord, the city of God and the Priesthood of all believers. This is the message of this great teaching priest – Ezra!

CHAPTER 34 - THE PRIESTHOOD IN MESSIAH'S TIMES

When Jesus came, He was born under the Law to fulfill the Law (Gal.4:4-5). In the cross, He would fulfill and abolish the temporal elements of the Mosaic Law and bring in the New Covenant.

From His birth to His death, Jesus upheld the laws relative to Moses and the Aaronic and Levitical Priesthood until that day that the same Aaronic Priesthood saw Him to His death on the cross. That very day the Mosaic Law was abolished. That old priesthood became one of the greatest enemies of the Messiah of God.

We note His fulfillment of the things pertaining to the Law.

A. The Lord Jesus Christ
1. **Priest Zacharias** – Lke.1:5
   Zacharias was the Priest fulfilling the course of Abia (also called Abijah) when he was visited by the angel Gabriel, the angel who gave Daniel the notable "Seventy Weeks Prophecy" (Dan.9:24-27). Zacharias was ministering at the altar of incense when Gabriel appeared. He gave him the revelation about the birth and mission of John, the Messiah's forerunner. Zacharias could not believe the word in his old age. As a result of his unbelief he was struck dumb until the birth and naming of the child, John, who became known as John the Baptist. Zacharias composed the magnificent Benediction when John was presented to the Lord in His Temple (Lke.1:67-79). No more is heard of this priest in Holy Scripture.

   It is significant that John was actually born a priest, as his father was, but the word of the Lord sent him to be a Priest-Prophet and the Messiah's forerunner. It was the beginning of a new dispensation.

2. **The Birth of Christ** – Matt.2:4
   The chief priests confirm that Christ would be born in Bethlehem.

3. **The Lepers sent to the Priests**
   a. Jesus sent the cleansed leper to the priests to show himself, offer the offerings as Moses said and this would be a testimony to them (Matt.8:1-4; Mrk.1:40-45; Lke.5:12-14).
   b. There were also ten lepers cleansed in similar manner. Jesus tells them to show themselves to the priest, offer the offering and this as a testimony to them. Only one of the ten returned

to thank Jesus for cleansing (Lke.17:12-19). One can only wonder whether the priests accepted their testimony.

4. **The Showbread**
Jesus justifies His disciples for plucking the corn on the Sabbath as David 'unlawfully' ate the showbread, which was only supposed to be for the priests (Matt.12:4, 5; Mrk.2:26; Lke.6:4).

5. **The Parable** – Lke.10:31
In the Parable of the Good Samaritan, Jesus mentions the priest, and the Levite, and their lack of concern for the 'certain man', and then the care of the 'good Samaritan".

6. **The Joint-Priests**
Annas and Caiaphas were joint-priests in the time of Jesus and both were responsible for His death under the Romans (Matt.26:3, 57; Lke.3:2; Jhn.11:49; 18:24; Acts 4:6). Refer comments in next chapter.

7. **The Death of Jesus**
Jesus, many times, foretold His coming rejection and death by the hands of the chief priests, the scribes and the religious leaders. These prophecies were duly fulfilled (Matt.16:21; 20:18; 21:15, 23, 45; 27:20; Mrk.8:31; 10:33; 11:18, 27ff; 14:1, 53-55; 15:1-3, 10, 11; Lke.9:22).

8. **Judas' Betrayal to the Chief Priests**
Judas betrayed Jesus to the chief priests. He sold Christ out to them for 30 pieces of silver, money he would never live to spend, but they were glad for His betrayal (Matt.26:3, 14, 47, 59; 27:1-12; Mrk.14:10; Lke.22:4-6). The Priests revealed their hypocrisy when the money Judas returned was used to buy a field and not be put back into the treasury as it was 'blood money!' (Matt.27:3-10).

9. **The Voice of the Chief Priests**
The chief priests were agitators and their voices prevailed above those of the people in the clamor for the crucifixion of Jesus on the cross (Lke.23:1-23).

10. **Mocking the Christ**
While Jesus hung on the cross in such agony, the chief priests mocked Him and His trust in the Father God (Matt.27:41-43 with Mrk.15:31). How cruel can 'religion' be!

11. **Making sure the Tomb**
    The chief Priests remembered the words of Christ that He would rise from the dead. They wanted to make sure that He never escaped the tomb. They made sure that the tomb was sealed (Matt.27:62 - 28:11). Then when Jesus did rise from the dead, they paid the soldiers large sums of money to lie about the resurrection scene (Matt.28:11-15).

12. **Enemies of their Messiah**
    The great tragedy is that the Chief Priests, along with the religious leaders, the scribes, the Pharisees and the Sadducees (the Fundamentalists, Theologians and Hermeneuticians of that day), were the strongest leaders of the nation and the greatest enemies and opposers of Christ. They stirred up the people against Him. They were great agitators, and this in spite of all the miracles, the signs and wonders Jesus had done. The root reason was envy of Christ (Mrk.15:10). Read also Jhn.7:32, 45; 11:47,57; 12:10; 18:3, 35; 19:6, 15, 21.

B. The Church, which is His Body

The further tragedy is that these same priests not only opposed their own longed-for Messiah, they also opposed the Church, the Body of Christ, after Jesus had gone to heaven. This is seen in the Book of Acts on several occasions.

1. Healing of the Lame Man – Acts 3:4 – 4:22. Caiaphas and Annas reject the healing of the lame man in the name of Jesus.
2. Many miracles, signs and wonders with great increase in the number of believers. Acts 5:17-33. Out of jealousy, they persecute the apostles.
3. The Death of Stephen – Acts 6:8-15; 7:1-60. They had him stoned to death.
4. Letters given to the Pharisee Saul – Acts 9:1, 14, 21. They gave Saul letters to kill Christians.
5. Rejection of Paul's testimony – Acts 22:5-22. They reject Paul's testimony of his conversion to Christ.
6. Paul apologizes to the High Priest – Acts 23:1-5, 14, 15. Probably the High Priest was not in his priestly garments.
7. Priests became believers – Acts 6:7. A great company of Priests became obedient to the faith once they knew the truth of the rent veil of the Temple and about Jesus.

The rejection of Christ and the Church thus filled up their "cup of iniquity" (See Gen. 15:16 for the principle) and brought judgment on the temple, the city, the priesthood and the people of Judah (Matt.23:32-38). This judgment was historically fulfilled in 70 AD when the Romans destroyed the temple and the city.

CHAPTER 35 - THE END OF THE LEVITICAL PRIESTHOOD

In the previous chapter, it was seen that, in Christ's time, there were joint-priests, Annas and Caiaphas (Lke.3:2). These are the last two priests ever mentioned in the New Testament as this Priesthood came to its timely end. It is predominantly with these two final High Priests that this chapter concerns itself.

A. Annas

Annas – his name means "Grace of Jehovah". Sad to say he rejected that grace that God revealed in Christ (Jhn.1:17). He was in office as a High Priest when John the Baptist began his ministry. The word of the Lord by-passed the current religious and political leaders and went to John the Baptist, "the voice crying in the wilderness" (Lke.3:1-6; Jhn.18:13, 14, 24; Acts 4:6). Annas took part in the trial of Jesus as well as the trial of Peter and John.

B. Caiaphas

Caiaphas – his name means "A Search" or "He that seeks with Diligence". He certainly did not live up to his name when it came to the person of our Lord Jesus Christ.

He was the son-in-law to Annas and was High Priest of the Jews for a number of years (Matt.26:3, 57; Jhn.18:13). Some expositors understand Caiaphas to be a Sadducee as to his belief system. If so, the Sadducees did not believe in angels, or spirit, or resurrection. They taught that the soul dies with the body (Matt.22:23; Acts 23:8). They also believed that all mankind was free to do good or evil. Tradition is not to be followed, only the Scriptures, especially the five Books of Moses, the Torah.

There are some seven significant passages in the New Testament that draw our attention concerning this evil High Priest, Caiaphas.

1. **The Resurrection of Lazarus**
   Caiaphas wanted to put Lazarus to death again after Jesus raised him from death, because so many people now were coming to believe in Jesus as the Messiah. It was evident he did not think that Jesus could raise Lazarus from the dead again (Jhn.11:1-49; 12:1-11).

2. **The Prophecy concerning Jesus' Death**
   After Lazarus was raised, the Jewish Council came together to discuss what to do with Jesus. As evil a man as Caiaphas was, God caused him to prophesy the death of Jesus, and the gathering

together of God's elect (Read Jhn.11:49-53 with Jhn.18:13-14). He prophesied: "You know nothing at all, nor do you consider that it is expedient for us that one man should die for the people, and not that the whole nation should perish. Now this he did not say on his own authority, but being high priest that year, he prophesied that Jesus would die for the nation. And not only for that nation, but also that He would gather together in one the children of God scattered abroad."

Read also Eph.2:14-18 in conjunction with this prophetic word. Caiaphas undoubtedly never realized the significance of what he was saying.

3. **The Trial of Jesus**
When the Sanhedrin met together at the trial of Jesus, Caiaphas evidenced his determination to find Jesus guilty of death. Because he was High Priest, his word was counted as authoritative. He violated Biblical law to see that Jesus was crucified (Matt.26:57-66; Jhn.18:19-24).

4. **The Rending of his Garment**
At the trial of Jesus, when Jesus refused to answer the false witness brought against Him, Caiaphas adjured Jesus with an oath as to whether He was the Christ, the Son of God. Jesus replied, giving His confession and prophesying of His second coming in the clouds of heaven. The High Priest charged Him with blasphemy and therefore worthy of death. At that moment, Caiaphas tore his clothes. This, for the High Priest, was forbidden by the Law. In doing so, he disqualified himself as High Priest and in actuality pronounced the 'death' or the cessation of the Aaronic and Levitical Priesthood (Read Matt.26:65 with Lev.10:6; 21:10; Ex.28:32).

It is significant that the soldiers who gambled for the garments of Jesus decided not to rend (tear) these garments. It was symbolic of Jesus' Priesthood being eternal, after the Order of Melchizedek (Jhn.19:23-24).

5. **The Trial of Peter and John**
Caiaphas was also involved in the trial of Peter and John after the healing of the lame man (Acts 4). Annas and Caiaphas could do nothing about this miracle of healing but command that the apostles cease to preach in the Name of Jesus, the risen Lord. This was done in spite of all they had witnessed under the ministry of Jesus and now of His apostles (Acts 4:6; 5:17-28).

6. **The Prison Rescue**
   With the healing of so many sick people under the shadow of Peter, and the unclean spirits being cast out of people (Acts 5:12-16) the High Priest, Caiaphas, rose along with the Sadducees and cast the apostles into prison. The angel of the Lord rescued them out of prison and told them to continue preaching the words of this life. The High Priest forbade them to preach in that Name (Acts 5:17-42). The Priests still refused to believe.

7. **The Trial of Paul**
   At the final chapters of Acts, Paul is standing before the Council. He is witnessing and testifying of Christ's saving power. Caiaphas commanded those around Paul to strike him on the mouth. Paul rebuked him, not knowing he was the High Priest. Undoubtedly he was not dressed in his garments for that occasion. Paul would not have done it if he had known who he was. Paul apologizes for his sin of ignorance. This was the final witness of the Lord to this Priesthood (Read Acts 22-23 chapters especially Acts 23:1-9).

Summary:
Caiaphas, along with Annas and the rest of the Priesthood stand condemned in the light of their rejection of Divine witness under Jesus and the apostles in the Acts.

When Jesus died on the cross, God the Father, 'rent' (tore) the veil of the Temple from top to bottom. It was a supernatural act of God. Man, if he had done it, would have torn it from bottom to top, but this was an act of God. It signified from the Divine side that the sacrificial system and its Priesthood was at an end. Believers in Christ may now enter "within the veil" into the Holiest of All through His sacrifice and Priesthood. This is the new Priesthood, after the Order of Melchizedek (Matt.27:50-51 with Heb.7:1-4; 10:16-20).

This was the Divine sign of the end and the cessation of the Aaronic and Levitical Priesthood. The new order had come in – Christ and His Church (Rev.1:6; 5:9-10; 20:6; 1Pet.2:5-9; Ex.19:6; Psa.110).

In AD.70 God allowed the Romans to come and destroy the Temple, the city of Jerusalem and scatter the people of Judah with its Priesthood. Jewry has been without the Temple and legitimate Priesthood since that time. If Jewry seeks to re-establish this abolished system, God will not endorse it. God will never re-institute or bless that which His Son has abolished forever! The cross signifies the END!

C. The Witness of the Book of Hebrews

A brief overview of the Book of Hebrews confirms more than any other New Testament Epistle that the Old Covenant economy and all involved in its ritualism had ended. All was finished at the death of Christ. He declared in His dying moments, "It is finished!" (Jhn.19:30). What was finished? His death on the cross along with all the Old Covenant sacrifices, priesthood, ritualism and ceremonialism. ALL was finished and put away by His death.

As to the Mosaic Covenant, Christ is better:
- Better than Aaron, the High Priest of the Old Covenant as He is Priest of the New Covenant.
- Better than the earthly Tabernacle for He ministers in the heavenly Tabernacle of which that on earth was the shadow
- Better than animal sacrifices, because His own body and blood supersedes any other and lower sacrifice of creatures. He is both Priest and sacrifice in the one person.
- Better than the Levitical Priesthood as He comes of the Tribe of Judah and is a King and Priest
- Better than the Old Covenant as He is the New Covenant personified
- Better than all Old Testament Prophets as He is THE WORD personified
- Better than Moses as Moses pointed and prophesied of Him who was to come
- Better than all the Heroes of Faith as He was and is the Source of all faith
- Better than the material Tabernacles and Temple as He Himself is God's Temple
- Better than earthly Jerusalem as He came from the heavenly Jerusalem
- Better than all Priests and Kings together as He is the eternal King-Priest after the Order of Melchizedek, living in the power of an endless life.

Christ is indeed better than all because of WHO He is, WHAT He said and WHAT He has done!

PART TEN - THE NEW COVENANT PRIESTHOOD

Chapter 36   New Covenant Times
Chapter 37   The Spiritual House
Chapter 38   The Spiritual Priesthood
Chapter 39   The Spiritual Sacrifices
Chapter 40   The Functioning Priesthood
Chapter 41   A Paradigm for the New Priesthood

CHAPTER 36 - NEW COVENANT TIMES

The Prophet Isaiah spoke a word to the people of his times which is also applicable to Messiah's times.

"Do not remember the **former things**, nor consider the **things of old**. Behold, I will do a **new thing**, now it shall spring forth: shall you not know it?" (Isa.43:18-19a).

In principle, the truth is applicable in every generation. It was true in the period of the transition from the Old Covenant to the New Covenant. The period of transition from the OLD to the NEW was a difficult time for man. The people of Judah, for too long, remembered "the former things", the things of the Old Covenant. The nation as a whole failed to make the transition. A faithful remnant made the transition and did not fossilize. It has been said that "a fossil is a living creature that failed to make a transition."

Many in Jewry took a long time to come into the things of the New Covenant, the "new thing" that God was doing in the earth, through His Son, the Lord Jesus Christ. They did not realize that these were New Covenant times and seasons (Eccl.3:1) and missed the purpose of God. God promised to make "all things new" (Rev.21:5).

A. The Former Things

Enough has been written on the things pertaining to the Old Covenant, "the former things". The reader is referred to the Bibliography for those textbooks dealing with the same. We note the major points of the Old Covenant.

1. The Old or the Mosaic Covenant
2. The Tabernacles of Moses, of David and the Temple of Solomon, the House of the Lord.
3. The Aaronic Priesthood and the Levitical Priesthood, or the Order of Aaron.
4. The Sacrifices and Offerings of the Law
5. The Feasts of the Lord.
6. The Sabbath Days and Years, and the Jubilee Years
7. The Law – Moral, Civil, Health and Hygiene
8. The Covenant Rite of Circumcision

All these things became "the former things", and what the Prophet Hosea called "the great (KJV) things of the Law" (Hos.8:12). All these things were part of the schoolmaster (tutor) to bring Israel to Christ (Gal.3:23-25).

The Book of Hebrews was written to wean the Hebrew believers from these "former things" to the realities now to be found in Christ Jesus. Those former things were the shadow, the type and the prophecy. Christ Himself was the reality, the substance, the anti-type and the fulfillment. Although the external form is abolished, the knowledge and the truth hidden in the form remains (Rom.2:20). The sad thing is that Jewry wanted to hold on to the external form and they missed the knowledge and truth in Christ. They wanted to remember the "former things", the things of the Old Covenant and they missed "the new thing" God was doing in the New Covenant!

B. All Things New

God promised to do a "new thing". This has been the workings of God over human history. He moves from that which becomes old to that which is new. This is true of those things pertaining to the New Covenant, when compared to the Old Covenant.

1. There would be a NEW Covenant, as foretold by the Prophet Jeremiah (Jer.31:31-34 with Heb.8:6-13).

2. There would be a NEW Temple or Sanctuary, which is the New Testament Church, when the old Temple was abolished (Eph.2:19-22; 1Pet.2:4-6).

3. There would be a NEW Priesthood, the Priesthood of all believers, and this would be a NEW Order, after the Order of Melchizedek (Rev.1:6; 5:9-10; Psa.110; Heb.7).

4. There would be NEW sacrifices; the once-for-all sacrifice of Jesus, and the spiritual sacrifices of the believer-priests (1Pet.2:5-9).

5. There would be NEW Feasts to celebrate with the Lord, fulfilled in Christ and the Holy Spirit (1Cor.5:6-8 and Acts 2:1-4).

6. There would be NEW days to celebrate the work of Christ, in the resurrection and the outpoured Holy Spirit (Col.2:16, 17; Rom.14).

7. There would be a NEW Commandment and NEW Tables where God would write His laws on our hearts and minds (Heb.8:6-13; Jhn.13:34).

8. There would be a NEW Covenant rite of circumcision, it would be of the heart and not merely of the flesh (Rom.2:25-29).

As the Lord prophesied, He was doing a "new thing" in the NEW Covenant. The believer is encouraged not to remember the "former things" and miss out on the "new thing" God did in the New Covenant. This was Paul's purpose in writing to the Galatian Churches as the Judaizers were encouraging them to have Moses in one hand and Jesus in the other hand. They were bringing the Galatian Churches into what might be called "covenantal confusion". They were confusing the Old and the New Covenants. Believers in Christ are under the New Covenant.

C. The New Covenant

Everything that was new belonged to and belongs to the New Covenant believers. Following is a listing of the wonderful "new things" in the New Covenant. For the serious student, this provides a wonderful study in itself.

1. The New Covenant was a new wineskin. Many Jews still believed "the old was better" (Matt.9:17; Mrk.2:22; Lke.5:37-39).
2. It was not possible to put the New Covenant into the Old Covenant wineskin.
3. In Christ, all believers are a new creation (2Cor.5:17; Gal.6:15).
4. The believer is given a new name, and this is received in water baptism (Rev.2:17; 3:12; Acts 2:36-39).
5. One could not sew the new garment on to the old garment, or else the tear would be made worse. The Old and the New Covenants just do not mix (Matt.9:16; Mrk.2:21; Lke.5:36).
6. A wise scribe (teacher) will use things from the old (Old Covenant) to illustrate that which is in the new (New Covenant). Matt.13:52.
7. Believers are under the New Covenant and not the Old Covenant (Matt.26:28; Mrk.14:24; Lke.22:20; 1Cor.11:25; Heb.8:8, 13). That which is old is ready to vanish away.
8. Jesus gave us the new teaching (Mrk.1:27).
9. Believers shall speak with new tongues (Mrk.16:17; Acts 2:13).
10. Jesus gave us a new commandment to love as He loves (Jhn.13:34; 1Jhn.2:7, 8; 2Jhn.1:5).
11. Believers are ministers of the New Covenant, of the spirit and not the letter of the Old Covenant (2Cor.3:6).
12. The Church, composed of both Jew and Gentile, is the one new man (Eph.2:15).
13. Believers are to put on the new man, as we are no longer "in Adam" (Eph.4:24; Col.3:10 with 1Cor.15:22).
14. We may approach God now through a new and living way, in the Lord Jesus Christ (Heb.10:19-20).

15. Believers look for a new heavens and a new earth, where righteousness dwells eternally (2Pet.3:13).
16. The overcomer has access to New Jerusalem, the new and heavenly city of God (Rev.3:12).
17. The redeemed can sing a new song (Rev.5:9; 14:3).
18. There will be a new heavens and a new earth and a new city of Jerusalem. The old will pass away (Rev.21:1, 2).
19. God will make all things new (Rev.21:5). The former things will pass away.

God will cause us to forget the former things on this earth. We will no longer consider the old because He will completely do a new thing for New Covenant believers! Old things will pass away and all things become new!

In keeping with the focus of this book, we are especially interested in the new priesthood. The old has finished; the new has begun.

CHAPTER 37 - THE SPIRITUAL HOUSE

Peter writes to the believers scattered abroad that we are "as living stones, being built up a spiritual house ..." (1Pet.2:5).

The basic proposition undergirding the studies presented in this text is that:

1. Where there is **Covenant,**
2. There is **Sanctuary,**
3. Which necessitates a **Priesthood,**
4. And this requires **Sacrifice** (Read again Heb.8:1-6 with 1Pet.2:1-10).

In the Foreword, we presented twelve pictures or types of the Church found in the Word of God. These types are to be found in both Old and New Testaments. The picture considered in brief in this chapter is the Church as God's House, God's Sanctuary in the earth.

A. Old Testament Types

In brief, we remind ourselves of several Old Testament types pointing to the New Testament Church, which is now the House of God.

1. The Tabernacle of Moses

The Tabernacle of Moses (the tent built by Moses) was the first particular habitation or house of the Lord. It was God's dwelling place among His people Israel. Its predominant message was that the only way of approach to a holy God in His manifest Presence was through blood sacrifice. The purpose of it being built teaches us that God wants to live with and among His people. The tabernacle of Moses was God's house, a material house, here on earth. The building was ordered by God in Ex.25:8 and He occupied the dwelling in Ex.40:33-35.

2. The Tabernacle of David

The next dwelling place of God among and with His people was the Tent or the Tabernacle of David (pitched by David). If the emphasis in the Tabernacle of Moses was the approach to God through sacrificial blood, the emphasis in the Tabernacle of David was the approach, firstly on the basis of blood, but from then on, through praise and through worship. Each Tabernacle had a Divine purpose in being built. God lives or is enthroned in the praises of His people (Psa.22:3). The decision to build the habitation is recorded in 1Chr.15:1. There is no specific time recorded as to when God "moved in" but we know God's presence went with the Ark of the Covenant (1Chr.13:6-12) and the Ark was installed in David's Tabernacle.

3. **The Temple of Solomon**
   The final habitation of God is found in the Temple that Solomon built. It is helpful to remind ourselves of the word that the Lord spoke to David through the Prophet Nathan (1Chr.17:5). David desired to build God a more permanent material house than the previous Tabernacles. The Lord said: "For I have not dwelt in a house since the time I brought up Israel, even to this day, but have gone from **tent to tent, and from one tabernacle to another …**"

   So the Lord had moved from the Tent of Moses, to the Tabernacle of Moses and He had moved from the Tabernacle of Moses to the Tabernacle of David, and now the Lord is about to move on again to the Temple built by Solomon, known more especially as "the house of the Lord". The Lord gave David the pattern of the Temple and Solomon built accordingly. This was God's final dwelling place in Old Testament times. The decision to build this habitation for God is recorded in 2Chr.1:1. It is completed (5:1) and God "moves in" in His glory to dwell amongst them (5:13-14).

B. **New Testament Reality**
   The Old Testament places of God pointed to the Church. Although the Lord commanded these structures to be built, that was never His real desire (Isa.66:1-2). His ultimate desire was to dwell IN His people, not just WITH them or AMONG them. This He desired both individually and corporately. That is, the Lord wanted to dwell in His people individually as His Temple (1Cor.6:19 where 'you' is singular, meaning each individual believer is a temple for God to indwell), but also corporately, in the Church, the Body of Christ (1Cor.3:16 where 'you' is plural. Also see 2Cor.6:14-18 for the corporate sense).

   Several Scriptures suffice to show that the New Testament writers all saw that the Church, the Body of Christ, became God's House, this side of the cross. The Church is God's dwelling place, His Sanctuary, His Tabernacle, His Temple, or "**a spiritual house**".

   1. We are being built up a spiritual house (1Pet.2:5).
   2. Judgment must begin at the house of God (1Pet.4:16-17).
   3. Every house is built by someone, but "Christ, as a Son over His own house … whose house we are …" (Heb.3:1-6).
   4. Paul writes, "I write so that you may know how you ought to conduct yourselves in the **house of God, which is the church** of the living God …" (1Tim.3:15). Paul interprets the symbol of the house to mean us being the Church of the living God.

5. We are "members of the household of God ... in whom the whole building being fitted together, grows into a holy temple in the Lord, in whom you also are being built together for a dwelling place (habitation) of God by (in) the Spirit" (Eph.2:19-22).
6. Jesus said, "Upon this rock, I will build My Church" (Matt.16:18).
7. At the conclusion of the "Sermon on the Mount" He talked about the "wise man who built his house on the rock" (Matt.7:24-27). Surely Jesus is the wisest of all men and His house will be built by obedience to the Word on the rock foundation.

These several **interpretative** verses from the passages of Scripture provide a hermeneutical foundation to use the Old Testament types or pictures as pointing to the New Covenant Church.

The Tabernacle of Moses, the Tabernacle of David and the Temple of Solomon, therefore, become great prophetic pictures of the Church in New Covenant times.

The Prophet Isaiah speaks of the "Lord's house" that is to be built in the last days (the latter days). To this house all nations will flow (Isa.2:1-4; Mic.4:1-2). It is a prophecy of the New Testament Church, as God's House, that is made up of disciples out of every kindred, tongue, tribe and nation (Matt.28:18-20; Rev.14:6). This is in great contrast to the Old Testament houses of God which were predominantly for the one and only chosen nation, Israel, and not for "all nations"!

The Church, the Body of Christ, is made up of all believers, out of every kindred, tribe, tongue and nation and this constitutes the "House of the Lord." It is a spiritual house, not a material house, in deed and in truth. This is the New Covenant house that God desired to live in all through human history, and not merely the material houses of Old Testament days.

[**Note**: For a fuller treatment of each of these habitations – the Tabernacle of Moses and David and the Temple of Solomon – the reader is referred to the Bibliography, as also "The Church in the New Testament"].

CHAPTER 38 - THE SPIRITUAL PRIESTHOOD

Woven throughout Peter's passage of Scripture (1Pet.2:1-10) is the language of Priesthood. Peter speaks of believers as being "a holy" (vs.5) and "a royal" (vs.9) priesthood.

The progression of thought is followed through:

1. New Covenant Times – emphasis on the NEW Covenant,
2. The Spiritual House – emphasis on the Church as God's New Covenant House,
3. The Spiritual Priesthood – emphasis on the ministering Priesthood, the Priesthood of all believers in the Church, the Body of Christ in the earth.

Because the burden of this textbook is the Priesthood of all believers, sufficient for this chapter will be to re-emphasize those New Testament verses that confirm that all believers in Christ are called to be priests of God and His Christ.

1. All believers are a Royal Priesthood before the Lord. They are "kings and priests" unto God and Christ (1Pet.2:9). A "Royal Priesthood" is a Kingly Priesthood.

2. All believers are part of that holy Priesthood (1Pet.2:5). "As He who called you is holy, you also be holy in all your conduct, because it is written, Be holy, for I am holy" (1Pet.1:15, 16 with Lev.11:44-45). "For without holiness, no one will see the Lord" (Heb.12:14). Holiness of character and life will be seen in those of this holy Priesthood.

3. "To Him who loved us and washed us from our sins in His own blood and has made us kings and priests to His God and Father ..." (Rev.1:5b, 6). Lit. "A Kingdom of Priests."

4. The twenty four elders sing a new song to God and the Lamb: "You have redeemed us to God by Your blood ... and have made us kings and priests to our God and we shall reign on the earth" (Rev.5:9, 10). Lit. "A Kingdom of Priests" (Refer again to Ex.19:4-6).

5. "... they shall be priests of God and of Christ and shall reign (as kings) with Him for one thousand years" (Rev.20:6c).

6. "... present your bodies a living sacrifice ... which is your reasonable service" (Rom.12:1-2). That is, in priestly service and the offering of a sacrifice. Or "rational, intelligent service and spiritual worship" (Amp. N.T.).

These several **interpretative** verses from these passages, as previously noted, provide a hermeneutical foundation in the use of the Old Testament Scriptures on Priesthood as being types and shadows of Christ and the Church, and the Priesthood of all believers.

Isaiah prophesies: "But you shall be named the priests of the Lord. They shall call you the servants of our God" (Isa.61:6a, b).

The New Testament teaches the Priesthood of ALL believers. The ministry gifts of Eph.4:9-16, apostles, prophets, evangelists, shepherds and teachers are given for one purpose. That is, to bring the saints into the work of their ministry, to build up the Body of Christ. They are not called to do the entire ministry but to equip the members to be functioning members in Christ's Church – to be a functioning Royal Priesthood. No one of the five-fold ministry are called to be any kind of a "priest-class", as they themselves are simply a part of that holy and royal priesthood.

CHAPTER 39 - THE SPIRITUAL SACRIFICES

Introductory:
As has been seen in our ongoing proposition, if there is a Covenant, then there must be a Sanctuary, and if there is a Sanctuary, there must be a ministering Priesthood, and this necessitates the offering up of Sacrifices (Heb.8:1-6 with 1Pet.2:1-10). The reader will bear with the repetition:

1. The Covenant is the New Covenant.
2. The Sanctuary is the Church, God's Spiritual House.
3. The Priesthood is the Priesthood of all believers, kings and priests unto God and Christ.
4. The Sacrifices are Spiritual Sacrifices, and this is what this chapter is about.

A. Old Testament Sacrifices
The reader is referred to the previous chapters concerning Old Testament sacrifices. Some additional and final thoughts are provided here. As we compare the Old Testament and New Testament sacrifice (whether of Christ and/or believers), we note these differences.

Old Testament Sacrifices	New Testament Sacrifices
Animal sacrifices	Divine/Human sacrifice of Jesus
Unwilling sacrifices – tied to altar (Psa.118:27b)	Willing to do the Father's will as He was nailed to the cross.
Lower order of creatures	Highest order of Beings
Some offerings compulsory	Necessity of Christ's death
Some offerings voluntary	He laid down His life voluntarily
	Christ was sinless
Sinless animals	Christ was innocent
Innocent victims	He died for sin once and for all
Died for sin and offered daily	Necessary to take away sin and sins
Necessary to take away sin	Jesus' blood cleanses sin, not covers
Covered sin, did not cleanse sin	
Offeror and offering separate	Offeror and offering all in one person
Priest and sacrifice separate	Christ is both Priest and sacrifice

B. New Testament Sacrifices
1. **The Sacrifice of Christ** – Heb.9-10 chapters
   The body and blood of Jesus was His sacrifice to the Father for our sins, transgressions and iniquities (Isa.53). The theme of Heb.9-10

is the blood and the body of Jesus offered for our pardon and cleansing. God was most particular with that which was done with the body and blood of Christ, as He was with all sacrifices and oblations in the Old Testament days. Jesus' sacrifice caused all animal sacrifice and oblation to cease, once and for ever (Dan.9:24-27).

2. **The Sacrifice of Believers** – 1Pet.2:5-9
The Church no longer offers animal sacrifices but "spiritual sacrifices" and these are acceptable to God through Christ, our great High Priest and Sacrifice. In the Old Covenant, all were acceptable to God through Israel's High Priest, Aaron. Now all is through Christ Jesus, our risen Lord.

C. Our Spiritual Sacrifices

We note twelve important spiritual sacrifices that the believing Priesthood may offer to God. Such must come from the heart, from the spirit of the inner man, and not just be external. There is much food for thought for all believers in order for them to serve in the Priesthood of all believers. All believers may check their spiritual offerings to the Lord as they meditate on these things.

1. **The Sacrifice of Thanksgiving**
Any Israelite could offer to God at any time the sacrifice of thanksgiving (Lev.7:11-15). We are living in an unthankful generation (2Tim.3:1-9). It is one of the characteristics of this age: an attitude of ingratitude, selfishness, ungratefulness and thanklessness.

- We enter into His gates with thanksgiving (Psa.100:4).
- We offer the sacrifices of thanksgiving (Psa.116:12-14, 17).
- We give thanks to God for all things (Eph.5:20).
- We give thanks to God in everything. This is the will of God concerning us (1Thess.5:18).
- Read also Phil 4:6; Col.3:17; Psa.107:22; Jonah 2:9. It cost Jonah to sacrifice thanksgiving to God when in the belly of the fish.

God speaks to Israel and tells them that He is really not after their animal sacrifices, but He would enjoy the "sacrifice of thanksgiving" (Read carefully Psa.50:7-13, and especially vs.14). It was not enough to offer the external; God was looking for the internal reality. When things may be rough and tough, it may cost us something to offer thanks to God, but with such He is well pleased. A thankful heart is pleasing to God.

2. **The Sacrifice of Joy**
David writes: "And now shall my head be lifted up above my enemies round about me: therefore will I offer in His Tabernacle, sacrifices of joy: I will sing, yes, I will sing praises unto the Lord" (Psa.27:6).

The apostles had been chastised and beaten for the name of Jesus. They had been disciplined by the religious leaders of the nation. But they responded with joy, counting it joy that they were worthy to suffer for the name of Jesus. Indeed a sacrifice that cost them (Acts 5:41).

The joy of the Lord is our strength (Neh.8:10), spiritually, physically and emotionally.

The kingdom of God is righteousness, peace and joy in the Holy Spirit (Rom.14:17). A healthy Church is a joyful Church. Joy is an infallible sign of the presence of God. As long as one lives in righteousness, there is peace, and when there is peace, there is joy.

It cost David something to rejoice and be joyful when he danced before the Ark of the Lord (1Chr.15:25-29). His wife despised him in her heart.

3. **The Sacrifice of Praise**
Paul and Silas offered the sacrifice of praise at the midnight hour when they had been beaten for the name of Jesus, fastened in stocks. They sang praises to God (Acts 16:22-25). To praise God over and against their feelings cost them something. They had been flogged and were in extreme pain and discomfort yet prayed and sang praises to God. God was pleased with such a sacrifice and sealed it with an earthquake and opening the prison doors. Salvation came to the prison-keeper's household.

We are to bring the sacrifices of praise into the house of the Lord (Jer.17:26 and 33:11; see KJV).

We are to offer this sacrifice continually unto God, through Christ, giving thanks to His name. This is the fruit of our lips (Heb.13:15). God gives us the garment of praise for the spirit of heaviness (Isa.61:3).

4. **The Sacrifices of Righteousness**
   Read Deut.33:19; Matt.5:10; 6:25-33; Rom.6:12-13; 6:16; 1Tim.6:9-11; Heb.12:5-11; 1Pet.3:14).

   It costs something to live a godly and righteous life before the Lord in an ungodly and unrighteous generation. Noah was righteous in his generation (Gen.7:1). We may be persecuted for righteousness sake (Matt.5:10).

   By one man's disobedience, all were made unrighteous; by one Man's obedience, all can be made righteous (Rom.6:12-21). This was through the sacrifice of Christ on the cross. We may suffer for righteousness sake (1Pet.3:14).

   God is pleased with the sacrifice of righteousness (Deut.33:19; Psa.4:5). David could have offered an animal sacrifice and the priest could pronounce him forgiven. But David knew the true sacrifice that God wanted was the sacrifice of righteousness (Psa.51:19).

5. **The Sacrifice of Obedience**
   Samuel's word to King Saul illustrates the truth of this sacrifice. Saul was called to destroy the Amalekites. He disobeyed and saved King Agag and the best of the cattle. He told Samuel he had obeyed the voice of the Lord and that he and the people would be offering a sacrifice to the Lord. Samuel replied: "Does the Lord delight in burnt offerings and sacrifices as much as in obeying the voice of the Lord? To obey is better than sacrifice, and to heed is better than the fat of rams" (1Sam.15:22).

   Samuel would rather sacrifice animals to the Lord than obey His voice. This was the wrong kind of sacrifice. Obedience is a costly sacrifice.

   It was by Adam's disobedience that the whole human race came under sin. It is by the obedience of Christ that all may be made righteous (Rom.5:12-21). Christ came to restore us back to the obedience from which Adam fell.

   If we are willing and obedient, God promises we shall eat the good of the land (Isa.1:19, 20).

   God blessed Abraham because he obeyed God's voice in offering up his only begotten son (Gen.22, especially vs.16-18).

Read also Psa.40:6-8; Heb.10:5-9; Matt.7:21; Jhn.7:17). Many Scriptures emphasize the importance of obedience which is a pleasing sacrifice to God. Human nature is prone to disobedience, doing one's own will.

6. **The Sacrifice of a Broken Spirit**
David illustrates the truth of this spiritual sacrifice. When David sinned in adultery, he was pardoned for his sins of adultery and indirect murder. such was punishable by the death penalty. God in grace pardoned and punished him (2Sam.12:1-13). David, as king, could have covered his sin and offered a sacrifice, but he knew the true sacrifice that was acceptable to God was a broken and contrite spirit (Psa.51:16-19).

Saul, when confronted by the Prophet Samuel, said, "I have sinned … BUT honor me before the elders" (1Sam.15:30). David, when confronted by the Prophet Nathan, said, "I have sinned …" No "but's" or excuses. He was of a humble and contrite spirit. This was the sacrifice that pleased God (Prov.28:13).

God dwells in the high and holy place, but He also dwells with him who is of a humble and contrite spirit (Isa.57:15).

7. **The Sacrifice of Hospitality**
"But to do good and to share, with such sacrifices God is well pleased" (Heb.13:16). Believers should be given to "distributing to the necessity of the saints" and "given to hospitality" (Rom.12:13).

Elders should be given to hospitality (1Tim.3:2; Titus.1:8). Sometimes it may be a sacrifice, but again, God is pleased with such sacrifices.

Widows who were supported by the Church in early times were those known for good works, faithful to her husband, bringing up the children, washing the feet of the saints, helping those in trouble, and given to hospitality (1Tim.5:9, 10).

8. **The Sacrifice of Giving**
The Lord called on His people to give of their tithes and offerings (Mal.3:8-12). The nation had failed to give to God in these areas.

- Israel gave generously to the work of the Tabernacle (Ex.35:22; 36:2-7).

- Israel gave generously to the work of building the Temple of the Lord (1Chr.29:3-9; 2Chr.24:10). David gave much to the work of the Lord.
- Believers are to be generous in their giving to the Lord (2Cor.9:6, 7). God loves a cheerful (or hilarious) giver.
- All we own belongs to the Lord. He is the owner, and we are but stewards of all He gives us (Psa.24:1; 50:10; Hag.2:8).

It is God who gives us power to get wealth (Deut.8:18). We give back to God what He has given us. At times there will be sacrificial giving (Phil.4:13, 19, especially vs.18). With sacrificial giving God is well pleased. Jesus said that the widow woman had given more than all the rich people, for they gave of their abundance. It was no sacrifice for them. For the widow it was a great sacrifice, although it was a small sum (Lke.21:1-4). Tithes and offerings, gifts and sacrifices were brought to the place where the Lord had recorded His name (i.e., the Tabernacle of the Temple). Read Deut.12th chapter.

9. The Sacrifice of Uplifted Hands
The lifting up of hands is as the evening sacrifice (Psa.141:1, 2).
- We are to lift up our hands in the Sanctuary as we bless the Lord (Psa.134-135). In the Tabernacle of the Lord, lifting of hands was as the evening sacrifice.
- Men are to pray everywhere, lifting up holy hands without wrath or doubting (1Tim.2:8).
- Read also Lam.2:19.
- Lifting hands is linked with the cry for mercy and help (Psa.28:2; 143:6).
- Lifting hands is also linked with expressions of praise (Psa.63:4).

When Israel fought in the battle with Amalek, Moses sat on the rock on the top of the Mount, Aaron and Hur upheld his hands when weary. As long as Moses' hands were uplifted, there was victory in the battle. His hands touched the throne of God (Ex.17:8-16). Without doubt, this was a sacrifice for Moses as an old man. But victory was assured. It was not just a demonstrative thing but a serious action in the presence of the Lord.

10. The Sacrifice of our Bodies
Believers are to present their bodies a living sacrifice, wholly unto God. This is our reasonable or priestly service. As the priest offered the dead bodies of animals on the altar of God, so the believer is to present his body as a LIVING sacrifice to God on His altar

(Rom.12:1-2). It is sometimes harder to LIVE for God than die in the faith, although both are a sacrifice.

Solomon illustrates the truth of this, as already noted in a previous chapter. Solomon, at the dedication of the Temple, built a scaffold the size of the brazen altar in the Court of the Tabernacle of Moses. He knelt thereon, lifted up his hands to heaven and prayed. He was, as it were, presenting himself a living sacrifice to God on that scaffold in the court (2Chr.6:13).

The Corinthian believers were giving their bodies over to immorality and self-indulgence. Paul reminds them that they were bought with a price. They were not their own. Their bodies were the Temple of the Holy Spirit (1Cor.6:19-20).

Our bodies, once the vessels of sin, are now "spiritual sacrifices" that we, as believer-priests, offer to God and His service to be used for His glory. Many martyrs also have paid the supreme sacrifice with their bodies physically on the altar of martyrdom.

11. **The Sacrifice of the Nations**
Isaiah prophesies that a time would come when God would gather the nations and tongues to see His glory. Some would be sent out to proclaim God's glory to the nations and many would come. Those who come would be like Priests and Levites offering to the Lord (Isa.66:18-21).

Paul applies this prophetic word to himself and his ministry to the Gentiles. He writes of: "...the grace (the unmerited favor) bestowed on me by God in making me a minister of Christ Jesus to the Gentiles. I act in the **priestly service** of the Gospel (the good news) of God, in order that the sacrificial offering of the Gentiles may be acceptable (to God), consecrated and made holy by the Holy Spirit" (Rom.15:15-17 Amp.N.T.).

The Gospel was to go to every creature. Disciples were to make disciples of all nations (Matt.28:18-20; Mrk.16:15-20). The coming in of both Jews and Gentiles would be the inheritance of the nations as fruit for the sacrifice of the Lamb. The Father said to His Son: "Ask of Me and I will give You the heathen for Your inheritance" (Psa.2). So, out of every kindred, tongue, tribe and nation, those who come to God through Christ are the fruit of the death of the Lamb (Rev.5:9-10). This is a "spiritual sacrifice" well pleasing to the Father.

12. **The Sacrifice of Prayer**
    Although there is no specific Scripture that speaks of prayer as a sacrifice, yet it is found that the two are linked in divine service.

    When Solomon offered himself "a living sacrifice" on the brazen scaffold, he offered the greatest prayer to God of his life (2Chr.6:13). He commences with praise and worship (vs.14, 15) and then moves into prayer for his nation.

    The prophetess Anna was a woman given to prayer. She worshipped day and night with fasting and prayer (Lke.2:37).

    In Rev.8:3-4 John sees the seventh seal opened and there is the golden altar of incense. It is the prayers of the saints. Though there was never animal sacrifice offered on the golden altar, once a year, this altar was touched with sacrificial blood, thus making the incense (the prayers of the saints) acceptable to God through blood (atonement). Read also Heb.8:5; 9:9; 10:2 and 13:10 where the services of the Tabernacle are linked through blood and incense; the brazen altar and the golden altar.

    Prayer is a costly sacrifice: costly in time and devotion to seeking the face of the Lord in intercessory ministry.

Conclusion:
David best expresses the true meaning of "sacrifice" when he bought the piece of land for the Temple site. He says: "I will not offer to the Lord that which costs me nothing ..." David paid the full price for the Temple site (2Sam.24:24; 1Chr.21:24). Sacrifice is really that which costs you something.

The rich young ruler wanted eternal life. He wanted a Christianity that costs him nothing! As soon as Jesus laid out the cost to follow Him, he walked away sorrowful and Jesus did not run after him. The real issue is: Did he really want eternal life or his own riches? (Matt.19:16ff; Mrk.10:17ff; Lke.18:18ff). What does being a believer-priest cost you? God asks for our time, our talents, our money, gifts, our life, our ALL!

These are twelve "spiritual sacrifices" that believer-priests may offer to the Lord. They involve our whole being, spirit, soul and body; spiritually, mentally, emotionally, intelligently, physically and materially! They involve all that we are, all that we have and all we ever hope to be. How can we give less than Him who gave us His all?

CHAPTER 40 - THE FUNCTIONING PRIESTHOOD

Our text is at an end, though not exhausted. The subject of Priesthood, like numerous other themes in the Bible, is one that is inexhaustible. In this final chapter, it may be seen that the believer-priest's ministry flows into a three-fold river. All ministry flows in and out of the river. Or, to use the Scripture from The Preacher, "A threefold cord is not quickly broken" (Eccl.4:12b). These three major areas:

1. Ministry to the Lord
2. Ministry to the Saints
3. Ministry to the World

Each area of ministry is dependent on the other. The more effectual ministry is to the Lord, the more effectual it is to the saints, and the more effectual it is to the saints, the more effectual it is (or should be) to the lost and dying world!

A. Ministry to the Lord – Worship
The first and primary ministry to the believer-priest is to minister to the Lord (Read again Ex.28:1-4). The Lord chose Aaron and his sons to "minister unto ME in the priest's office", repeated at least four times.
- Samuel ministered before the Lord and Eli (1Sam.2:18; 3:1).
- Elisha ministered to the Prophet Elijah (1Kgs.19:21).
- The Levites ministered before the dwelling place of the Tabernacle of the Congregation with singing until Solomon built the Temple (1Chr.6:32).
- The Church at Antioch ministered to the Lord in prayer and fasting (Acts 13:2).

Ministry to the Lord is first and foundational. It includes both the individual and the corporate expression of relationship.

In 1Chr.23:30 and 2Chr.29:11 it is spelt out in a more personal way. The Lord had chosen the Levites as Priests:

- To stand before Him
- To serve Him
- To minister to Him
- To burn incense to Him
- To stand and thank the Lord
- To offer sacrifices to Him

It is to HIM all true worship is given, both in the Old and the New Covenant times. Whether of Aaron and the Levitical Priesthood or the believer-priests of the New Covenant, worship is first of all ministry to Him! Ministry to Him includes:

1. Worship in Spirit and in truth (Jhn.4:20-24; 17:17). John tells us WHO to worship and HOW to worship. We worship God who is a Spirit Being. We worship Him in the spirit and in truth. We do not worship after the traditions of men (Mrk.7:7-9).
2. Love is worship. We are to love the Lord our God with all our heart and soul and mind and strength (Mrk.12:30).
3. Fear the Lord in reverence and true fear of grieving or displeasing Him (Prov.1:1-7). The fear of the Lord is the beginning of wisdom.
4. Prayer and intercession are part of Biblical worship. "My house shall be called a house of prayer for all nations" (Isa.56:7; Matt.21:13; Mrk.11:17). We prepare by pre-prayer!
5. Thanksgivings are also part of our worship. We thank God not only for what He has done but simply for who He is!
6. Communion time is also an expression of worship as we remember His Son, Jesus Christ (Matt.26:26-28; 1Cor.11:23-24).
7. Giving of our substance to the Lord is an act of worship. We give back to Him what He has given us, for all things come of Him (Mal.3).
8. Praising the Lord through various expressions is part of our worship to the Lord (Psa.22:3; 33:1).
   - Singing (Psa.47:6; Col.3:16)
   - Shouting (Isa.12:6)
   - Standing (Psa.135:1, 2)
   - Bowing or kneeling (Psa.95:6)
   - Dancing or rejoicing (Psa.149:3)
   - Clapping (Psa.47:1)
   - Lifting hands (Psa.134:2; 1Tim.2:8)
   - Instruments (Psa.150)
9. Serving is part of worship. The Scriptures clearly show the relationship between "worship" and "serve" the Lord (Read in KJV: Deut.4:19; 5:9; 6:13; 8:19; 11:16; 12:32; 17:3; 26:20; 29:26; 30:17; Josh.24:14-24; Lke.4:8). We worship who we serve, and we serve who we worship, whether the true God or false gods. It is, "Worship precedes service", not, "service precedes worship"!

All life lived as unto the Lord is the believer-priest's first reasonable service (Rom.12:1-2).

B. Ministry to the Saints – Fellowship
The next area of ministry is ministry to the saints, or to "one another". There are many "one another" references in the New Testament, all of which point to believer-priests in the Body of Christ, ministering to each other as members of that Body. This also is one of the great pictures in the New Testament setting forth the fellowship in the Church (1Cor.12:12-27).

The human body, with its millions of cells and members, all working together in harmony, unity and life, illustrate that harmony, unity and life which is to flow in the Church, the Body of Christ, or, as in our present study, the Royal Priesthood. There are no idle members or cells. In the body every member lives for the other members. Sickness and disease come in the cells that are in rebellion or out of harmony with the rest of the members, thus causing pain and distress. Following are a number of Scriptures setting out the privileges and the responsibilities of members one to another. Members should have mutual care one for another (1Cor.12:25; Eph.4:25). Members should:

1. Love one another – Jhn.13:34-35; 15:12, 17; 1Pet.1:22; 1Jhn.4:7, 11-12
2. Comfort one another – 1Thess.4:18
3. Consider one another – Heb.10:24
4. Exhort one another – Heb.3:13; 10:25
5. Edify one another – Rom.14:19; 1Thess.5:11
6. Admonish one another – Rom.15:14; Col.3:16
7. Minister to one another – 1Pet.4:10
8. Forbear one another – Col.3:13; Eph.4:2
9. Forgive one another – Col.3:13; Eph.4:32
10. Submit to one another – Eph.5:21
11. Be subject one to another – 1Pet.5:5
12. Teach one another – Col.3:16
13. Prefer one another – Rom.12:10
14. Pray for one another – Jas.5:16
15. Give hospitality to one another – 1Pet.4:9
16. Greet or embrace one another – 1Pet.5:14
17. Salute one another as friends – Rom.16:16
18. Fellowship one another – 1Jhn.1:7
19. Have peace with one another – Mrk.9:50
20. Be like minded one with another – Rom.12:16; 1Cor.1:10; Phil.1:27; 2:2; 4:2
21. Bear one another's burdens – Gal.6:2, 5
22. Confess our faults one to another – Jas.5:16
23. By love serve one another – Gal.5:13 with Ex.21:1-6

24. Be kindly affectionate one to another – Rom.12:10. Eph.4:32
25. Receive one another – Rom.15:7
26. Have compassion one for another – 1Pet.3:8

Things that we are not to do to one another:

1. Let us not judge (criticize) one another – Rom.14:13
2. Do not bite or devour one another – Gal.5:15
3. Do not provoke one another – Gal.5:26
4. Do not envy one another – Gal.5:26
5. Do not hate one another – Titus 3:3
6. Do not go to law courts with one another – 1Cor.6:6-7
7. Do not lie (deceive, or be untruthful) to one another – Col.3:9
8. Do not speak evil one of another – Jas.4:11
9. Do not grudge (sigh, murmur or groan) one against another – Jas.5:9

The Scriptures give both positives and negatives as pertaining to relationship with one another in the Body of Christ. The positive attitudes bring life, peace and harmony. The negative attitudes bring death, upheaval and dis-harmony. Members are to be the expression of Christ's character, nature and life.

John exhorts: "Let us not love in word, neither in tongue, but in deed and in truth" (1Jhn.3:18). Each of these Scriptures lend themselves to a study of the particular words used (Refer Strong's Concordance).

Besides these exhortations, the Lord has provided many ministries in the Body of Christ to bring that Body into a functioning one in the earth.

- God has set in the Church apostles, prophets, evangelists, shepherds and teachers for a three-fold purpose.
- They are given FOR the adjusting and the equipping of the saints.
- They are given FOR the work of the ministry, that is, to bring the saints into the work of their ministry, NOT to do the entire ministry themselves. If the fivefold ministries fail to do this, then they have failed to fulfill the purpose of their existence.
- They are given FOR the edifying or the building up of the Body of Christ (Eph.4:9-16).
- God has given the gifts of the Spirit to various members in the Body. It is the gift in the member which makes that person a functioning member (e.g. sight to the eyes, hearing to the ears, speech to the mouth, etc) 1Cor.12-13-14.
- There are other giftings and operations of the Spirit the Lord has set in the members of the Body (Rom.12:1-8).

Within the various gifts in the Body of Christ, there is great variety within each. It is the responsibility of each member to discover their place and their particular gifting in the Body of Christ, and then to function accordingly. There is variety, diversity and yet unity (Psa.133 with 2Chr.5:11-14; Acts 1:14; Jhn.17:21, 22; Isa.65:8). This is the Royal Priesthood functioning in the earth as God intended it to.

(Note: the reader is referred to Bibliography to the text "**The Church in the New Testament**" for fuller details).

C. **Ministry to the World – Discipleship**
The third area of ministry is that which pertains to the world. Jesus came to die on the cross to redeem a lost and dying world from sin and the kingdom of darkness. After His death, burial and resurrection, and before His ascension, He gave commandments to His disciples.

1. They were to preach the Gospel (the Good News) to every creature and as they preached the Word, the Lord would follow that Word with signs (Mrk.16:15-20).
2. They are to teach all nations and make disciples of all nations. This is spoken of as the Great Commission (Matt.28:18-20 with Acts 1:8).
3. Believers have a burden for the world, even as Jesus did. In John 17, the "world" is mentioned some 19 times. God so loved the world that He gave His only begotten Son (Jhn.3:16). He sent His disciples into the world to seek the lost.
4. Believers are to be as watchmen and warn people both within and without of things to come (Ezek.3:17-21 with 33:1-16).
5. Believers are to be ambassadors for Christ (2Cor.5:18-21). We represent another country, a heavenly country, and represent the King and Government of that country.
6. Believers are to be as shepherds looking for sheep that are lost (Jer.23:1-8; Ezek.34:1-16; Lke.19:10; Jhn.9:35).
7. Believers have been given the ministry of reconciliation, beseeching people to be reconciled to God through Christ (2Cor.5).

In order to do this, believer-priests need to be moved with the compassion of Christ, as He was when he saw the multitude as sheep without a shepherd. This is priestly ministry to a lost and dying world (Matt.9:36; 14:14; 15:32; 18:27; 20:34; Mrk.1:41; 5:19; 6:34; 8:2). Compassion moved Jesus to meet the needs of people, whether the individual or the multitude. "Find a need and meet it with the answer" was the lifestyle of Jesus, our Great High Priest.

The Scriptures show the state of the unsaved, as the following list indicates:

1. People are Lost – they can be Found
   The Son of Man is come to seek and to save that which is lost (Lke.19:10). Think of the Parables of the Lost Sheep, the Lost Coin and the Lost Son (Lke.15).

2. People are Unsaved – they can be Saved
   "…that the world through Him might be saved" (Jhn.3:17 with Acts 2:21; 4:12; 11:14). "What must I do to be saved?" (Acts 16:30). "Look unto Me and be saved, all the ends of the earth" (Isa.45:22).

3. People are Unbelievers – they can become Believers
   He that believes and is baptized shall be saved, and he that believes not shall be damned (Mrk.16:16). His portion will be with the unbelievers (Lke.12:46). God wants all to believe.

4. People are Sinners – they can become Saints
   I came not to call the righteous but sinners to repentance (Matt.9:13).
   Jesus was called the friend of sinners (Matt.11:19).
   "This man receives sinners" (Lke.15:2).
   "O Lord, I am a sinful man" (Lke.5:8).
   God wants them to be saints. There is joy in heaven over one sinner that repents (Lke.15:2, 7 and 10).

5. People are Outside of Christ – they can be In Christ
   One is either "in Adam" or "in Christ" (1Cor.15:22; Rom.5:12-21).
   The wages of sin is death (Rom.6:3).
   If anyone be in Christ, they are a new creation (2Cor.5:17).
   In Adam, the old creation, there is sin and death. In Christ, there is a new creation of righteousness and life. Out of Adam into Christ. God sees two men on earth and all mankind in one or the other.

6. People are dead in Trespasses and Sins – they can be Resurrected
   Having been dead in trespasses and sin (Eph.2:1, 5; 5:14; Col.2:13). Some are dead while they live (1Tim.5:6). They need the resurrection life of Jesus.

7. People are under Condemnation – they can come to Justification
   He that believes not is condemned already (Jhn.3:18). This is the condemnation; men love darkness rather than light (Jhn.3:18-19). There is no condemnation to those in Christ (Rom.8:1-2). He did

not come to condemn the world as the world was already condemned because they do not believe (Rom.5:12-21). In Adam, condemnation came on all. In Christ justification is available for all.

8. People are under God's Wrath – they can come into His Love
   The wrath of God abides continually on him (Jhn.3:36, and vs.16 with vs.36; Rom.1:18). "Hide us from the wrath of the Lamb for the great day of His wrath is come" (Rev.6:16-17). God wants them to come from under His wrath to experience His love.

9. People are Perishing – they can receive Everlasting Life
   Except you repent, you shall likewise perish (Lke.13:3-5). Whoever believes on Him shall not perish but have everlasting life (Jhn.3:15-16). We preach the cross, which is foolishness to those who are perishing, but to those who believe, it is the power of God to salvation (1Cor.1:18).

10. People are going to Hell Fire – they can go to Heaven's Glory
    People are hell-bound, going to a Christ-less eternity, the lake of fire and brimstone. "And whosoever was not found written in the book of life was cast into the lake of fire" (Rev.20:11-15). Depart, you cursed into everlasting fire, prepared for the devil and his angels (Matt.25:41). If men serve the devil in time, they will be with the devil in eternity. The opposite is true. Serve the Lord in time and live with Him in eternity. God wants people to come to heaven and live with Him and Jesus forever.

11. People are Blinded by Satan – they can have their Eyes Opened
    The god of this world has blinded the minds of them that believe not (2Cor.4:4). They are in the Kingdom of Darkness (Col.1:13; 2Cor.3:14). Their minds are blinded in the reading of the Old Testament. God wants to open their eyes, as He did for Saul (Acts 9). He wants to turn them from darkness to light and from the power of Satan to forgiveness and inheritance with the saints (Acts 26:18).

12. People Matter to God – they should Matter to Us
    God saw the state of mankind and sent His Son to die for them. He saw their need. God so loved the world that He gave His only Son (Jhn.3:16). People are loved by God. They may not want God, but they need God. God can do without them, but they cannot do without God. People matter to God therefore they should matter to us. We are living in an "it does not matter" generation, but people matter to God.

This is what the believer-priest's ministry means to a lost and dying generation. This is the compassion that moved Christ to forgive sins and heal those who were sick.

Thus, the believer-priest, in order to fulfill the purpose of his redemption, needs to walk in this three-fold area:

1. Ministry to the Lord,
2. Ministry to the Saints and
3. Ministry to the World.

CHAPTER 41 - A PARADIGM FOR THE NEW PRIESTHOOD

In our studies so far we have considered the history, Scriptural basis and function of the New Covenant Royal Priesthood of God. In this supplemental chapter we set forth a living example of one who lived out that ministry. While some sections of Church Denominations debate whether women can be priests unto the Lord or not, this woman becomes a great example to all believers, men and women, in every nation and culture.

Our living example is a woman, chosen because some will still find it difficult to put aside the cultural conditioning that has given the masculine gender a mortgage on ministry.

- She is one who, to use a common expression, was "from the other side of the tracks", and thus many of us will be able to identify more readily with her. We don't know much about her background, but she was obviously not always a paradigm of perfection due to the demonic possession problem from which she desperately needed deliverance.
- She had no spectacular charismatic gifting that we know of. This means she went about her work of the ministry with only those basic things which are available to all of us so-called "ordinary people".
- Finally, we are aware that she lived and ministered under the Old Covenant, so, technically speaking she wasn't a true member of the New Covenant Priesthood. But she lived in the time when the two covenants met. After her encounter with Jesus she based her whole life and ministry on His teaching. She lacked the spiritual rebirth which was ushered in by the death and resurrection of Christ and the coming of the Spirit on the Day of Pentecost, but she showed forth to a remarkable degree the characteristics of the new priesthood which was about to be let loose on the world. She did what God had originally required all of Israel to do, and that was to minister as a royal priesthood should minister.

We speak of Mary of Magdala, or as she is often known, Mary Magdalene.

"Mary" is one of the many forms which come out of a concept meaning "bitter". Some Dictionaries attach to it the idea of bitterness through troublesome experience or rebellion.
"Magdala" means "a high tower" or "a castle." See Boyd's Bible Dictionary and "All the Women of the Bible" by Herbert Lockyer.
So, symbolically, within her name we have someone who was born to live in a high tower or castle but has suffered in life's bitter circumstances.

A. **Mary in Travelling Ministry**
   Luke 8:2 gives us the earliest record of Mary's life and ministry. Jesus had delivered her from seven demons (either a literal number seven, or seven being God's seal of completeness, she was so far under demonic possession that her case was about as bad as it could possibly be). Here we find her in the company of Jesus, the twelve disciples and an unknown number of women. She, along with the other women, was ministering to Jesus and providing for Him out of her own substance. This means she had left any home comfort which she may have had to take part in a travelling ministry. By modern standards this would have meant a lot of self-sacrifice and hard work.

   1. Mary ministered to Jesus.
   2. Her ministry involved great commitment.
   3. She gave of her own substance and resources.
   4. She was in the company of the twelve disciples and many other women and was thus involved in mutual support and ministry of fellow believers.
   5. Her ministry was integral with Jesus' mission, which we see from vs. 1 was preaching and showing forth the glad tidings of the Kingdom of God to those outside the Kingdom.

   So she is ministering to Jesus who is God incarnate, fellow believers who were soon to become the Church, and the cities and villages of Israel who in post-Pentecost language would be the world. These are the three areas of ministry of the N.T. royal priesthood…God, the Church and the world.

B. **Mary at the Cross**
   After her deliverance, the next time we see Mary she is at the cross. Along with other women she is witnessing all Jesus' torture and suffering. See Jhn.19:25.
   1. Mary's ministry to Jesus had been continuous from the time she was delivered, through the time in Galilee right up to the cross Matt.27:55-56; Mrk.15:40-41.
   2. She stands with Mary the mother of Jesus. There is a strong bond here between her and the earthly family of Jesus.

C. **Mary at the Tomb** See Matt. 27:61 and Mrk.15:47.
   1. She followed Him up to the point of death.
   2. Now her faithfulness extends even beyond death.

D. **Mary, Faithful in Service, even in His Death.**
   See Mrk.16:1-2 and Matt. 28:1

1. Well before dawn on the Sunday morning. Nothing else matters. Jesus is the consuming passion of her life now.
2. Still in faithful service to Jesus, still in the company of her fellow believers, the two no doubt mutually ministering to and supporting each other…partners in the same traumatic situation.

E. Mary and the Resurrection See Mrk.16:5-11 and Jhn.20:1-18
1. She is one of the two women who were first to enter the tomb.
2. She had the encounter with the angels.
3. She is first to see Him after the resurrection.
4. She became the first messenger of the resurrection.

Summary:
The above sets out all that we may know of Mary and her ministry. As stated in our introduction, she pre-figures the ministry of the New Testament priesthood which had been in the mind of God from the beginning and which was just about to be finally realized on the earth.

She had experienced great grace and as a result loved much (Lke.7:47). Therefore her ministry was motivated totally and utterly by love.

There was no desire in her for power, position, privilege or recognition, but just an insatiable passion to minister to the One who gave her life. He had given her life back to her and she was intent on giving it back to Him.

Mary was not a loner driven by some possessive disorder. She was always in the company of others of like mind. As a natural consequence of her service to Jesus she served those around her.

Her eyes were opened to the supernatural realm. She saw and communicated with angels.

She encountered the risen Christ and communicated with Him.

She proclaimed His resurrection to others. As a woman in a male dominated culture, this made her vulnerable to their unbelief and criticism, but she did it anyway.

She had no formal or recognized qualifications to be "in the ministry" but she had faith, hope and love and was thus qualified by the Master to be in His service.

So it is for us. There is a place for formal qualifications. We certainly don't want to discourage those who undertake such pursuits. **But every man,**

woman and child has the right, duty and privilege to minister as a member of God's Royal Priesthood.

What a wonderful example Mary becomes to all believers, whether men or women, in the Church, the Body of Christ!

SUMMARY

As we come to the end of our study it is appropriate to revise and further clarify some of the main issues.

A. God's Purpose for the New Testament Church

Just as under the Old Covenant, so under the New Covenant, God desired a Kingdom of priests. Under the Old, Israel was supposed to be His royal priestly nation. The very name "Israel" means "one who prevails with God" or "prince who has power with God". Every Israelite was to be a prince and priest. Individually and corporately they were to demonstrate God's nature, characteristics and principles such that the nations of the world would be drawn to the light of God. They missed their high and royal call and God settled for an imperfect situation where one of the twelve tribes, the Tribe of Levi, would function as priests to represent God to Israel and vice versa. It was not His perfect will, but He suffered it to be so.

However His original purpose was not thwarted. It was merely set aside for a later time. When the high priests of Israel rent their clothes and crucified their Messiah, they brought an end to that dispensation. A new dispensation was born where once again every member of the royal family of God (the New Testament Church) was invited to be a priest. The ministry and mode of operation of this new priesthood may clearly be seen in the book of Acts. Fishermen, servants, tent makers and some of those who were priests under the old order joined together to do the work of the ministry with great effect. For a few short years God's purpose seemed to have been fulfilled. His glory was displayed in and by the New Testament Church and the nations of the world began to flow into the house of God.

B. The Decline

It had long been foretold by the prophets that a time of apostasy would come. The New Testament apostles and prophets confirmed those prophecies. With the passing of the pioneers of the long-awaited royal priesthood, ecclesiastical, hierarchical structures and man-made positions of authority soon took over and in flat out opposition to God's design, they over-rode and minimized the priesthood of every believer. A priestly caste was re-established. The people of God were once again relegated to approaching and hearing God via a mediating class of leadership, the clergy.

What started out on the day of Pentecost (Acts 2) in power, glory, fruitfulness and life, soon became subdued, powerless, unfruitful and almost dead. To be sure, there was great expansion in Christendom. The

Church gained great numbers, credibility, political and even military influence, but as far as reflecting and demonstrating the nature, character and qualities of God goes, it was an abject failure. As we look across the centuries of Christian history we see more of the nature and characteristics of the kingdom of darkness than we do of the kingdom of God. This situation continued for approximately 1400 years, which interestingly enough was nearly the same length of time Israel continued under the Old Covenant after they rejected their call to the royal priesthood.

C. The Reformation

Just as the apostasy and decline had been prophesied, there had also been glimpses of a time of glory which would come. The Old Testament king and priest Melchizedek was a living prophecy – a glimpse of a time when the two mutually exclusive roles of king and priest would somehow come together in peace and harmony (Zech.6:13). This had never been allowed since Israel let their opportunity slip by. Kings who tried to operate as priests had been dealt with severely by God. With hindsight it seems God was saying to all who tried, "You refused to take the opportunity when it was offered. You cannot presume to take it up now!"

But there were prophesies and hints of the rising of a new order of royal priesthood where the functions of ruling and mediating would come together. This order was named after the king-priest Melchizedek (Psa.110). Jesus was the inaugural king-priest of that order but was soon followed by a great company who were raised up into the same order.

For a long period of time the so-called "dark ages" seemed to have repressed that order, but God had already twice suffered the putting aside of His perfect will. It was not going to happen the third time. The Reformation started a process that will never again allow the people of God to be subjugated under the rule of a body of specialist religious authorities. It has not been an instantaneous, all embracing liberation movement. It has been a slow and hard-fought process in some nations and religious denominations. But as surely as day follows night, God will finally establish His royal priesthood in the earth. Since the Reformation, truth has been progressively restored into the Church. The births of many Christian denominations are history markers of specific truths of God being restored to the body of Christ on earth. Refer to Bibliography for the text on "Restoration Theology" for a detailed treatment of this concept. The authors of this text believe now is the time when the church must begin to fully embrace the truth of the Priesthood of All Believers.

D. Royal Priesthood ... both Doctrine and Demonstration
Two Aspects of Truth ... Both Essential to the Royal Priesthood

Legal Truth	**Experiential Truth**
Position	*Condition*
What God declares about us	*What God does in and through us*
The place we live	*What we do there*
Us in Christ (Phil.3:9)	*Christ in us (Col.1:27)*
Risen with Christ (Col.3:1)	*The daily transformation of our lives (2Cor.3:18 and Rom.12:2)*
Already	*Not yet*
What we claim when under spiritual attack...purchased and cleansed by the blood, I am the righteousness of God	*What we tell our neighbor when he sees our faults ... yes, I'm a Christian but am still a work in progress*

An understanding of these two aspects of truth is important if we are to function as kings and priests before God and man.

Consider the example of a young princess who has left her father's palace to follow her vagabond lover. He has deserted her and now she is living in the gutter, homeless and hungry. What is the truth about her situation? Is she royal born? Yes! Is she rich? Yes! Can she call herself a princess? Yes! Does she have a throne set for her? Yes! Those things are all ***legally*** true. That is the ***position*** she was born to occupy. It is hers by birth-right. It is her legal status. But of what use is that in her life situation? The man in the hamburger van doesn't want to hear the legal truth. He just wants his five dollars, and she can't produce it, so she spends another hungry night on the street. What she needs to do to enjoy her privileged position in life is to go home to her father the king and to actually live like a princess. Her ***condition*** needs to be brought into line with her ***position***. She needs to "become in experience what she already legally is".

We have taken time to explain this because some Christians have a propensity to always and immediately apply the legal and positional truths to their life to such an extent that the experiential, conditional aspects of truth are never allowed to challenge them.

The reader should be very clear that claiming the legal and positional truth of membership in the Melchizedek priesthood is insufficient in itself. When we address Rom.5:17; Rev.1:6 and other references, we are talking about *how we live and what we do*. The legal truth of our birthright is of course our starting point. All that we do springs out of that heritage. Like the princess in our above example, we are born into the royal priesthood and nothing can change that. But reliance on that legal truth without any serious attempt at moving on in the experiential and practical truth is simply not an option (Rom.8:9-14). Everyone born from above is born into the royal priesthood, but God's overall desire is for us to *fully become* what we *already are*. We have been reborn as baby royal priests, but we must learn to live in the royal household and grow up into fully functioning kings and priests.

Being a king and priest is not just a matter of what we believe. It is largely to do with how we live. The royal aspect involves ruling and overcoming. This doesn't mean holding some legal position of authority. It means living the Christian life as it is meant to be lived in the face of a world which is intent on knocking us off such a course to follow its corrupt and Godless ways (Eph.2:2-3).

E. God's Care for Detail Regarding His Royal Priesthood

We saw in our study of the Old Testament the amazing degree of detail God prescribed for the priests, their garments, functions, sacrifices and consecration. By itself all that has little meaning for anyone. However, when we see how every last detail was given, firstly to pre-figure the Messiah and secondly as an object lesson for the nature, character, function and consecration of the new order of priesthood which was to come (us, the N.T. believer priesthood), we cannot fail to be amazed at the wisdom and foreknowledge of God. We should also be impacted by just how important this whole concept of an "every-believer royal priesthood" is to God. Our priesthood takes it role from its founder, Jesus Christ. We share in that same ministry and are therefore key figures in what God is going to do in the closing days of this present age.

Perhaps we need to say a special word on the issue of consecration. The Old Testament priests wore special garments, all of which spoke of the time to come when the New Testament priesthood (us) would stand before God clothed in the glorious pure garments of righteousness. In those garments we can stand before God Himself. This is positional righteousness. It is the righteousness given to us by God. It is the wedding garment spoken of in Matt.22:12. It is something we are given, and we put it on. It is not to do with our inner condition. But the priestly consecration went beyond this with various washings and rites of purification. As the robes typify our positional righteousness, so the washing, purification and behavior of the priests typify our conditional righteousness … the things we do! In a time when some powerful people in Christianity are preaching on the grace of God to a point where sin and repentance are non-issues, we could perhaps give these things fresh thought. (Psa.15; Psa.24:3-6; Isa.33:13-17).

F. We can and must learn from the old order
A study of where God's first order of priests either failed or succeeded will greatly assist our self-understanding. Those priests who God commended should be of special interest to us. Eleazar, Phinehas, Zadok and Ezra stand out as examples for us to imitate.

G. The Tabernacles of Moses and David
Much can be learned from a study of these, especially in considering the differences between them and how each had a certain order of approach and worship of God.

H. Chapter 39, The Spiritual Sacrifices should be of special interest
These are not doctrinal concepts but are a call to a spiritual priesthood to live and exist on the basis of spiritual sacrifices. The very purpose for the existence of the Old Testament priesthood was to offer up sacrifice. So it is for us. We have no higher purpose for our existence than to offer up the spiritual sacrifices mentioned in that chapter.

I. The Transition of the Call of God from One Priesthood to Another
As we saw in our text, the Old Testament priesthood destroyed itself, made itself redundant and found itself in opposition to God when they crucified their Messiah. This should be a powerful lesson to us. Throughout the history of the Church we have failed this test. We have not transitioned well. In the restoration of Bible truth which has been going on since the reformation, when God has established a truth and moved on to the next phase of His grace upon us, it has usually been the most recent move of God which has opposed that which God did next. If we are protective of our denomination or our emphases, and if we have invested much effort into it and are not big hearted enough to lay it all down before God, it seems we all too easily fall into this trap.

J. In particular, note the three areas of priestly ministry as outlined in Chapter 40
Our call is to minister to God, the Church and the World. Some specialized ministries may be involved with one of these areas more than another, but all of us are called to minister in all three areas to one degree or another, starting first and foremost with our ministry to God.

K. A Check List for Church Leaders
1. Is there anything in the way we "do Church" which might aid and abet the establishing of an elite class of ministry, thereby widening the gap between our pulpits and pews?

a. The use of honorific titles is one such way. Matt.23:8-12 seems a plain warning against such language. Our churches abound with reference to title and position. We address people as "Your Eminence", Bishop Bob, Pastor Peter, Reverend Ray, etc. Mostly we do this with good motives but every time we do it, we emphasize an imaginary and illegitimate dividing line between God's ministries ... further dividing the so-called clergy and laity.

b. The limiting of certain functions within the church to the "ordained ministry only" is another such way. Should not all ministries within the church be fulfilled by those with the required gifts? In general we would hope that the ordained have been so chosen because of their gifting, but there are many multi-gifted people employed in a secular vocation who have not chosen to go the way of ordination. If these people are not used because they don't have the required paperwork, the church is the poorer for it. Based on this model, Jesus would be called a carpenter and would lack the qualifications to speak in the church or have any governmental role. He could of course contribute by fixing up the furniture.

c. Undue emphasis on our "ministry team" which mostly consists of the "ordained", is a way of saying to the "unordained" that they are recipients of ministry rather than givers.

d. Frequent platform reference to "the leadership" as a separate group within the larger group helps to maximize the pulpit-pew gap. Everyone knows we must have leaders, but many churches don't need to put as much emphasis on them as they do.

e. There are many such ways leaders can emphasize and magnify a divide between the so-called "clergy" and "laity". At the very root of the matter are the attitudes of the heart. Any who wish to establish themselves as being in some way greater than or different to the multitude will find a way. They may not do any of the above but will still set themselves apart from the rest of the Body. Any who truly see themselves as ministering from within the Body rather than from a position above the Body, will minimize the gap between pulpit and pew even while still using divisive language like the above.

2. We need to realize that many of the reformers paid the price of their life (literally) to see this truth (along with others) restored to the Church.

   In eternity we will stand alongside these people, some of whom suffered dreadful tortures, burning at the stake, etc. Will we be able to say we took seriously and lived out the doctrine and truth they died for? Or will we realize that in some of our practices we tore down and opposed the establishing of the true royal priesthood of Christ?

3. As leaders, do we respect …? … really respect the members of the Body of Christ on earth?

   It is so easy to justify an aloof, brisk attitude when dealing with people. Everyone wants to talk to the preacher and give him/her the benefit of their knowledge and it is hard to get things done in our busy schedules if we mix too much with the congregation. So we can easily slip into a mode of disrespect toward others where they are "below us on the scale of importance". The antidote? If we had the opportunity to minister to the hurting, physical and literal body of Christ on the cross, what tenderness and care we would display. The last thing we would want to do would be to hurt Him more. Yet when we touch the sometimes dysfunctional, divided and hurting people of the Church, we are touching the very Body of Christ on earth.

   Before his Christian conversion Paul, at that time called Saul, was destroying the Church (Acts 9:1-5). Jesus struck him down on the Damascus road and said, "Saul, Saul, why do you persecute me?" Of this very verse, Augustine said, "It was the Head in heaven crying out on behalf of the members still on earth". There is a powerful organic bond between Jesus and His Church (Matt.10:40; 18:5; 25:40; Lke.10:16; 1Cor.8:12). To touch its members is to touch Jesus. Do we respect it as we should? If we do, we will have no trouble releasing its members into their divinely sanctioned ministries and tasks.

4. What can church leaders do to empower the emerging priesthood of God? Some suggestions are given below. They are given, not to be normative, but to get leaders thinking about ways to release the priesthood that may lie dormant in their churches.

a. We can change preaching and teaching topics from pastoral and successful living type stuff exclusively and include some Bible content. In this era of the Church we are placing huge emphasis on empowering the individual to live successfully and get through another week, and that is very good and necessary. But what we have bred is a Church where in many cases our pastors and leaders know very little of the Bible. Bible knowledge in and of itself is viewed negatively and has become irrelevant. This woeful lack of biblical understanding has set the Church and its members up to fall. Where are our future leaders and teachers going to come from? Too often we choose our leaders on the basis of charisma, ability to lead and inspire, etc., but they can't lead anyone into a deeper walk with God because they haven't been there themselves. Turn on Christian television any time of the week and you will have no difficulty finding rank heresy being preached from some of the most popular platforms in the world. It is inspirational! It is well preached! ... but it is often simply wrong.

    If our leaders don't know enough Bible to cover and protect the flock of God, we become very vulnerable as the winds of doctrine blow across the Body of Christ. In these days every believer needs to have enough Bible education to sense truth and balance. Our churches even now are being swept by "winds of doctrine" which have little resemblance to a homeless, foot-weary carpenter preaching repentance and faith towards God ... and some who are leading our churches don't know any different. They are good and faithful people. They can handle the church business brilliantly. They can set vision and unite the body with their considerable leadership skills, and all this is commendable, but they don't know enough Bible to get their people to walk close with God. They see God's acts, but they don't know His ways (Psa.103:7). There is a huge difference.

b. Bring back some emphasis on the spiritual disciplines of prayer, fasting, meditation and study. Build our people up in these things. Without them many gifted leaders will simply fall by the wayside because they were not adequately prepared for the battle. Becoming a functioning member of the royal priesthood involves spiritual formation, real discipleship and being transformed into Christ's image. Depending on our starting point, this can be a slow and painful path. Who preaches on these things today? Training people to be kings and priests cannot be accomplished by training them to do things or perform certain functions and procedures expected of good leadership. It can't be done in a "ten-week course".

That is what we might expect in a school of leadership. Training people to be kings and priests involves training people to walk with God, hear His voice and obey it. This only comes with a sustained emphasis on spiritual formation for every member.

c. Think outside the box when it comes to setting up leadership and ministry structures. The pastor being the key and almost sole voice into the church is necessary if we are to run churches as they are today ... the leader as captain of the ship or CEO of the company.

But while there are similarities, the Church is neither of those things. It is a living organism which needs the real and valid contribution of every living cell in its body. Perhaps in some smaller churches, depending on their sociological setting, instead of having the leader as the first person on the payroll, we might be better to release a home handyman into full time ministry so that the members of a struggling community can be looked after materially with home repairs, gardening, etc.

d. If Church leaders really want to see their members flourish, live and minister as kings and priests, they will find ways to bring it to pass. If they just want to build a big following, they won't see the need.

e. Perhaps some might think about re-evaluating the worship service, including the type of songs we sing. Worship is an all-of-life thing of which music is just a part. Nonetheless there is a strong link between the two. In some of our Churches of today, music plays little part in worship. Christian music has never been so professional yet conversely, in some streams of the Church it has probably never had so little to do with actual worship of God. It may enthuse and entertain but it sometimes has little to do with worship. It is a simple thing to evaluate. All we need to do is look around and see how many people-priests are being drawn into a state of worshipful reverence, or on the other hand, how many are listening to the music just as a spectator at a concert would.

For some Churches the Sunday worship service is about interfacing with an unchurched culture, so real worship in music and song is minimized. That is to do with the local vision of that Church and warrants no comment here, but if music/worship doesn't fit the Sunday agenda, can we fit it in elsewhere? Perhaps a mid-week prayer and worship service might work. Somewhere, somehow, the body of people-priests we are helping along in the process of spiritual formation need to be led in worship. They don't need music and song performed for them; they need it to be done in such a way that they can easily take part. To quote Soren Kierkegaard, "Worship is an expression of the community, not something done to the people by worship leaders … (in) the image of the theater … in worship the people are the actors, the worship leaders are the prompters, and God is the audience" (See Greg Ogden, The New Reformation, p24).

L. Practical Things for All Christians to Consider

1. We should prepare ourselves with the spiritual disciplines of prayer, fasting, study, etc. When the need for ministry arises, we must be built up, spiritually strong and ready to minister as God leads.

2. Just like our leaders we should handle the Body of Christ carefully and with great respect. See K.3 above.

3. We should respect Church leadership as exhorted by the scriptures but personally walk close to God and take responsibility for our own lives before God. The Israelites were very happy to send Moses up the mountain, so they didn't have to deal with God direct. Life was more comfortable that way. It is a disturbing thing that some Christians follow that line of thinking. Some will attend meetings, give of their money and even volunteer their services in some things, but their bottom line is, "We pay the pastor, and he hears from God for us." Such an attitude is fine if we have joined a club or are working for a business, but it doesn't meet the required standard for one who has taken a place in the Melchizedek priesthood of God.

4. Always be ready to minister but cultivate a heart which will do that gently and sensitively. One of the problems we constantly must face is that a person who is a hammer thinks everything and everybody in life is a nail. Every other believer/priest in the body does not need our ministry all the time. Employed in the gentle leading of God, our gifting can do great good. Employed as an outworking for our ego the same gift can do great harm.

CONCLUSION

In the story of Samuel and Eli in the house of God at Shiloh we saw the glory of God withdrawing from His chosen nation. Ichabod was born as the glory departed. It was because of a corrupt priesthood that God brought judgment to the house of God.

In Ezekiel we have a fascinating but tragic picture of the glory of God hovering around the temple and the city, unwilling to leave but unable to stay amidst such idolatry and rebelliousness. Especially note Ezek.8:6. The priests, prophets and leadership of the nation were the main propagators of that apostate condition. We can see God's progressive departure in the scripture chain: 1:28; 3:23; 8:4-6; 9:3; 10:3-4, 18-19; 11:22-23. However, in the same prophetic book, we see the promises and prophecies of the glory returning. See 39:21; 43:1-2, 4, 5, 7; 44:4, where the glory returns to a temple with a faithful priesthood, the sons of Zadok.

This is a prophetic picture of what lies ahead of us in what the scriptures call the last days. The royal priesthood, the order of Melchizedek, the company of Christians where all are kings and priests, are not the reason the glory will return. There are many factors and truths involved in that process, the main one being the grace and mercy of God. However, there will be such a priesthood functioning as world history as we know it draws to a close. Each of us has the choice to be part of that company. Let us choose wisely.

BIBLIOGRAPHY

- Bulley, Colin. *The Priesthood of Some Believers,* Paternoster Press, 2000.
- Cohu, J R. The Evolution of the Christian Ministry, London, 1918.
- Conner, Kevin J., *The Tabernacle of Moses,* Blackburn, Victoria, Acacia Press. 1975.
- Conner, Kevin J., *The Tabernacle of David,* Blackburn, Victoria, Acacia Press, 1976.
- Conner, Kevin J., *The Temple of Solomon*, Blackburn, Victoria, Acacia Press, 1988.
- Conner, Kevin J., *Interpreting the Symbols and Types,* Blackburn, Victoria, Acacia Press, 1975.
- Conner, Kevin, J., *The Feasts of Israel*, Blackburn, Victoria, Acacia Press, 1980.
- Conner, Kevin J., *The Church in the New Testament,* Blackburn, Victoria, Acacia Press, 1982.
- Conner, Kevin J., *The Book of Hebrews,* SRM Productions, Malaysia, 2002.
- Conner, Kevin J., *New Covenant Realities*, Blackburn, Victoria, Acacia Press, 1990.
- Conner, Kevin J., *Kings of the Kingdom,* Boronia, Victoria, Razer Graphics, 2008.
- Conner, Kevin J., *The Lord Jesus Christ, our Melchizedek,* Boronia, Victoria, Razer Graphics, 2008.
- Conner, Kevin J., *Restoration Theology*, Blackburn, Victoria, Acacia Press, 1998.
- Donavan, Vincent J. Christianity Rediscovered: An Epistle from the Masai, SCM Press LTD, 1976.
- Dowley, T Editor, *A Lion Handbook: The History of Christianity*, England, Lion Publishing, 1988.
- Elwell, WA Editor, *Evangelical Dictionary of Theology,* Grand Rapids, MI, Baker Books, 1984.
- Frend, WHC, *Creeds, Councils and Controversies*, Cambridge, University Press, 1989.
- Green, Michael, *Evangelism in the Early Church,* Grand Rapids, MI, Eerdmans Publishing Co., 1970.
- Green, Michael, *Freed to Serve,* Great Britain, Hodder and Stoughton, 1994
- Jones, Brynmor P., *Voices from the Welsh Revival*, Evangelical Press of Wales, 1995.
- Muthiah, Robert A. The Priesthood of All Believers in the Twenty First Century, Oregon, Pickwick Publications, 2009.

- Ogden, Greg, *The New Reformation,* Grand Rapids, MI, Zondervan Publishing House, 1990.
- Pauck, W., *The Heritage of the Reformation,* Oxford, University Press, 1961.
- Rowthorn, Anne, *The Liberation of the Laity*, Harrisburg, PA, Morehouse Publishing, 1986.
- Stevens, R Paul, *The Abolition of the Laity*, Paternoster Press, 1999.
- Stevenson, J Editor, *A New Eusebius*, Cambridge, University Press, 1987.
- Whittaker, Colin, *Great Revivals*, Basingstoke, UK, Marshall, Morgan and Scott, 1984.

About the Author

Born in Melbourne, Australia in 1927 and saved at the age of 14, Kevin Conner served the Lord in the Salvation Army until the age of 21. At this time he entered pastoral ministry for several years. After that, he was involved in teaching ministry in Australia, New Zealand and for many years at Bible Temple in Portland, Oregon. After serving as Senior Minister of Waverley Christian Fellowship for eight years (1987-1994), he continued to serve the church locally as well as ministering at various conferences and the continued writing of textbooks.

Kevin is recognised internationally as a teaching-apostle after his many years in both church and Bible College ministry. His textbooks have been used by ministers and students throughout the world. He has been in great demand as a teacher and has travelled extensively. Kevin passed away peacefully in Melbourne, Australia in February 2019 at the age of 92.

Visit Kevin's web site at www.kevinconner.org for more details about his life and ministry, as well as information about his 75+ books, his video courses, and his audio teaching podcast.

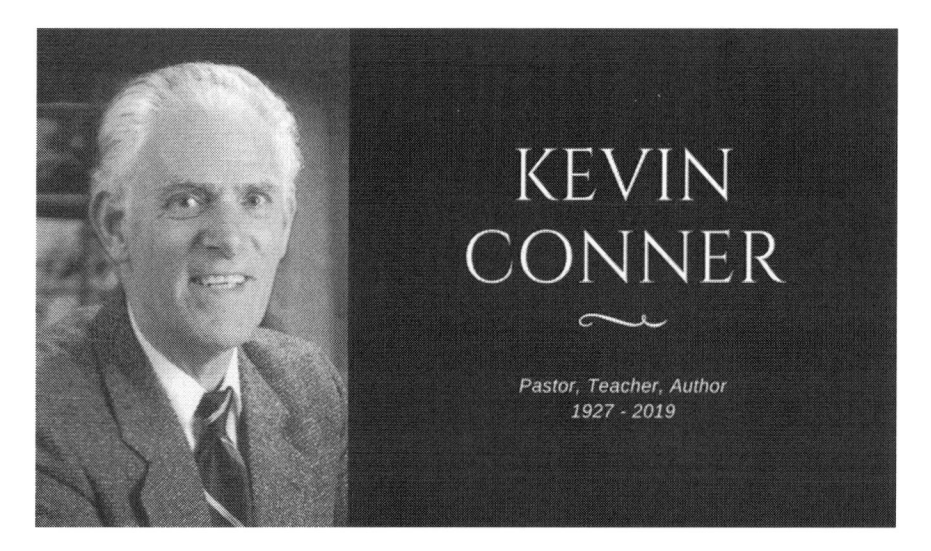

KEVIN CONNER

Pastor, Teacher, Author
1927 - 2019

Kevin's Autobiography

Kevin Conner is known by many people around the world as a theologian, Bible teacher, and best-selling author of over 75 biblical textbooks. Although thousands of people have been impacted by his ministry and his writings, only a few people know his personal story. Kevin took the time to detail his own life journey, including lessons gleaned along the way, in his auto-biography "This is My Story" back in 2007. It is now available in the following formats:

- PDF download - visit www.kevinconner.org/shop
- International paperback or eBook from Amazon.
- Australian paperback from WORD books (www.word.com.au).

Kevin was an orphan who never met his dad or mum. He grew up in boy's homes before coming to faith in Jesus Christ in the Salvation Army in his teenage years. From there, his life took many turns as he continued to pursue his faith in God and his understanding of the Scriptures and church life. Follow his journey and gain wisdom for your own life and ministry as you read his intriguing life-story.

Other Books by Kevin Conner

Acts, A Commentary
An Evaluation of Joseph Prince's Book 'Destined to Reign'
Are Women Elders Biblical?
Biblical Principles of Leadership
The Christian Millennium
1 & 2 Chronicles, a Commentary
1 Corinthians, a Commentary
The Church in the New Testament
The Church of the Firstborn and the Birthright
1 & 2 Chronicles, A Commentary
Colossians and Philemon, A Commentary
The Covenants (with Ken Malmin)
Daily Devotions (or Ministrations)
Daniel, An Exposition
The Day After the Sabbath
The Death-Resurrection Route
Deuteronomy, A Commentary
Esther, A Commentary
Exodus, A Commentary
Ezekiel, A Commentary
The Feasts of Israel
First Principles of the Doctrine of Christ
Foundations of Christian Doctrine
Foundations of Christian Doctrine (Self Study Guide)
Foundational Principles of Church Membership
Foundation Principles of the Doctrine of Christ
Frequently Asked Questions
Galatians, A Commentary
Genesis, A Commentary
Headship, Covering and Hats
Hebrews, A Commentary
The House of God
Interpreting the Book of Revelation
Interpreting the Scriptures (with Ken Malmin)

Interpreting the Scriptures (Self Study Guide)
Interpreting the Symbols and Types
Isaiah, A Commentary
James, A Commentary
Jeremiah and Lamentations, A Commentary
Joshua, A Commentary
Jude, A Commentary
Judges, A Commentary
Keep Yourself Pure
The Kingdom Cult of Self
Kings of the Kingdom - Character Studies on Israel's Kings
Law and Grace
Leviticus, A Commentary
The Lord Jesus Christ our Melchizedek Priest
Maintaining the Presence
Marriage, Divorce and Remarriage
Messages from Matthew
Methods and Principles of Bible Research
Ministries in the Cluster
The Ministry of Women
The Minor Prophets, A Commentary Mystery
Mystery Parables of the Kingdom
The Name of God
New Covenant Realities
New Testament Survey (with Ken Malmin)
Numbers, A Commentary
Old Testament Survey (with Ken Malmin)
Only for Catholics
Passion Week Chart
Philippians, A Commentary
Psalms, A Commentary
The Relevance of the Old Testament to a New Testament Church
Restoration Theology
Restoration Theology
Revelation, A Commentary
Romans, A Commentary

The Royal Seed
Ruth, A Commentary
1 & 2 Samuel, A Commentary
Sermon Outlines (3 volumes)
The Seventy Weeks Prophecy
Studies in the Royal Priesthood
The Sword and Consequences
The Tabernacle of David
The Tabernacle of Moses
The Temple of Solomon
Table Talks
Tale of Three Trees
1 & 2 Thessalonians, A Commentary
This is My Story (Kevin Conner's autobiography)
This We Believe
Three Days and Three Nights (with Chart)
Tithes and Offerings
Today's Prophets
To Drink or Not to Drink
To Smoke or Not to Smoke
Two Kings and a Prince
Understanding the New Birth and the Baptism of the Holy Spirit
Vision of an Antioch Church
Water Baptism Thesis
What About Israel?

Visit www.kevinconner.org for more information.
Visit www.amazon.com/author/kevinjconner for a list of other books by Kevin Conner.

Video Training Seminars

Kevin Conner's popular "Key of Knowledge" Seminar is now available as an online teaching course. Part 1 covers 'Methods and Principles of Bible Research' and includes over 6 hours of video teaching, the required textbooks, extra hand out notes, and a self-guided online study program. The first lesson, 'Challenge to Study' is FREE.

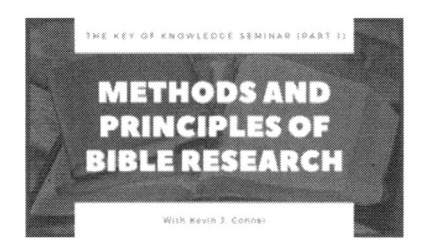

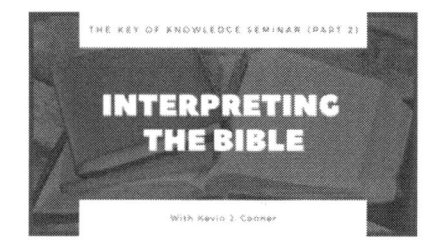

The second part of Kevin Conner's "Key of Knowledge" Seminar is about 'Interpreting the Bible' and includes over 7 hours of video teaching, two downloadable textbooks, extra hand out notes, and a self-guided online study program. These two courses can be taken as stand-alone courses, in succession, or simultaneously.

Also available at www.kevinconner.org/courses is Kevin's extensive teaching on his best-selling book The Foundation of Christian Doctrine, which includes 67 videos which can be purchased in 4 parts.

Visit the courses page at www.kevinconner.org for all the details.

Kevin Conner's Audio Teaching

Dozens of Kevin Conner's messages are available on his FREE teaching podcast - 'Kevin Conner Teaches'. This podcast is accessible from Apple Podcasts, Google Podcasts, or Spotify Podcasts (if you are a subscriber), as well as at www.kevinconner.podbean.com (including on the Podbean mobile App).

New messages are published weekly, selected from messages Kevin has given over the years at various churches, conferences, and training seminars. Be sure to subscribe so you are notified of recent releases.

Visit https://www.kevinconner.org/audios-by-kevin/ for a full list of podcast titles and series.

PDF Versions of Kevin Conner's Books

All of Kevin Conner's books are now available to purchase in quality PDF format. This digital format is in addition to the Kindle eBooks and paperback/hardback versions currently available. A PDF is a 'portable document format' used on all computers for reading documents. Books in this format can be read on a computer, laptop, or handheld device and/or printed out for your personal use (even stored in your own binding of choice). Many PDF readers also allow you to 'mark-up' and add your own notes to the document. PDFs of Kevin's books are for your personal use and are not for copying or redistribution.

You can purchase PDF books at www.kevinconner.org/shop. Upon payment, a download link will be sent to you via email along with your receipt.

Resources by Mark Conner

Kevin Conner's son, Mark Conner, worked closely with him in the church ministry for many years (as music director and youth pastor), before succeeding him in 1995 as the Senior Minister of what was then Waverley Christian Fellowship (now [CityLife Church](#)) Mark transitioned out of that role in early 2017 and since that time has been giving himself to speaking, training, coaching, and writing.

Here is a list of Mark's books which may be of interest to you:

- *[Transforming Your Church - Seven Strategic Shifts](#)*
- *[Money Talks: Practical Wisdom for Becoming Financially Free](#)*
- *[The Spiritual Journey: Understanding the Stages of Faith](#)*
- *[How to Avoid Burnout: Five Habits of Healthy Living](#)*
- *[Prison Break: Finding Personal Freedom](#)*
- *[Pass the Baton: Successful Leadership Transition](#)*
- *[Successful Christian Ministry](#)*

These can be purchased from:
- [Amazon.com/author/markconner](#) in paperback and eBook format.
- [WORD books](#) in Australia ([www.word.com.au](#))
- [www.kevinconner.org/books-by-mark-conner/](#) in PDF format.

Mark also has an active BLOG and teaching podcast. Visit [www.markconner.com.au](#) for more information.

Made in the USA
Columbia, SC
05 April 2025

361c1466-8767-4983-8829-426cfe5a1a99R01